AT THIS TIME

THEOLOGICAL EDUCATION BETWEEN THE TIMES

Ted A. Smith, series editor

Theological Education between the Times gathers diverse groups of people for critical, theological conversations about the meanings and purposes of theological education in a time of deep change. The project is funded by the Lilly Endowment Inc.

Daniel O. Aleshire
Beyond Profession: The Next Future of Theological Education

Elizabeth Conde-Frazier
Atando Cabos: Latinx Contributions to Theological Education

Corwin Malcolm Davis and Ted A. Smith, editors
At This Time: Dialogues in Theological Education

Keri Day
Notes of a Native Daughter: Testifying in Theological Education

Willie James Jennings
After Whiteness: An Education in Belonging

Mark D. Jordan
Transforming Fire: Imagining Christian Teaching

Maria Liu Wong
On Becoming Wise Together: Learning and Leading in the City

Colleen Mary Mallon, OP
Inclusivity and Institutional Change in Education: A Theologian's Journey

Ted A. Smith
The End of Theological Education

Chloe T. Sun
Attempt Great Things for God: Theological Education in Diaspora

Amos Yong
Renewing the Church by the Spirit: Theological Education after Pentecost

Mark S. Young
The Hope of the Gospel: Theological Education and the Next Evangelicalism

At This Time

Dialogues in Theological Education

Edited by
Corwin Malcolm Davis and Ted A. Smith

William B. Eerdmans Publishing Company
Grand Rapids, Michigan

Wm. B. Eerdmans Publishing Co.
2006 44th Street SE, Grand Rapids, MI 49508
www.eerdmans.com

Published 2026
Printed in the United States of America

32 31 30 29 28 27 26 1 2 3 4 5 6 7

ISBN 978-0-8028-8521-0

Library of Congress Cataloging-in-Publication Data

A catalog record for this book is available from the Library of Congress.

Contents

CONTENTS

Introduction

Conversations from and for This Time

Ted A. Smith: I think of this book as an attempt to let some extraordinarily rich conversations spill onto the page. Conversations like these have been the lifeblood of the whole Theological Education between the Times (TEBT) project. As the project developed, authors in the project's series—myself included—found ourselves doing many presentations. Generous invitations brought some great exchanges, but they were also brief encounters. We'd fly in for a day or Zoom in for an hour. I missed the depth of relationships that had emerged over eight gatherings of the authors of the first books in the series. Those relationships are intrinsically valuable; they also have done a lot to help each of us see and understand more about the meanings and purposes of theological education. And so I was glad when you were willing to work with me, Corwin, to convene a new group of authors. Time and budget allowed for only three three-day meetings. But friends and friends of friends helped us invite some profound scholars and leaders. And the group came together quickly. It was a joy for me to share in these times with these friends.

Corwin Malcolm Davis: I experienced great joy in these gatherings, too. Each time this group of authors gathered for our sessions, I could feel the energy and the connections building. Writing together, and then talking about our writing, helped us give voice not only to our personal experiences in ministry and the academy but also to some insights we wanted to share with our wider communities.

Ted: One of the highlights of the gatherings came when John Kartje called our collective attention to the Gospels' emphasis on the moment of fulfillment. I'm sure you remember it, too. It was itself an arresting moment. He first reminded us how the prophet Anna had been fasting and praying in the temple for a very long time when Jesus's parents brought him to the temple. "*At that moment*," the text says, she broke into praise (Luke 2:38, emphasis added).[1]

The moment of divine presence has consequences, John continued: time is different before and after that moment. John followed the thread of this insight through multiple passages in the Gospels. In the Fourth Gospel, for instance, Jesus gives his mother and the disciple whom he loves to one another just before he dies on the cross. "Woman, here is your son," he says to Mary, even as he says to the disciple, "Here is your mother." "And *from that hour*," the Gospel says, "the disciple took her into his own home" (John 19:26–27, emphasis added).

God's active presence makes a difference in time. Christian life depends on discerning the difference God makes and then responding in fitting ways. Our responses happen in time, too. And when we try to respond, John reminded us, we are not on our own: "When they bring you before the synagogues, the rulers, and the authorities," Jesus teaches the disciples, "do not worry about how you are to defend yourselves or what you are to say; for the Holy Spirit will teach *at that very hour* what you ought to say" (Luke 12:11–12, emphasis added).

This book is our attempt to say what God has given us to say at this time.[2] The authors do not pretend to speak timeless truths. There are no promises of eternal blueprints for theological education in every age. These are words from and for these times between the times.

Corwin: I agree with you that the book is not an attempt to offer timeless truths. I would add that the book is also not an attempt to offer *universal* truths. Our gatherings gave voice—literally and figuratively—to the many different ways that we were uniquely experiencing the "times between the times" that you describe in

The End of Theological Education.[3] While we are also experiencing the times collectively, the book is an attempt to offer individual perspectives and responses that attend to the diversity of those experiences.

When the prophet Anna recognizes in Scripture what time it is, I can imagine how that discernment might be received differently by persons from various social locations. What does the time mean for the other widows or for Simeon? What does it mean for the religious and political leaders? How might *that* time offer hope and delight to some while simultaneously bringing confusion and disappointment to others?

The authors in this collection present their own unique experiences of the current times in theological education and the complex emotions and possibilities therein. This book does not shy away from ambivalence, nor does it strive for a forced unity of vision. Diversity matters for the richness of our own spiritual lives, and certainly for theological education.

After all, a recognition of diversity has been central to the TEBT project. We have encouraged one another to write with a spiky particularity out of our different identities, experiences, traditions, and institutional locations. These differences are not fetters or hindrances to our shared work: they are essential opportunities to the gifts of theological education.

Ted: I confess I flinched a little when you suggested that these essays do not contain "universal truths." Whole libraries have been written on the nature of the claims theological speech makes, and we don't need to reproduce them here. We have a different mission. But I will say that I absolutely share your sense that the plural and complex social locations of the authors matter very much for the theological work they do. As you say, recognition of the significance of these different locations—and the different things that can be known and spoken from each of them—has shaped every part of the TEBT project. These are writings from particular times *and* from particular places, in a broad sense of that term. Which is just to say that they are writings from particular people.

What I want to preserve from talk of "universals" is the insistence that the voices here make claims on one another—and on all of us as readers. These voices say things that are true not only for people who happen to share the particular temporal and social locations of the authors. Those things are not confined to particular silos of identity; they speak to and make claims upon all of us. They do this when they speak about a God who is the creator of all things, visible and invisible. And they make these wider claims when they insist on the particularities of their locations, which are always intertwined with other locations. The particular location from which Juan Molina writes, for instance—the Mexican American Catholic College (MACC)—has been formed in relation to white Anglophone Catholic traditions; Latine Pentecostal communities; an Association of Theological Schools whose criteria did not easily fit MACC's mission; liberation theologies that crossed between Africa, Europe, and the Americas; and more. When Juan speaks from the particularities of his location, he is in conversation with all the other communities to which his location is already connected. These connections become visible when we think about identity historically, rather than in essentialist terms. Seeing these connections, and tracing the ways connections lead to other connections, opens each piece to a universal horizon. That horizon appears not through abstraction but through attention to social and historical particularities.

In trying to understand these questions, I have learned a lot from Keri Day's account of the practice of *testifying* in the Black Pentecostal churches that did so much to form her. She describes testifying as an act profoundly rooted in the particular time, place, and person offering the testimony. It is a kind of prophecy: it is from, for, and about God. It is an ethical discourse: it makes moral claims on people in and beyond the circle of immediate hearers. And it is never just the work of an individual. As Keri writes, "Testifying was a communal act; it forged a truly democratic community drawn together by filial bonds of love, care, and accountability. We trusted that God would speak through our sisters and brothers as they testified to God's goodness, mercy, and grace. We uttered our stories in hopes that we would experience the power of the Spirit to be healed and made whole."[4] While testifying is profoundly particular, it is not solipsistic. It grows out of and forges community with other people and with God. Testifying invites response; it invites dialogue. That's why this book takes the form it does.

Corwin: Ah! Your teasing out of "universal truths" helps me clarify what I mean. I absolutely agree that the voices make claims on one another, and on all of us as readers. And, as you argue through your reference to Keri Day, the various ways that the authors in this book testify invite dialogue and foster connection. In response to your saying that the book does not offer "timeless truths," I mean to stress that the truths of these testimonies are not "universal" in the sense of having an objective, abstract existence apart from any particular community. A unique gift of this book is that it is a collection of voices that do not all offer one impartial conclusion about theological education. Instead, the authors offer us the gifts of their experience and invite us to linger and explore them.

I think this is especially important to emphasize when we consider how the "universal" or "objective" Western claims about theology have historically been the concomitant claims of coloniality and of whiteness. The diversity that this book presents is one that is not defined by the same schemas of education that have often listed theologies from other populations as alternative, at best, or at worst, aberrant. I am reminded of how Willie James Jennings writes in *After Whiteness* about the fragments formed of colonial power. Drawing upon the gospel lesson of the feeding of the multitude, Willie remarks that God works with the fragments, including the ones left by colonial power, fragments through which many of us are "trying to tie together, hold together, the witness of our peoples."[5] But, as Willie recognizes, theological education sometimes takes the fragments that could facilitate connection and instead "aligns them with colonialist aspiration, and invites us to compositions that drain life."[6] This book resists both the "universals" that allow only one conclusion, only one fitting theological response, and the claims that singularity is something objective to be applied to all other situations. That's why it is so important that the perspectives in this book come not only from a variety of identities but also from a variety of institutional locations.

And so I think we're saying similar things: that the theological claims in this book are intentionally personal and subjective, and that it is exactly in that particularity that they make claims in and beyond their contexts. Each section of this book begins with particular lived realities of religious life and simultaneously offers to the reader a vision of the meanings and purposes of theological education that extends to other communities and contexts. In other words, the authors offer their particular and unique experiences that also present reflections that transcend those experiences. Grace Kao's essay, for example, on the unique technological and social platform of Progressive Asian American Christians (PAAC) is not the only way of thinking and reasoning about the communal balance between tradition and innovation. What narratives like Grace's offer us, instead, is a situatedness in the social and historical particularities of her community, and the blessings and burdens of trying to create something new. The author then invites readers to respond for themselves—as Grace's dialogue partners Julian Davis Reid and Joanne Solis-Walker do—to the gifts of Grace's experience and to her claims.

Ted: Yes. We're hoping for testimonies in conversation: speech that is deeply located, seeking to respond to God, and in conversation with all kinds of other particular voices with other locations. We're hoping for connections that don't seek a lowest common denominator in an attempt to erase difference but find contingent points of similarity even as they bring difference into bolder, appreciative relief. That can only emerge in conversations. And those are the kinds of conversations that broke out in our gatherings with the writers of this project. It's what made those gatherings so distinctive. And it's why we wanted to build dialogues into the structure of the book.

I should add, for readers' sake, that the dialogues printed here are excerpts of conversations that happened as part of the writing process. Each participant in that process committed to writing an essay. Authors were constantly reading and responding to one another. As we moved to publication, we asked each author which conversations with other authors had been most generative for their writing. We then tried to gather authors into groups with those insights (and our own listening) in mind. In this published product of the process, each author hosts one dialogue with two other authors and then joins two other dialogues as a respondent. Our hope is that the book displays a dense web of overlapping conversations like the ones that stretched across our gatherings. The dialogues on the page are not mere transcripts of in-person conversations. They are samples of much longer exchanges. They have been lightly edited for clarity and consistency. But most of them started in speech. And all of them grow out of relationships.

The relationships behind this book grew to be thick and interconnected in many different ways, like a tangle of roots below a thriving grove of trees. Because that's the way these essays grew, it did not make sense to impose a topical ordering of them. And so we've tried to emphasize the arbitrariness of the order, gathering them here in alphabetical order by author's last name. A reader could start anywhere—and then go to any number of connected places from there. There are many paths through the book.

Corwin: Keeping that tangle of relationships in mind also helps connect us to one of the main priorities of this book, and of the larger TEBT ethos: to make room for the work of the Spirit. Each of our three gatherings featured shared times of worship that made manifest the diverse ways we connect to the Divine. Our days began and ended with prayers and rituals that reflected the unique traditions of each particular facilitator. We framed our time together in worship in order to remind ourselves of—and experience anew—the communion that unites our fragments, the work that God invites us to join together. This book reflects not only the authors' experiences but also the ways in which the Spirit transcends all things and helps us to hear one another more clearly. To put a spin on a Pauline claim, "we do not always know how to [write] as we ought, but the Spirit intercedes for us with groanings too deep for words" (adapted from Rom. 8:26–27). While we do not all share the same contexts, the Spirit moves in ways that help us to hear and see each other better. The testifying might sometimes require translation, and for that we trust that the Spirit intercedes in our gatherings and in this book.

Ted: Amen. And I'd add that the prayers for conversation continue. The TEBT project was never about cooking up some smart plans for theological education and then retailing them to schools as if we were consultants. Former TEBT associate director Lucila Crena helped me come to see the project more as a dynamic social process of study, friendship, prayer, and writing. Just as other authors in the series sparked the reflections in this book, I hope these pieces will spark readers to reflections of their own—from their own places, their own times. And *for* all of us.

Corwin: The dynamic nature of the project is what has been the most rewarding for me. Together, we lean into the catalytic nature of thinking and learning. And in so doing, we join the ongoing process of those who came before us, and of those yet to come. The writing is our attempt to linger alongside each other and alongside the God who desires to be known.

1

The Rise and Recalibration of Progressive Asian American Christians (PAAC)

Grace Y. Kao

On December 22, 2016, a writer from the Detroit suburbs named Liz Lin penned a blog with which I deeply resonated, titled "The Loneliness of the Progressive Asian American Christian."[1] She described how her evangelical, ethnic-specific church had been a place in her youth that had not only taught her about a gracious God who loved her unconditionally but had also served as a site of deep community as she came to terms with her racial identity. She also recounted how taking classes in Bible and theology later in graduate school had "blown open" her world by enabling her to see Jesus no longer merely as her "personal Savior" but as a "revolutionary who came to set the oppressed free (Luke 4:18)."

This powerful transformation came at a cost, however. Lin reported growing uncomfortable in Asian American churches since they did not tend to share her developing commitments to feminism, racial justice, and LGBTQIA+ advocacy. Her loneliness consisted of constantly having to "choose between shared theology and experience." She could either be a racial minority in a largely white or Black church where others shared her political commitments but not her cultural experiences, or she could draw some comfort in Asian American churches but still feel out of place due to their social conservatism. She dreamed of meeting up with like-minded folks who wouldn't "feel the need to turn down the volume on either our ideology or our cultural experiences." She concluded her blog with a call to action: "If you're interested in such a space, here's a start: Join the *Progressive Asian American Christians* group on Facebook, curated by Lydia Suh [now Shiu], a pastor at City Church San Francisco. We're still figuring out what the group is, but at the very least, it's a place to know that we aren't alone."[2]

Within a day of her post's publication, a friend added me to that newly constituted PAAC Facebook group. Apparently three hundred others also joined that day.[3] Lin's piece went viral approximately two weeks later after the *Huffington Post* reprinted it. PAAC grew to two thousand members within six weeks of creation. As my colleague aptly described the situation, Lin essentially sent out a "bat signal"—and thousands of us heeded her call.

Lin's call had everything to do with "theological education" in the fullest sense of that phrase. After all, it was her intensive seminary study of the Bible and theology that had ultimately led both to her more expansive view of Jesus and to her diminished sense of community. And her blog's call was for like-minded folks to meet up for times of colearning and conversation for the sake of developing both individual identities and communal bonds. Lin was essentially inviting us to come together to imagine a kind of theological education that did not end in alienation but in a new kind of progressive Asian American Christian community.

THE EMERGENCE OF PROGRESSIVE ASIAN AMERICAN CHRISTIANS (PAAC)

There was tremendous energy in PAAC in those early weeks and months. We members shared our stories and invited responses to all sorts of matters. One member's post from October 2017 asked anyone to comment in "humorous, serious, [or] cringe-worthy [ways] . . . [on] beliefs about God or our relationship with God . . . we don't believe anymore." Popular among the 358 responses were references to "purity culture" teachings about women being responsible for men's lust, and to fears that mundane activities would cause spiritual harm (e.g., that reading Harry Potter books would expose readers to or even incline readers toward witchcraft). Thus PAAC quickly became a welcome space for many to process the churches, fellowships, and belief systems they had outgrown.[4] Individual members also turned to the community to ask for advice about personal predicaments, such as how to handle a racially insensitive colleague or a difficult relationship with a family member who disapproved of their gender expression or sexual identity.

Even though PAAC served as a vibrant online community, members began to press for in-person gatherings. The first took place within one month of the first request in Minneapolis. Within the next three months, members took it upon themselves to organize regional hangouts, with corresponding Facebook regional subgroups, in eight more cities or regions.[5] Within just six months of the main Facebook group's creation, PAAC even hosted its first in-person conference in San Francisco, "Progressive Asian American Christians: The Conference [Forging Our Identity]."[6]

I was amazed that the winning combination of one well-written blog and one newly created Facebook group under the leadership of two very capable women could so quickly blossom into a meaningful space where self-identified progressive Asian American Christians could explore new ways of thinking and being. Individuals posed questions that some of my MDiv students continue to ask: Why have many Asian American Christians been captivated by white male celebrity megachurch pastors (like Rick Warren, Tim Keller, and John Piper)? How can we understand Jesus's death and resurrection in ways other than the violent atonement theories (satisfaction, penal substitution) that had once been pivotal to our turn to faith? Other members asked how to rebuild after deconstruction, wondering, for instance, what a progressive Christian sexual ethic could be beyond total license on the one hand and the traditional sexual mores in which they had been raised but had outgrown on the other.[7]

Across the years, I especially enjoyed processing our community's reactions to current events. Our spirited discussions included the positioning of Asian Americans as pawns in affirmative action debates, our mixed reactions to the success of the film *Crazy Rich Asians*,[8] solidarity with Black Lives Matter as a matter of social justice, and individuals' support for certain Asian American candidates (like Rep. Andy Kim of New Jersey's Third District) and grave concerns about others (like Rep. Young Kim of California's Fortieth District).

In PAAC's first several years, it seemed as if members were constantly rolling out new initiatives. In addition to creating regional subgroups, folks formed their own affinity groups, such as PAAC Fam (the LGBTQIA+ group), the Parenting PAAC, and Progressive Asian American Clergy. Some ethnic-specific groups (PAAC Filipinx Caucus, Taiwan Interest and Advocacy) also developed loyal followings. On June 1, 2017, PAAC launched a regular podcast.[9] Several PAAC members also started an online magazine, *Diverging*, that housed Lenten and Advent devotionals, original and reprinted articles from PAAC authors about the work of justice, sermons from PAAC clergy, and even an advice column.[10] There were several iterations of an online book club mostly featuring Asian American authors. There was even a short-lived private group and dating app for single PAACs with the tongue-in-cheek name STUMBL.

The group's strength and vibrancy likely peaked at our second annual conference. Held at the Immanuel Presbyterian Church in Los Angeles's Koreatown in May 2019, the conference gathered some 170 of us from across the United States for a rich time of worship, workshops (on mental health, spirituality, sexual ethics, clergy reflections), fellowship, and great food.[11]

I largely experienced PAAC as a space where gifts were freely offered and warmly received: members with theological training could draw from their expertise, persons in ministry could relate to others in need pastorally, those with particular professional expertise (in higher education, mental health fields, medicine, public policy, the arts) could share their knowledge and insights, and anyone so inclined could pose questions to the group, organize in-person gatherings, or roll out new initiatives.

Theological education was central to the whole movement. It was theological in a way that kept it neither narrowly concerned with the institutional church nor attached to models that involved formal accreditation, faculty and staff on payroll, and recognized degrees. It was more like the consciousness-raising groups of second-wave feminism or even the freedom schools of the civil rights movement—it was a "for-us-by-us" effort at teaching and learning together. The PAAC community was complex, with many different practices and purposes. It was always more than an educational project. But it was never less.

Indeed, the closest approximation to structured, formal education that PAAC provided was the PAAC Fellowship—a ten-month intentional online community that aimed to educate PAACs about "our histories, intersectionalities, and activism with the goal of developing a more integrated PAAC identity and deeper relationships with fellow PAACs." The Fellowship offered a monthly two-hour live webinar with an expert, then weekly meetings in online small groups in which the fellows processed the reading and discussion questions curated by that month's expert. To join, applicants answered three essay questions and provided two reference letters. Those accepted were charged $550 for tuition, though scholarships were offered to those for whom the fee would be a heavy burden. In all, PAAC ran four separate cohorts (2017–2018, 2018–2019, 2019–2020, and 2021–2022) and recruited esteemed Asian American theological educators among their experts (e.g., Kwok Pui Lan, Timothy Tseng, Jessica ChenFeng, and Tisha Rajendra).[12] Essentially, PAAC served the needs of its members by providing them multiple avenues and spaces in real life and online both to explore and to express who and what they were and were desiring to become.

BUILDING AND DEFINING THE PARAMETERS OF THE PAAC COMMUNITY

As much as PAAC had an inclusive ethic because it was designed for "lonely" persons, the PAAC community nonetheless experienced growing pains as we worked out in real time the limits of the topics—and persons—we could handle. Put differently, with a group that quickly grew to over six thousand members within one year of its founding, our interactions with one another were not all smooth sailing. Our different temperaments, points of departure, and online personas led to occasional misunderstanding and defensiveness in some scenarios, and combative, all-out flame wars in the worst cases. As cofounder Liz Lin has acknowledged in a podcast, "Interacting with somebody online who you have no relationship with in real life sometimes means the interactions don't have the same level of care or the same level of empathy that an IRL (in real life) interaction would have. Things like tone are really hard to read online."[13]

Indeed, the need to appoint moderators and develop group rules and norms arose within the first several months. Some members willingly engaged with the full range of questions asked especially by newcomers, including about the propriety of Christians living noncelibate queer lives or of women exercising spiritual authority over men. Others grew weary of discussing "clobber passages" and wanted this self-identified community of progressives to move beyond these "basic" questions about prohibition or permission.[14] Cofounder Liz Lin explained in a podcast interview that she had originally hoped that PAAC would be a space that had "room for everyone at any stage of the journey," because she understood "progressive" to mean "not so much that you meet x, y, z criteria" but to signal "an orientation . . . of what direction you are heading in."[15] Still, the PAAC leadership concluded that real harm was being inflicted on some vulnerable members and so some questions (e.g., about the appropriateness of women serving at the highest rungs of church leadership or of the good and beauty of LGBTQIA+ Christian lives) would no longer be permitted.[16]

PAAC eventually settled on this statement of its mission and identity: "PAAC is a community for socially, politically, and theologically progressive Asian/Pacific Islander/Desi American and diaspora Christians to support each other and discuss faith, identity, and current events. It is an LGBT-affirming, feminist, justice-oriented, anti-racist, pro-immigrant, anti-ableist space that holds a wide range of theologies." Once these norms had been set, anyone who wished to join PAAC was asked to answer three member-request questions and to abide by the group's rules. As cofounder Lydia Shiu explained in an October 2017 post that I quote at length:

> *We post an iteration of something like this every few months, because as new people join every day, it seems like it helps to over communicate our intention in this group! . . .
>
> Welcome! This is a place for Progressive Asian American Christians. Glad you've found us and decided to join! If you don't identify as progressive (politically, socially, AND theologically liberal), AND you are not Asian American, AND you don't identify yourself as Christian, this might not be your jam! You are still welcome to be here and listen in. However, *this group has become what it is for the sole purpose of creating a safe community for PAAC* (yes all 4 of those), so that we can support one another, vent about being a minority in most churches, console and help one another, have conversations about things we can't talk about in other Asian spaces, or in white spaces, or dominant systems (*i.e.* patriarchy, heteronormative).
>
> We have this space because we desperately need each other. *If you don't desperately need other PAACs . . . this place may not be the right fit for you.* But still, if you are interested, to just learn and see, you may, but . . . because the PAAC voice is raised here to offset the outside environments in which PAACs are usually minorities . . . you may even be very very confused. *If progressive theology is new to you, if feminist thinking is something you haven't studied, if LGBTQIA rights and the full acceptance and embrace of LGBTQIA by God and the church is still in question, this group may*

> *be difficult for you to be a part of. These are just some of the topics that will be assumed in this place. If any of these are questioned, in validity of argument theologically, or if it's in line with Christianity, or your understanding of world views, then it will not be tolerated due to the harm it's caused . . . to PAACs for even talking about these things everywhere else.*
>
> . . . I started this group and I'm a pastor. I'm a Presbyterian pastor's kid, and ordained in the PCUSA. I have learned a lot since I started co-leading this group with Liz Lin. Heck, I've grown a lot as a pastor from moderating this group. I wanted a learning space. . . . *I'd love for conservative AAC, like one of my friends, to listen in and learn and open their minds, expose them to other kinds of Christians. . . . But I'm saddened every time my longing for this space to be that comes at the cost of my LGBT friends who just came to terms with "Jesus loves me," women who are newly finding strength in an oppressive world, those who are trying to forge their AA identity, are hurt and getting comment thread wars.* This is supposed to be a safe space for lonely PAACs and I feel protective, and responsible, and guilty, for not being able to protect them better. And I think I have to kind of come to terms with something: *I wanted to welcome everyone here like a church. But . . . This is not a church. Or maybe it's a different kind of church-like community that's needed. A refuge. A grieving hole. An underground gathering. . . . I wanted everyone to join and love one another!* Too much to ask lol. *I still hope and dream that there's a greater space where we can learn, listen, disagree, vent, without being rude, or mean, or hurting others. And I hope this place can be that. But I guess, honestly, it is not all things to all people. It's a place for PAACs. So I guess what I'm trying to say is, I want to re-center us on being a place for PAACs. . . .*
>
> Oh and PAACs, I LOVE YOU!!!!!! [emphasis added]

Even with this clarification, the moderators still occasionally had to caution rule-breakers and others who appeared to be engaging in bad faith. What's more, new persons not necessarily aware of recent clarifications or past discussions continued to join and post variations of these questions in PAAC, and even long-term members did not always heed the group's norms before posting. In addition, whenever a member would inquire about churches in a particular area, whether because of a relocation or because of impending vacation plans—a very popular information request that continues to this day—a moderator would quickly post a reminder that *any* recommendation of a church that either did not permit women clergy or excluded queer and trans members from full inclusion would be deleted.[17] All told, serial offenders were warned that they would be removed; church recommendations that failed to meet the criteria were scrubbed; and I vividly recall some members being expelled or voluntarily leaving in a huff after some heated exchanges.

PAAC and the Pandemic

Given the energy and excitement generated online in the main Facebook group, the aforementioned initiatives, and the well-attended second conference in Los Angeles, I would never have expected that PAAC would begin to lose its vibrancy and momentum sometime during COVID-tide. The third PAAC conference, "Rooted Together," which Seattle PAAC had been organizing for May 2020, had to be postponed in an era of stay-at-home orders and lockdowns. The PAAC podcasts' two-part interview with feminist theologian Rita Nakashima Brock (March 31, 2020, and April 14, 2020) and with PAAC members Melissa and Serena Cerezo-Poon on their same-sex parenting journey involving the use of reproductive technology (May 26, 2020, and June 9, 2020) ended up being their last ones until PAAC rolled out a new initiative (to be discussed below) several years later.[18] *Diverging* magazine published its last original article on January 17, 2021. To be sure, Seattle PAAC regrouped and was planning to host the postponed conference in June 2021, but that, too, painfully had to be canceled several weeks prior to the scheduled start in the interests of public health.

To breathe new life into PAAC and also to provide much-needed spiritual care, the PAAC cofounders and moderators launched a PAAC sermon series on January 20, 2022, that promised to "feature a series of monthly livestreams where invited speakers . . . will share stories and messages of hope, sorrow, joy, and contemplation."[19] Sermon speakers included Rev. Lydia Shiu, Rev. Sandhya Jha, Rev. Laura Chefeitz, Rev. Kevin Kim Wright, Rev. Emily McGinley, Pastor Mira Sawlani-Joyner, Rev. Joshua Young, and Rev. Mihee Kim-Kort. While I am uncertain how many persons listened to those sermons through the podcast's free and publicly accessible platforms, the comment threads in PAAC about each did not generate much internal discussion.

Social scientists have studied how relationships of various kinds were put on hold, impaired, or even severed during the pandemic, with some never being fully restored when the crisis eased. Both public health guidelines on social distancing and restrictions on in-person gatherings disrupted people's social networks and routines such as going to school, work, the grocery store, or other activities that would have put them into regular contact with others.[20] While many churches and other religious organizations that had paused their traditional, in-person worship services in the early months of the pandemic had resumed offering some type of regular service by March 2022, one Pew Study found that only 43 percent of attendees reported that the services and attendance at their place of worship had returned to their prepandemic levels.[21]

The PAAC community was not immune to these disruptions. I had originally thought that a community that had begun online, had built a genuine sense of community online, and had hosted many significant and meaningful activities online would have been better positioned to survive the massive upheaval that was COVID-19, but I was wrong. Liz Lin has speculated that while PAAC was able to sustain itself for the first year of the pandemic, when *everything* went online—work, school, church, even significant family events like weddings and funerals—the prospect of spending even more discretionary time online likely became unpalatable to many and they simply checked out.[22] I cannot recall when I myself started to disengage, but sometime during the pandemic I no longer participated as much as I had in those early years. Lin's thoughts helped me to make sense of my own diminished engagement, and I suspect her explanation worked equally well for others, too.

PAAC's Uncertain Future

While PAAC has lost some of its original momentum, neither the need nor the hope that gave rise to the movement has gone away. Instead, PAAC leaders have been eagerly recalibrating what it would be, or become, postpandemic. Over Labor Day weekend in 2023, PAAC convened its first in-person conference/retreat since summer 2019 at Stony Point Center in upstate New York. It was cohosted with HA:N United Methodist Church—a progressive Asian American church with many core members, including their first pastor, from PAAC. Some seventy-two members, including myself, attended. Many of us had not seen one another in years.

In addition to reconnecting with one another in a retreat-like setting and sharing how many of our religious practices (e.g., church attendance) or even sense of religious identity had since shifted, we held sober discussions about PAAC's next steps. It was clear that PAAC still held value to many persons even as many of PAAC's various programs had been put on pause. To breathe new life into our once-active regional groups, several of us volunteered to host regional gatherings within three months.[23] We also discussed the wisdom of moving off Facebook, given Facebook's reputation as the "bastion of the older generation" and some members' ethical concerns about the platform.[24]

The future of PAAC as an organization remains uncertain. While fewer people engage regularly in the main Facebook group than before the pandemic, there are relational networks beyond the regional subgroups and institutional structures that endure. Two of the three churches that began thanks to the organizing efforts of regional PAAC members continue to meet regularly with a core group of faithful parishioners, even as they are undergoing growing pains of their own: the aforementioned Ha:N United Methodist Church in New York formed in December 2018 and First Progressive Church in Los Angeles, which held its first service in October 2018.[25] Prior to the fall 2003 conference, PAAC even incorporated as its own nonprofit, which means it now has a board and is no longer under the fiscal sponsorship of another organization.[26] In 2024, PAAC hosted its first ever Board retreat, funded in part by their receipt of a capacity-building grant from the Lilly Endowment. At the time of this writing, planning is under way for our third national conference to be held in Seattle from July 11 to July 13, 2025.

PAAC and Theological Education

While it remains an open question what will become of PAAC, the emergence, pandemic easing, and current reestablishment of PAAC hold several important takeaways for theological educators. Of course, the particularities of the PAAC community matter, as PAAC's rise and recalibration will not automatically translate across meaningful lines of difference. Still, the PAAC experiment, precisely in its particularity, can spark reflection and conversation that might prove helpful for other communities.

1. **The benefits and limitations of seminaries for theological education.** The first insight is that there remain a deep hunger and need for theological education, with PAAC as a case study showing how the traditional seminary has been both important and insufficient in meeting that need. On the one hand, the teacher-experts in the successive cohorts of the PAAC Fellowship, most PAAC clergy, and many academic speakers at PAAC conferences have been seminary trained. On the other hand, the structure of the PAAC Fellowship itself, the self-organized book clubs, and the vibrant exchange of ideas in other online and in-person spaces demonstrate that the dissemination and co-construction of this knowledge require neither a formal classroom with clearly demarcated teachers and

students nor a physical library. As a case study, PAAC also shows that there are more people interested in theological education than are willing or able to become officially enrolled students in a school. Institutions of higher learning might accordingly offer shorter-term nondegree programs, lifelong educational opportunities for all people, or even just hubs that convene people in resource-rich spaces for sharing, study, and connection.

Likewise, given its adaptability, the PAAC Fellowship model especially merits further consideration by other communities hungry for theological education outside of the conventional, degree-granting model. Because PAAC fellows pledged to participate in a ten-month intentional community with one another—a period longer than a standard academic year—they could build even deeper trust and intimacy with one another than they could in the main, seven-thousand-plus-member-strong PAAC group. Yet the primarily online life of PAAC made dealing with internal differences challenging, since much of human communication is tied to body language and tone—not just the actual words used—and an individual's digital persona might not reflect their true self. Thus, in discussion threads where members could enter into and out of conversations, sometimes the only connection people had to one another or even the topic under discussion was a hastily written post and equally hasty replies. In contrast, in the ten-month PAAC Fellowship, the fellows' relationships with one another could develop over time. And though they were not meeting in person, they were interacting in real time (synchronously) and thus their virtual interactions could better approximate the ordinary back-and-forth of an in-person conversation, with visible facial expressions and more detectable tones. Schools accredited by the Association of Theological Schools (ATS) and increasingly offering online education—including some schools offering fully online degrees—might do well to learn from the PAAC Fellowship example both about the liabilities of purely asynchronous versus synchronous instruction and about adopting a cohort model to help students build a sense of community and trust among themselves.

2. Online communities and theological education. As the example of the PAAC Fellowship demonstrates, there are both benefits and risks to developing what cofounder Lydia Shiu earlier called a "learning space" primarily online.

Consider, for instance, PAAC's emergent rules, its evolving list of banned topics, and its expulsions of repeat offenders—all things about which I have had mixed feelings. Prior to joining PAAC, I had been fairly new to the world of online Facebook groups or virtual chat rooms, and the groups in which I participated did not require heavy moderation. Moreover, as a theological educator, I have generally taken the position that it is my job to work with *any* person who has a desire to learn, even if I find their assumptions or premises offensive. Thus, some of the PAAC conversations that were shut down and some of the "cancellations" of rule-breakers painfully cut against my own pedagogical sensibilities, even as I understood the rationale behind them. Relatedly, I have felt unsettled about PAAC's church recommendation policy, for this policy, designed in the interests of normalizing LGBTQIA+ Christians and women church leaders, means that no one can *ever* recommend attending a Catholic or an Orthodox church (until and unless their church policies change). Another way of putting this is that PAAC as an organization can never recommend that its members experience Christianity in the fullness of its ecumenical spectrum.

Many other communities or institutions that consider themselves progressive might make different choices than PAAC did—in tolerating or even welcoming the range of topics that were ultimately banned, and in not restricting the types of churches they could recommend. This is not to suggest there is only one right way to define the limits of acceptable speech and that PAAC got it wrong. Rather, it is to say that the parameters of what is and is not appropriate will need to be determined contextually. For instance, my employer, Claremont School of Theology (CST), is known as a progressive interreligious school that is United Methodist in origin and affiliation. We have had an LGBTQIA+ inclusion statement since 2010—years in advance of the denomination finally voting in May 2024 to lift the bans on clergy identifying as LGBTQ and on pastors officiating at same-sex weddings. While the campus ethos in the interim was much more progressive on issues of gender and sexuality than was the denomination as a whole, our students from more conservative backgrounds who had never encountered queer biblical hermeneutics or theology before could still ask the types of questions that PAAC ultimately ruled were *verboten*. While PAAC eventually settled on a list of banned questions and topics, CST decided not to do so, beyond their standard harassment policy and diversity and inclusion statement. Perhaps that is because CST stakeholders could more readily "see" the sincerity behind the questions and desires to learn, whereas the PAAC leadership and moderation team has had the more difficult task of discerning tone and intentionality online as well as protecting the community from unsavory elements like Internet trolls.

3. Progressive Asian American Christians as a demographic. The third and final takeaway is that we Asian American Christians with progressive sensibilities are here to stay, and that we have distinctive ministerial needs that are easily met neither in existing progressive churches where Asian Americans remain a minority nor in existing Asian American churches that skew more conservative. How small or large this group will be remains unknown. Much, for instance, has been made of the fact that Asian Americans are the fastest-growing racial or ethnic group in the United States, with its size doubling between 2000 and 2019. The number of Asian Americans is projected to surpass 46 million—more than 10 percent of the total US population—in 2060.[27] In addition, while Christianity is still the largest faith group among Asian Americans (at 34 percent), growing numbers of Asian Americans are identifying as religiously unaffiliated. Similarly, while Asian Americans have historically supported the Democratic Party, the 2020, 2022, and 2024 elections showed some evidence of vote swings to Republican Party platforms and candidates in areas with large concentrations of Asian American residents.[28] It is an open question whether our current institutions can provide the type of contextual and culturally competent education to equip the next generation of leaders to serve these communities. In cases where they prove insufficient, we should not be surprised if PAAC, or other grassroots organizations like PAAC, step in to bridge the void.

CONCLUSION

The PAAC story is one in which a discrete collection of individuals found one another to create a space of their own. Whether PAAC as an organization stands the test of time is yet to be seen, but we have produced art, podcasts, liturgies, writings, and other expressions that did not exist before and will take on new lives in the years to come. Furthermore, in contrast to many forms of academic publication, many of these works are freely available to the public and may prove influential for successive generations of progressive Asian American Christians. In other ways, too, PAAC continues to offer a different model for theological education—one in which a vibrant exchange of ideas can occur without formal classrooms or formal teacher/student roles and where participants of all ages are welcome to colearn and cocreate with one another. On a more personal note, PAAC effectively served as my church in the years I was most active. I thank God so many of us heeded Lin's "bat signal" as we came together to live and be in the world while drawing upon the fullness of our PAAC identities.

Dialogue

Grace Y. Kao, Julian Davis Reid, Joanne Solis-Walker

Julian: I was fascinated by the story of PAAC's growth and also by the tensions that came up. That was my favorite part—the way you were trying to complicate what spaces were opening and what spaces were closing. I think that's core to the body of Christ. I mean, you don't get any of the Epistles without there constantly being openings and closings.

Joanne: Yes, yes, exactly.

Julian: I also love the way you said that as a theological educator, you don't engage—or try not to engage—in cancel culture. You didn't say "cancel culture," but you did use the word "cancellation." The cancellations seemed to be foreclosing possibilities of encounter: of rigor, engagement, and hospitality. You didn't use any of those words exactly, but I think you were getting at them when you referenced your "pedagogical sensibilities."

Joanne: Yes, you refer to the original hope that PAAC would have "room for everyone at any stage of the journey"— not just be a space for people that met "x, y, z criteria."

Grace: Yeah, that quote was from cofounder Liz Lin.

Joanne: While PAAC sought to embody progressiveness, it's possible that this approach may have also contributed to its difficulties. This tension is apparent throughout the text.

Grace: Yeah.

Joanne: I think that might also [have been] part of PAAC's demise. Sometimes we fall victim to the very thing that we're trying to defend and stand for, and then we ourselves become the oppressor. So I love Lin's concept of progressive theology being more of an "orientation" and a "direction" where the community is heading, not a set of orthodoxy tests.

Julian: And where theological education is a place where you must actually contend with the person in front of you. . . . I can't cancel a student, even if their premise, like you said, is "offensive." I love that line. I love that line. That line is hot!

Grace: Thank you, Julian! But, real talk: I felt some kind of way about those moderator decisions. I mean, I appreciate and affirm why PAAC moderators eventually disallowed some questions and topics. But still, I run my classroom differently. Are you in spaces where some questions and topics just can't be broached?

Julian: I'm in different kinds of spaces, but cancel culture is real. So, to Joanne's point: the irony is that I have been in evangelical spaces that function the same way but in the opposite direction. And maybe that gets to a deeper meta-claim about religion and enforcement. Because I don't think you can have religion without some kind of enforcement.

What I was curious about was how you regarded this as theological education. After all, PAAC didn't have a formal curriculum. It didn't have a formal structure. So what does it mean for us to create these kinds of communities that are Internet-based but also have these in-person components?

Joanne: Yes, what do you think this means for theological education, beyond just the future of PAAC? It seems like you're speaking to both theological education and the Asian American community. Liz Lin's vision of creating a space where people wouldn't feel the need to "turn down the volume on either our ideology or our cultural experiences" is not only inspiring but also fundamental.

Grace: For sure. In having experienced PAAC as a space where many of us could finally bring *all* of ourselves to the table without needing to self-censor or conform to alien standards, one wonders why any of us stayed with inferior alternatives for so long. And, going forward, what kinds of local communities we will or won't be willing to invest in.

Julian: Grace, could there be a seminary that comes out of PAAC?

Grace: Oh, interesting! I have literally never thought of that! I mean, creating a seminary would involve creating a new institution. With degrees. And accreditation. And payroll. But PAAC is so grassroots where the model is basically gig work: give one sermon and receive an honorarium, lead a ten-week intentional community and receive a stipend, etc.

Joanne: It's possible to discuss the idea of a theological institution, but I believe more emphasis should be placed on the theological education that has already occurred through the existing model. When you consider the names, participants, and individuals involved, it becomes clear that PAAC was already offering remarkable theological education.

Grace: Yeah.

Joanne: I mean, you're referring to theological educators who were already writing and influencing.

Julian: I love what you were saying, Joanne! I don't know how the connective tissue is really being threaded between all the essays [in this volume]. After all, there are different stakes in the ground, but think of Juan Molina's essay about MACC [the Mexican American Catholic College]. Now MACC is more fully institutionalized and has been around longer. But there are similarities. Such as that MACC came from the community it serves. It saw a need. It was more interested in serving that community than in securing ATS accreditation. I think that's what I care about more than a seminary—surfacing the theological education already present.

Joanne: Absolutely.

Julian: And MACC continues to train people to be faithful lay leaders. Some people go on to become priests, but it's not like the school is only valid because of them. The fact is that MACC is committed to educating the full range of leaders—of every kind—that the community needs. It is doing faithful work within a slightly different matrix of concerns than other schools. So I really want to hold to what Joanne is picking up about PAAC: there was no formal training for it, even though people were formally trained. And there's also no formal end. There's no certificate from PAAC that says you are done, qualified, trained. So as I think about it, that's so critical to hold on to, because once a movement becomes institutionalized as something like an accredited school, then you have to have some sort of end point. Perhaps what you're after is a less goal-oriented kind of formation then, a "direction" or "orientation," to harken back to a point in your essay.

On another note: Is there any way you can talk about a theology of technology? It's a huge piece of where theory is going. A real question that emerges for theological education, and Willie Jennings talks about this in his work *After Whiteness*, is the extent to which we are beholden to the places where we are. Now the Internet problematizes that, because in a way it is placeless but then also creates a new place. So you have the space that was this Facebook group. But even you saw that being contested because younger cats like me ain't really on Facebook.

Grace: Yeah.

Julian: But like, Yo!, what does Facebook mean for theological education? Facebook? What does this kind of digital platform do, given the way it's been connected to all of these alt-right movements? It's helped foment all kinds of dissent. It censors people, it has algorithms. How is this a way of creating what's important in theological education? And how does it sever people's relationship to where they are?

So this I found really fascinating. Facebook was this oasis for all these cats who felt marginalized and maybe in some ways disaffected in their respective local communities. And all these Asian cats are standing up for racial justice and other social justice concerns. But the conversation about racial advocacy or trans folk in LA is gonna look real different than it does elsewhere. And if people are spending their discretionary time on Facebook, what does it mean for the people that they're with day to day?

Grace: I've so much to say in response! This is also something we've been talking about in another group I'm part of—PANAAWTM (the Pacific, Asian, and North American Asian Women in Theology and Ministry network). It's not simply that the younger generation are on Snapchat or Instagram instead. It's like, do you really want Facebook to be the holding space for community when it has been guilty of various things, like pushing out misinformation or harvesting personal data, as in the Cambridge Analytica scandal? But what are the alternatives? Instagram is popular, but it's not really a space where you can build community. I do know of some groups (e.g., Evolving Faith) that are using something called "Mighty Networks" to build community; it's run on a subscription service, so it's not free, but it's an amazing platform. So the future of PAAC might be connected in this other way to the future of theological education, especially since so much of what we're doing in both is hybrid. I mean, I myself went from teaching 100 percent in-person when I started working at my seminary in 2009 to now teaching primarily online, with only occasional in-person intensives. This hybrid model seems to be here to stay.

Joanne: I'd like to challenge that idea a bit—hear me out.

Grace: Yeah, okay, bring it!

Joanne: I believe the absence of a theology of technology that Julian is addressing may have contributed to the gradual decline of the work being done in PAAC. . . . You suggest "The reason behind that was COVID."

Grace: Right.

Joanne: That could be the main reason. . . . But if there had been a theological framework supporting PAAC's theology of technology, then that structure—even if loose—could have strengthened the bonds of community among PAAC members. This relational capital could have enabled PAAC to better withstand the challenges posed by COVID and even thrive in the aftermath of the pandemic.

Julian: Ultimately, Grace, what are the theological claims you want to make? It's very easy to read this story through the lens of sin and fall. It's the Garden of Eden, or it's Jericho, or it's Jerusalem. People are getting kicked out. People are struggling. People are in need of God's grace.

But these cats were still contending with wherever they were living, and had to figure out, okay, can we go to this Presbyterian church today or this year? Then, you know, the First Progressive Church of LA opened. So there were brick-and-mortar places. But in some cases, the churches that some individuals were a part of were more conservative.

Grace: And they couldn't or can't, and I can't—

Julian: I can't cancel them, and they can't cancel me [in a brick-and-mortar place] in the same way that a cat who asked a certain kind of question about sex and marriage online may get canceled. I'm not interested in cancellation, because I think all of us, you know, any one of us could or should be canceled if based on some shifting dynamic or metric. I'm just thankful that God hasn't canceled me!

Grace: I love it. Oh, I love it. That might make it into the dialogue for the book!

Julian: I'm thankful that God hasn't canceled me.

2

Restoring Self-Gift to Catholic Priestly Formation

John Kartje

> The scribes and the Pharisees brought a woman who had been caught in adultery; and making her stand before all of them, they said to [Jesus], "Teacher, this woman was caught in the very act of committing adultery." (John 8:3–4 NRSV)

We begin this chapter with a cautionary parable.

On a late summer day, the seminary faculty and administration had gathered as they did every year before the start of the fall semester for what was labeled a "retreat." In spite of the expectation that all should attend, several had customarily found reasons to be absent. After the celebration of Mass, the order of business was typically just that: administrative business to be tended to, like updates in policies and procedures, the introduction of new committee chairs, etc.

But then something happened. *Someone* happened.

Right after lunch, seminary leaders invited a young woman into the meeting to address the group. The gathered assembly clearly did not recognize her, although she had worked for several years at one of the parish pastoral placement sites used by the seminary and had even given a public witness talk at a recent fund-raising event for the school. She introduced herself by noting that, after attaining her master of divinity degree, she had worked her entire professional career for the church, serving in multiple capacities at four parishes within the diocese. She listed impressive accomplishments that included the founding of new school programs and the rapid growth of young adult ministry. Now, as a mother of two young children, she was striving with her husband to raise their family on a firm faith foundation within the church she loved.

This was the sort of narrative in which the seminary delighted—happy, accomplished men and women, serving their parishes and working alongside their pastors for the betterment of the church and the wider community. The faculty could take pride that their graduates were helping to form faith environments in which such people could thrive.

And then, at first with a soft, nervous laugh, the woman slowly found her voice and in measured tones shared that she had been abused by several priests at multiple assignments over her relatively brief tenure. Not "that kind" of abuse, she was quick to add, but abuse nonetheless: verbal, emotional, spiritual, and psychological. She had been yelled at by priests in parish staff meetings, humiliated before school boards, and told that she did not bring adequate value to the parish for her part-time position to be elevated to full-time, despite working well over forty hours most weeks. And she had witnessed others receiving similar or worse treatment from these same priests: lack of availability, harsh and condescending attitudes, dismissiveness and anger when approached with legitimate criticism, and so on.

Eventually, her voice started to shake, and she fought hard to hold back tears. She kept reaffirming that she loved her church and wanted nothing more than to share it with her family—but she was now seriously doubting whether that same church could be a place where she felt safe and nurtured, or a place where her gifts would be welcomed and stewarded.

She knew enough of theology to realize that this was not the fruit of the Holy Spirit animating the body of Christ. She knew enough of humanity to realize that such abusive behavior evinced a terrible lack of freedom and compassion, likely rooted in unresolved shame and fear of vulnerability. She knew enough of the church to realize that it ought not to require a lone messenger standing before an entire seminary faculty for this revelation to emerge.

All those in the room were visibly moved. One asked in what year these priests had been ordained. "None more than ten years ago," she said, upending the common perception that such behavior is typically found among older priests who did not receive such quality seminary formation as is given today. Another asked which seminary these priests had attended. "Yours," the woman replied softly. Someone asked whether these bad experiences had all happened at one parish—thinking that perhaps we were hearing about the influence of one bad pastor on his resident associates. No, the woman's experiences had been with different priests at different sites.

The encounter was as brief as it was profound. For just a slight moment the faculty and administrators had the opportunity to discern whether they bore any responsibility for what was transpiring before them. Then the moment was gone. The woman thanked them for listening and left the meeting, alone. Back in the room, the members shared a few comments of shock, anger, or disappointment over the behavior of "these young priests." But none bent down to write in the sand. And none arose to leave, one by one, in contemplative silence.

A Systemic Problem

The above encounter has haunted me from that day to this. When I invited the woman, one of my spiritual directees, to join our meeting, I knew that all of us collectively needed to be in the room. There could be no space for a comfortable escape into divisions of "teaching faculty versus administrators" or "ordained versus laity." We had each played a role in the painful life experience of this dedicated servant of the church, even as each of us lived within our own complex history as seminary formators (e.g., the laywomen faculty in a Catholic seminary have journeyed, and continue to journey, on a road markedly different from that of their priest faculty colleagues).[1]

While the Catholic Church has been wracked by the emergence of egregious scandals concerning the sexual abuse of minors dating back many decades, the type of abuse described above is, I fear, even more widespread and pervasive, and often overlooked or reluctantly tolerated. It was not until I began serving as a seminary rector, and complaints of such poor behavior regularly made their way to my in-box, that I fully realized how infrequently faculty or administrators acknowledged or addressed these abusive encounters with recently ordained—or not-so-recently ordained—priests. Because they often manifest only after ordination, such behaviors can too easily be blamed on circumstances outside of a priest's seminary tenure.[2]

The very fact that it is often difficult to identify priest candidates who are likely to react in such emotionally abusive ways after ordination ought to alert us to a potential flaw in the seminary system itself. Although the reasons for such behavior can certainly not be traced solely to a seminary formation program, it would be a mistake to focus only on the failings of particular problematic seminarians. Rather, we ought to be questioning whether the entire program of classroom pedagogy and human formation within the Catholic seminary tradition (largely unchanged since the Council of Trent in the sixteenth century) is somehow lacking in significant ways.

The identification of systems-wide failings in the church is not new. In their recent study of clergy-perpetrated sexual abuse, Julie Rubio and Paul Schutz from the Jesuit School of Theology at Santa Clara University argued that this tragic problem does not spring from the actions of lone "bad apples" within an otherwise healthy organization, but rather that it is the product of systemic "clericalism," a condition they define as "a structure of power that isolates clergy and sets priests above and apart, granting them excessive authority, trust, rights, and responsibilities while diminishing the agency of lay people and religious."[3] While not claiming that clericalism inevitably leads to sexual abuse, Rubio and Schutz note that it significantly contributes to an ecclesial foundation from which such abuse can arise, and that it is always contrary to the intended mission of the church of Jesus Christ. Catherine Clifford, professor of theology at Saint Paul University in Ottawa, describes clericalism as "a sad distortion of priesthood, an attitude of exceptionalism that conceives of the ordained as belonging to a separate caste, untainted by the quotidian holiness of ordinary Christian discipleship. As [Pope] Francis describes it, clericalism tries to 'replace, or silence, or ignore, or reduce the People of God to small elites.'"[4] Although I do not intend to address clericalism per se in this essay, the type of behavior that the guest at our faculty meeting had endured provides a striking example. If clericalism is a problem that grows out of systemic shortcomings in the church, then any systemic reform ought to include the seminary system. In particular, seminary formation programs ought never to foster an environment in which a priest's clerical "authority, trust, rights, and responsibilities" are perceived as standing over and above those of the laity for whom, and with whom, he serves.

While great strides have been made in recent decades regarding attention to the healthy emotional and psychological assessment and development of priest candidates, more remains to be done. My intention here is to look beyond those programs within seminary formation that are specifically focused on human development—such as counseling, psychological testing, or preparation for healthy celibate living—and seek out more foundational issues, exploring to what extent an accurate understanding of Christian anthropology pervades the basic pedagogy and community life within Catholic seminaries today. By focusing on some of the core documents and teachings surrounding the structure of seminary education, we shall find that many of the most significant principles proposed within the last fifty years for the process of priestly formation have yet to be fully developed and integrated into the Catholic seminary system.

INTEGRAL FORMATION: WHOLE PERSON, WHOLE CHURCH

Nearly sixty years ago, the Second Vatican Council produced a document on the training of priests, *Optatam Totius*. It describes a seminary as the "heart of the diocese" that it serves.[5] Relating this metaphor to Paul's image of the body of Christ comprising multiple members, none of which is freestanding or self-sufficient (cf. 1 Cor. 12:20–23), we might conclude that the heart is the organ most intimately related to all other parts. If the seminary is truly to function as the heart of the local church, then it must be intimately connected to it. Ideally, that relationship is meant to be mutually enriching, with the seminarians receiving critical formation from their interaction with parish congregations in a way that they could never receive within the seminary's walls. In short, there would be an ongoing symbiotic connection between the seminary and the diocese that transcends both parish and seminary boundaries.

This vision is vividly manifested in the Catholic Rite of Ordination for Priests. During that liturgy, the ordaining bishop engages in a scripted exchange with the seminary rector, who tells him: "After inquiry among the Christian people and upon the recommendation of those responsible, I testify that they [the *ordinands*] have been found worthy [to serve as priests of Jesus Christ]." It is assumed that "those responsible" include the seminary faculty. But actually the language of the rite is much broader than that: it refers to an inquiry "among the Christian people." If taken seriously, this reply can only be made in good faith if the seminary and the parishes of the diocese are working in close cooperation to accompany the man along his formational journey.

To accomplish this vision, what we need is a process that has come to be known in seminary formation documents as *integral formation*. "Integral" in this context refers to both the interior integration of the seminarian himself (i.e., his mature emotional, psychological, intellectual, and spiritual development) and the integration of the seminary formation process into the diocese(s) that it serves (i.e., the quality of the coordination between the seminary's mission, objectives, and pedagogical methodologies and the diocese's parishes and administration/leadership—and vice versa).

The Catholic Church hierarchy has only recently acknowledged the centrality of integral formation. This acknowledgment calls for an accurate understanding of the human person, which in turn should produce effective teaching methods throughout the seminary system. The Congregation for the Clergy's document *Ratio Fundamentalis Institutionis Sacerdotalis* (*The Gift of the Priestly Vocation*), which outlines the governance of all Catholic seminaries worldwide, underscores this point: "The concept of integral formation is of the greatest importance, since it is the whole person, with all that he is and all that he possesses, who will be at the Lord's service in the Christian community. The one called is an '*integral subject*,' namely someone who has been previously chosen to attain a sound interior life, without divisions or contradictions. It is necessary to adopt an *integrated pedagogical model* in order to reach this objective: a journey that allows the formative community to cooperate with the action of the Holy Spirit."[6] Insofar as pedagogy builds upon anthropology, the fact that a proper understanding of Christian anthropology has yet to be fully woven into Catholic priestly formation has greatly impeded the design and implementation of an integrated seminary pedagogy. Sadly, both shortcomings have contributed substantially to the type of abusive behavior described at the start of this essay. In what follows I will first expand upon the church's call for the seminarian to be an "integral person" and will then explore how an "integral pedagogy"—executed by "integrated *pedagogues*" (i.e., an integrated faculty)—can help achieve that end.

BECOMING AN INTEGRAL PERSON: FROM SELF-KNOWLEDGE TO SELF-GIFT

Consider the well-known foot-washing scene in the Gospel of John.[7] When Jesus approaches Peter with the seemingly compassionate and generous desire to offer him a kind service, Peter abruptly responds with a rude rebuke: "You will never wash my feet" (John 13:8 NRSV). He is so overcome by the power of his feelings (which may include confusion, disappointment, or shame) that he openly rejects Jesus's intentions and undercuts the possibility for authentic relationship and connection with him at that moment. He is incapable of grasping the central lesson of Jesus's self-sacrificial love because he cannot make sense of it within his own personal worldview in which his master ought never to wash his servant's feet.

In the language of the *Ratio Fundamentalis*, one could say that Peter is "poorly integrated" insofar as his present emotional experience cannot be properly assimilated with what he knows about Jesus from his shared relationship with him over the entire time they have been together. When his familiar relationship is challenged by a new experience, the vulnerability of the trust he had developed with Jesus is exposed and stretched to the breaking point.

The exchange between Jesus and Peter at the foot-washing scene illustrates a core principle of Christian anthropology, which is still not adequately appreciated by seminary formators: affective movements of the heart are as constitutive of the human person as are the intellect and the will. This is not a mere philosophical footnote, for it underscores the entire trajectory that programs of priestly formation have historically been designed to follow. A seminary formation program with a poor grasp of the foundational importance of human affectivity can result in priests who are emotionally underdeveloped and often unable to relate compassionately to the people to whom they have been sent and whom they are to serve and care for. When that condition is combined with the remarkable power of governance that Canon Law assigns to Catholic priests in their parishes, priests can visit serious spiritual and emotional harm upon the people of God.

For centuries, following Aristotelian/Thomistic theories, the Catholic Church basically understood the identity of the human person to be located in the faculties of the intellect and will, powers then presumed unique to human beings.[8] The emotions or passions the church relegated to the "sensitive" powers, which humans share with animals. With the development of phenomenology and personalist philosophy in the nineteenth and twentieth centuries, this perspective was increasingly challenged. Writing in 1965, Dietrich von Hildebrand lamented that "the secondary place assigned to the sphere of affectivity and to the heart have remained, strangely enough, a more or less noncontroversial part of our philosophical heritage. The entire affective sphere was for the most part subsumed under the heading of passions, and as long as one dealt with it expressly under this title, its irrational and nonspiritual character was emphasized."[9]

By assigning a lesser importance to the affective sphere (compared to the intellect and will), seminary formation programs in the years prior to the Second Vatican Council placed an excessive emphasis on strict obedience to what was known as the seminary "rule," which included a code of conduct as well as the daily *horarium*. Beyond classroom studies, adherence to the rule constituted the primary form of priestly preparation. In his study of the history of human formation in Catholic seminaries, Robert Anello, former associate director of human formation at Sacred Heart Seminary in Wisconsin, noted that the rule was "associated with an emphasis on obedience and docility . . . governing every hour and aspect of seminary formation. A classic saying regarding obedience to the rule was, 'if you keep the rule, it will keep you.'"[10] The church placed little emphasis on emotional or psychological development, and it sought to keep seminarians largely isolated from life outside the seminary walls, with tight restrictions on visits from family or friends and limited involvement in parish ministry.

While most of these restrictions were considerably relaxed in the years following the Council, and seminary faculty paid increasing attention to psychology and other understandings of basic human development, the church still implicitly and predominantly adhered to the traditional Thomistic anthropology.[11]

Thus it woefully undervalued the significance of affectivity in the human person.

Such an anthropology is incomplete, even deficient. The feelings of the heart are not "wild horses" to be constrained, but rather unique powers, along with those of the intellect and will, to be fully integrated into one's personhood. This truth is grounded in the biblical concept of the human person created in the image and likeness of God (Gen. 1:26), the human person for whom relationship with God is as constitutive of their personhood as is the earth and divine breath from which they are made (cf. Gen. 2:7). A seminal document from the Second Vatican Council, *Gaudium et Spes*, strongly affirms this sentiment: "God did not create man [*sic*] as a solitary, for from the beginning 'male and female he created them' (Gen. 1:27). Their companionship produces the primary form of interpersonal communion. For by his innermost nature man is a social being, and *unless he relates himself to others he can neither live nor develop his potential.*"[12] A person's affectivity—their affections—without which authentic relationship with another is impossible, is an essential part of their humanity.

One of the most influential voices at the Council, particularly in the drafting of *Gaudium et Spes*, was that of the young philosopher and archbishop of Krakow, Karol Wojtyla, who, upon being elected pope in 1978, took the name John Paul II. In the homily of his inaugural Mass as pope he included the powerful line: "The absolute and yet sweet and gentle power of the Lord responds to the whole depths of the human person, to his loftiest aspirations of *intellect, will, and heart.* It does not speak the language of force but expresses itself in charity and truth."[13] It is likely that a philosopher as accomplished as Karol Wojtyla intentionally added "heart" to the traditional pairing of "intellect and will" as a means of drawing attention to the centrality of affectivity within the human person. This would be in keeping with the entire trajectory of his academic writing, a unique strain within the larger scope of personalist philosophy for which philosopher Juan Burgos of the University San Pablo CEU, Madrid has coined the name "integral personalism."[14] He contends that Wojtyla was creating a new path "based on an integral concept of experience, meaning that experience contains, simultaneously, objective and subjective elements. The *objective* elements come from the knowledge and perception of the world external to the subject, and the *subjective* elements come from our own intimate world of subjectivity. . . . And that there are two different levels of primary knowledge: experience and understanding."[15]

After his election as pope, Wojtyla applied his integral personalism in a call to advance the reforms of the Catholic seminary system that had begun with the Second Vatican Council. In 1989 he gathered the world's Catholic bishops to a synod "on the formation of priests in the circumstances of the present day." A preparatory document drafted by the bishops before the synod met warned that "nothing is more dangerous, nothing is more harmful, than the priest who has little or minimal maturity—'Woe to the nation whose prince is a little child,' we read in the Book of Ben Sirach (10:17)—on account of his [the priest's] youthful spirit, he is able to corrupt human consciences and lives."[16]

The summary document produced by the synod was titled *Pastores Dabo Vobis* (the opening words of the Latin Vulgate translation of Jer. 3:15, "*I will give you shepherds* after my own heart"). The document is a landmark among the modern seminary formation literature insofar as it elevates the goals of human formation (which encompasses the principles of Wojtyla's integral personalism) as "the basis of all priestly formation."[17] Thus, the foundational aim of seminary formation is the fundamental development of the human person, upon which are based all other aims such as the acquisition of theological knowledge, growth in the practice of contemplative prayer, etc.

In his writings on seminary formation, John Paul II noted that to achieve a high level of personal integration one must reach a state of "affective maturity." While this term is used widely in seminary literature, it is rarely explicitly defined. Thomas Cheruparambil, a formator at St. Joseph's Pontifical Seminary in Aluva, India, defines it thus: "Affective maturity is the capacity to manage emotions constructively and smoothly. It requires awareness about one's emotions, especially negative ones, due appreciation and acceptance of them as part of self and the ability to control them reasonably. Many of the pastoral problems arise due to the mismanagement of emotions."[18] John Paul II contended that "affective maturity, which is the result of an education in true and responsible love, is a significant and decisive factor in the formation of candidates for the priesthood," and that it "presupposes an awareness that love has a central role in human life."[19] Nearly twenty-five years later, the Congregation for the Clergy reaffirmed this, saying, "It would be gravely imprudent to admit to the sacrament of Orders a seminarian who does not enjoy free and serene affective maturity."[20]

Affectively mature persons know themselves well enough that they can recognize the emotions and feelings that well up within their heart in a given situation. In addition to recognizing their emotional state, they are also aware of how such emotions affect their own personal proclivities and vulnerabilities (e.g., their emotional "triggers"), which are the product of numerous influences over the course of their life, such as family of origin and traumatic encounters. Armed with this self-knowledge, affectively mature persons can appropriately regulate their emotions and feelings and properly integrate them into their reaction to the situation at hand. Thus, affective distress does not "hijack" or overwhelm them and render them either immobile or out of control. If they are interacting with another person, they are able to respond with empathy or compassion.

Affective maturity therefore is a requisite quality for the exercise of pastoral charity. For John Paul II, pastoral charity is the singular unifying principle at the heart of the priesthood, for it unites the priest to Christ himself: "The internal principle, the force which animates and guides the spiritual life of the priest inasmuch as he is configured to Christ the head and shepherd, is pastoral charity, as a participation in Jesus Christ's own pastoral charity,"[21] he wrote.

Thus the well-formed priest is an integral person who embodies affective maturity and loves with pastoral charity. The fruit of exercising such charity is the ability to adopt Christ's own radical gift of self in love for the other: "Pastoral charity is the virtue by which we imitate Christ in his self-giving and service. It is not just what we do, but our gift of self, which manifests Christ's love for his flock. Pastoral charity determines our way of thinking and acting, our way of relating to people. It makes special demands on us."[22]

It is noteworthy that, twenty years before *Pastores Dabo Vobis*, the Second Vatican Council had already affirmed that to live as self-gift is not only a means by which to imitate Christ but also a constitutive element of fundamental anthropology: "the human person . . . can attain its full identity only in sincere self-giving (cf. Luke 17:33)."[23]

Drawing upon the writings of the Council, *Pastores Dabo Vobis*, and the *Ratio Fundamentalis*, the Catholic bishops of the United States integrated the qualities of affective maturity, pastoral charity, and self-gift into their *Program of Priestly Formation*, formulating the triad of "Self-Knowledge, Self-Possession, Self-Gift." The progression from self-knowledge to self-gift provides a map for the entire journey through seminary, which "is a gradual process of growth that integrates both the human and spiritual life of the man and leads to a deepening of interior freedom."[24] With this freedom, one can embrace in one's own life the self-sacrificial love manifested by Christ in the paschal mystery (cf. John 13:34 and 15:13).

Presumably none of the priests who abused the woman described at the beginning of this essay woke up one morning and decided that they wanted to cause harm to the body of Christ. They likely never envisioned that they would react with such bitterness and spite toward colleagues in ministry, or that they would so abuse their privileges of gender and authority. But somehow, they left seminary formation with a clear lack of affective maturity. Perhaps they were overwhelmed by stresses in their ministry; perhaps they felt embarrassed or ashamed in the face of more accomplished nonordained colleagues; perhaps they were simply acting out of attitudes of selfishness and entitlement. Whatever the reasons, they are not excuses but egregious instances of clericalism. These priests' behaviors evinced their inability to recognize and regulate negative emotions or attitudes within themselves. And they certainly failed to offer love self-sacrificially and become a gift of self to others.

Over the last half century, the Catholic Church has provided eloquent and beautiful documents describing the desired outcomes of priestly formation. While many of these outcomes are being met, there yet remains an elusive goal: an *integral pedagogy* that respects a true sense of integral anthropology, that is, a pedagogy that presumes that every facet of seminary formation necessarily contributes to the development of an integral person, possessed of affective maturity, and willingly embracing the opportunities to live as a gift for others while receiving the other as a gift to himself.

INTEGRAL PEDAGOGY: CLASSROOM AS PARISH, PARISH AS CLASSROOM

An authentic integral pedagogy for Catholic seminaries must be predicated on the fact that the laity have an irreplaceable role in the formation and theological education of their priests. And yet this truth is implicitly undermined by the very language used to describe priestly formation. The word "seminary" itself implies a pedagogical model that is easily overlooked because it has become so familiar. Etymologically, the word means seedbed or nursery, a place where seedlings are carefully protected and nurtured in a manner they would not likely receive "in the wild." Only when the gardener deems them sufficiently hardy are they transplanted into the more natural environments for which they are intended. From that point on, they will either thrive or fail in their new territory; neither their familiar seedling neighbors nor their benevolent gardener is with them anymore.

True to this image, the Catholic Church often operates its seminaries in the same way. Seminarians spend most of their time on the seminary grounds, living only with each other and their priest formators. They likely spend a few hours each week serving in a local parish, but faculty often regard that time as depriving the students of precious hours they could (or should) be spending in the classroom or library. The expectation is that seminarians spend their time "being prepared" at the seminary. Then, after ordination, they are ready to be sent out to be with the people.

This mind-set not only falsely assumes that "pastoral time" in the parish somehow competes against "intellectual time" in the classroom, it also fails to honor the anthropology described above. There is no better environment for the future priest to engage in encounters that are likely to push him to seek deeper self-awareness than among the very people (priests and laypersons) among whom he is preparing to live and with whom he will be serving.

Far from making the seminary less relevant, more intentional time in parish ministry would significantly enhance the efficacy of the seminary's unique function. As a seminarian gains self-knowledge about his strengths and vulnerabilities, he can better leverage the unique formational assets that only the seminary can provide (such as spiritual directors, counselors, and priest mentors) to grow in the ability to manage and integrate his emotions in a healthy way. He will profit much more from these services by processing real-life experiences than case studies or staged scenarios that are only encountered in the classroom. Furthermore, his intellectual formation will be significantly enhanced insofar as his parish encounters will give rise to more relevant questions and observations with which to engage the theological tradition.

Most important of all, by being among the people of God in a parish setting, the seminarian will learn to offer, and to receive, self-sacrificial love in a manner more configured to the heart of Christ than he would by only interacting with the population of his classmates, all of whom are living within the highly structured, homogenous environment of the seminary campus. The diversity of encounters in the parish will expose him to the joys and struggles of marriage, parenting, career changes, grieving losses, intergenerational issues, and the like. The value of these encounters is not simply (or even primarily) that he will gain valuable experience and pastoral skills, important as those are. The primary value of these encounters is that they are the catalyst for the seminarian to progress in his mastery of self-knowledge, self-possession, and self-gift. Rather than recoiling from the vulnerability that is demanded in any authentic interpersonal engagement, a seminarian who has been formed as an integral person will be more willing to give of himself to another in pastoral charity and to receive the other as a gift to himself.

And yet, even if more focused time were devoted to acquiring and processing parish encounters, the seminary formation system would fail to provide a fully integrated pedagogical model unless the academic faculty and intellectual formation programs were also reformed. Notwithstanding the encouraging language of seminary formation documents about the equal importance of academic, pastoral, and spiritual pursuits within priestly formation,[25] the reality is that most time, energy, and importance in priestly formation programs are devoted to academic pursuits, as much as 70 to 80 percent, according to a recent study.[26] The solution to any such imbalance is not necessarily to spend less time in the classroom, but rather to do a better job at integrating how knowledge is being conveyed and received.[27]

Furthermore, faculty members themselves often need to grow in their embrace of self-knowledge, self-possession, and self-gift. They were almost certainly not trained to have this mind-set as they pursued their own advanced studies. The seminary faculty described at the opening of this essay clearly had little capacity for extending themselves in compassion as a gift to the suffering woman before them. Until faculties begin experiencing this kind of paradigm shift within their own ranks, the integral pedagogy called for by the *Ratio Fundamentalis* will remain elusive.

CONCLUSION: THE SELF-GIFT GIVEN AND RECEIVED

Any priest who fails to practice self-knowledge and self-possession will invariably fail to bring the gift of self-sacrificial love to others, often with the abusive consequences that my colleagues and I witnessed at our faculty meeting. It is only from within the worldview shaped by self-gift that a seminarian can be formed as a true disciple of Jesus Christ. Only from such an embrace of authentic personhood might a stressed priest look with compassion at a parishioner who presents to him a challenging pastoral need or an angry demand. This ability of a priest to extend his own compassionate heart as a gift, and to receive the cries of a wounded heart—also as gift—provides the powerful antidote to the type of clericalism decried earlier.

The embrace of identity as self-gift does not happen automatically. It begins with a seminary formation program that requires an integral pedagogy that is built upon a proper anthropology, one that assumes an integral person. Only then can the Catholic Church be receptive to the fulfillment of God's promise: not just that "I will give you shepherds," but that the shepherds given will truly be "after my own heart."

Dialogue

John Kartje, Ann Killian, OP, Caleb Maskell

Ann: I was struck by the interplay between the story of the woman caught in adultery and your opening story about the faculty retreat. The woman in your story isn't really the equivalent of the woman in adultery because she hasn't done anything wrong. It's the young priests who have misbehaved who are equivalent to the adulterous woman, but then the story seems to be really indicting the seminary faculty and administrators. Like the seminarians, they are somewhat contained within a seminary bubble, with limited connection to the outside world of the church. And they're in a position of considerable power over the men they are forming. What should we do about that?

John: That's a key concern, and it's the reason why we focus so much on facilitating the encounters between the seminarians and laypersons in actual parishes, to try and expand (even if we can't entirely burst) the bubble to which you refer.

But to return to your observations about the opening story. I agree that it's complex in its relation to the account from John's Gospel. There is no intentional one-to-one mapping between the various characters, but I was struck by the nature and (ab)use of power, as well as the opportunity for compassion, in both scenarios. And in every case the dynamic flow of the narrative is driven by encounter: whether between the elders and the woman in adultery or between our faculty and the laywoman. The difference is whether the encounter leads to the ability to look at yourself honestly or not.

Caleb: I'd like to follow up on that and get to the heart of the affective maturity framework that you construct. As a non–Roman Catholic, one of the things I love about the Catholic Church is its ability to formulate such clean, lovely, lapidary phrases to describe a concept as complex as "affective maturity," and I find that very helpful. I'm thinking of the definition of affective maturity that you quoted [from Fr. Thomas Cheruparambil]. On the one hand, I can see that in the eyes of the pope and the Congregation for the Clergy it would be gravely imprudent to admit to the Sacrament of Orders a seminarian who does not enjoy free and serene affective maturity. But on the other hand, I think about my own, often stumbling, journey toward maturity as a man in his forties. I'm aware that there remain many things I'm still learning about myself in that arena to which I don't think I had any access for even asking the right sorts of questions when I was in my twenties. So, to be blunt, do you really think that anyone—Roman Catholic seminarian or not—should be allowed to be a pastor before they reach about the age of forty? Perhaps the deeper question concerns how age and experience play into any of this cultivation. Are there limits to what a seminary can accomplish in light of that larger anthropological challenge?

John: Well, I have about fifteen years on you, and I wouldn't say that my own journey toward affective maturity is anywhere near completed! You are putting your finger on an important point: the language in these church documents often seems a far cry from reality. And yet, that's partly the point. It serves as an ideal or a goal, to provide both guideposts and an objective for the formation process. Maybe its best use would be to induce some healthy humility. That's why we're trying to draw in the lay parishioners to function as formators themselves. Such a self-image is very foreign to most of them, largely due to the great authority that Canon Law cedes to the ordained pastor in a parish. It can create a mind-set in which the laity are overly passive. For example, I've seen the CEO of a highly successful business totally defer to the decisions of his young parish priest in areas in which he has vastly more experience and wisdom, such as finances or personnel management. That culture of deference can be devastating, both materially and spiritually. We need to build up a parishioner identity in which the laity can confidently convey to the pastor that he has much to learn, and that they—while totally respecting his ordained charism—can help support him and guide him. As I note in the essay, the laity have an irreplaceable role in the ongoing formation of clergy.

Ann: So I'm wondering to what degree this reflects the lack of a supportive community with whom newly ordained priests can interact. It seems that once they leave the seminary, they are largely on their own. I know that I, as a fairly new teacher, am invested with much authority in the classroom. But if I make a decision that seems problematic, or that I have a question about, I can come home to a community of sisters who are my peers, to help me do the self-reflection and processing I need. These young priests need support, and I wonder whether they are getting it as part of the postseminary system.

Caleb: As part of that support, I'd like to return to what you were saying earlier about empowering the laity to be formators of the seminarians, and I presume, also to provide ongoing formation for their ordained priests. How do you think that would be facilitated? In an earlier conversation we were discussing the Synod on Synodality that Pope Francis has been leading. Its aim seems to be for everyone to become able to say what they have to say to each other, and for everyone to listen in the ways they ought to listen, and then to synthesize what they're hearing. But that very process seems vulnerable to breakdowns along political lines or along lines dividing who has, or lacks, authority and ruling status. So how do you actually make this *work*?

John: I would point us toward another of those idealized concepts in the Roman Catholic tradition: subsidiarity. Basically, it is the idea that every issue ought to be first addressed at the local level, and only then broadened from the bottom up. While synodality can be a huge challenge on the global scale, it has a much better chance of succeeding when it's based on interpersonal encounter among folks in a parish or neighborhood setting. But once again, the authority ceded to the pastor by Canon Law affects the success or failure of the synodal process. Ultimately, the pastor has the freedom to accept or reject what he is hearing from his parishioners, if he is listening at all. That's why affective maturity is so critically important: it takes an affectively mature person to be willing to impose self-limits to his or her vested authority in the interests of benefiting from the collective wisdom of a community. Moving outward—in the spirit of subsidiarity—from the scope of an individual parish to that of an entire diocese, the local bishop has a great deal of authority over how the parish priests govern their own congregations. But every bishop is himself the product of a seminary formation process. Hence the importance of getting this formation right, from the outset, cannot be overstated.

Ann: A common thread that is surfacing from the synod in Rome is that a lot of people are heartbroken. The church has really broken their hearts. But they love the church, they love their faith, they love being Catholic, and they truly care about the church. That's why they are coming to these synodal conversations. Their stories remind me of the harm that priests' emotional mismanagement can cause. So I'm wondering whether something like a "harms exercise" could be helpful here—yes, to think about a time that I have harmed someone through the abuse of my own power or social location, but also to reflect on when I have been harmed by others. Seminarians obviously love the church, but perhaps they also need to reflect on any times that the church has broken their heart, or that of someone they care about. When I think of my peers in religious life, a lot of us have been heartbroken by the church at some level. Knowing and admitting that can open you up to compassion, as well.

John: Absolutely. And one of the keys to a compassionate response in the face of hurtful behavior is the ability to hit the pause button, recognize what is happening within your own heart and mind, and then recalibrate your emotions. Those are skills you can teach. Sure, only in a limited way by the age of twenty-five or twenty-six, but you can build the foundation for a lifetime of ongoing formation.

Caleb: That is really accurate in my experience. You *can* learn how to get better at this process. But you don't see the need for it until you see it.

John: Which brings us back to the woman in adultery or my guest at the faculty meeting.

3

Experiencing Theological Education in Vowed Religious Life

Ann Killian, OP

Vowed religious life offers an experiential approach to theological education in which together members of a community come to know the living God. Since becoming a sister, I've found that our practices of contemplation, truth seeking, and collective care open our hearts to receive the Spirit's gifts of knowledge and understanding so that we may respond to the call to conversion. These spiritual practices are central to fulfilling our vows. They have a particular meaning in the context of vowed life, yet they hold wisdom for Christian theological education more generally because they are a way of imitating Jesus.

As sisters, we try to live as much like Jesus as possible in a twenty-first-century world. We read in the gospel that Jesus prioritized time to be alone before God. He centered his life on intimate relationship with the Father. Likewise, sisters spend time each day praying personally and in community. We take a vow of obedience, a word rooted in the Latin verb meaning "to listen." Listening for God's voice in the silence of our hearts, we ask to manifest God's love in and for the world. Following Jesus involves commitments that make no sense according to the capitalist logic of (re)production and consumption. In the gospel we read that Jesus made a highly unusual decision for a Jewish man born in first-century Palestine: he didn't marry or start a family. He left his father's carpentry trade and departed from his hometown to travel around preaching the good news that the poor are "to be poor no longer."[1] In a similar way, sisters take a vow of celibacy. We give over our lives to Jesus's mission, remaining totally available to go wherever God calls us to accompany, advocate, and care for the needs of Earth and our neighbors.

Now, Jesus didn't go around preaching on his own. He invited disciples to hit the road with him, including women, who shared their resources and extended hospitality. Jesus called his disciples friends and loved them as his chosen family until the end. They shared everything in common. Similarly, we sisters live together in community and take a vow of poverty, renouncing personal ownership of all goods. Upon profession, we close bank accounts, cancel credit cards, and liquidate personal assets. Our salaries go directly to the community. Economically, religious life models an equitable redistribution of wealth: each sister gives as she is able and receives according to her needs. We try to live simply and sustainably to walk lightly on Earth. By practicing the vows, and through the quality of our communal life, we bear witness to God's dream for a flourishing future.

Throwing in my lot, materially, with the women of my community was a radical choice—one that brings me surprising joy and freedom. Growing up, I never would have imagined dedicating my life to the gospel in such a countercultural way. When initially deciding to enter the community, I was not consciously setting out to imitate Jesus as closely as possible. Rather, I was looking for Catholics who were responding creatively to the Second Vatican Council's teaching that all the baptized are sent to carry on Christ's mission in the world. That search led me to sisters who had fully embraced the conciliar spirit of renewal. I thrilled to hear their stories of ministering in Catholic spaces as women leaders. What captured my heart, though, was the affectionate care they showed for one another and the warmth with which they embraced the people among whom they ministered. What I had seen and heard in their presence made real for me Jesus's words: "The Kingdom of God is among you" (Luke 17:21 NABR).

To say that sisters try to live as much like Jesus as possible is my best attempt to explain the vows as a path to joy and freedom.[2] Fewer women may elect this path today, yet those of us who do remain convinced that vowed life is a gift of the Spirit to our church and world. I write at a pivotal juncture, both in my personal journey and in our collective history as women religious. As a sister in temporary profession, I am integrating my experience of initial formation and preparing for final vows. This moment impels me to "give a reason for my hope" that God is calling me and my age-peers to this life for some definite purpose.[3] This essay attempts to name our desire for the future of vowed life and to trace the contours of our mission for this time in history. That mission has a tripartite shape: we are called to contemplative listening in a world of noise, to seeking and speaking truth in community, and to caring collectively for the whole of life. This threefold mission resonates with Pope Francis's exhortation to witness to the joy of the gospel and cultivate an integral ecology. In fidelity to that mission, we trust that vowed life will remain a vital and attractive option for Christian discipleship into the future.

To carry out this mission, women religious need a transformative theological education. Over the past ten years of discerning my vocation, I've received one both informally through tutorials with elder sisters on Scripture, Christology, and the Second Vatican Council and formally through graduate-level coursework. The goal of these studies is not to prepare me for a particular ministry but to provide a solid grounding for lifelong, vowed commitment. As an educator myself—I teach college writing—I've found that religious formation has changed my approach to teaching, emboldening me to bring spiritual practices of introspection and contemplative dialogue into the classroom. As a Dominican Sister, I've inherited the order's charism: to contemplate and share the fruits of one's contemplation. Embodying that charism means engaging in a theological education that invites my students into the communal search for Truth.

Ann Killian, OP

Attraction and Desire in Theological Education

Implicit in the Dominican charism is a belief that humans desire to learn truths about themselves and the world, and through this search they may come to know the One who is Truth. That desire for learning draws Christian disciples to theological education and opens them to its transformative possibilities. The gospel stories of Jesus calling the first disciples convey the attractive power of his person and teaching. A motley crew of fisherfolk and tax collectors, the first disciples respond to Jesus's invitation with unhesitating alacrity, a sign that they shared his ardent longing for the coming reign of God. Their life on the road with Jesus was as much of a theological education as was his ministry of preaching and healing. The experience of traveling together—unlikely companions on the journey—gave shape to their desire for communion, justice, and liberation.

The disciples' experience resonates with my own journey through initial formation, which has been impelled by desire for God and attraction to vowed life in community. When I first met the Dominican Sisters of Peace, their joy drew my heart like a magnetic force. That joy came from their intention to live in right relationship with God, each other, and Earth community. The sisters had recently opened a new house to welcome an incoming candidate, a woman in her thirties discerning whether God was calling her to enter. Six sisters moved in, ranging in age from thirty to eighty; they were Anglo, Vietnamese, Mexican, and Tanzanian. Together, they prayed, shared meals and conversation, and enjoyed life. Their prayer fostered mindfulness of the deep interconnectedness of life throughout the cosmos. They celebrated the gifts of their diverse cultures and held house meetings to work through different understandings of timeliness, hospitality, and prudent stewardship. They gardened, composted, and repurposed materials to reduce waste. The common life, I could see, provided support and accountability for individual and collective transformation. I joined them outside city hall to advocate for our migrant neighbors, for dinner on Tết to usher in the lunar

New Year, and for a talk on liberation theology by our Dominican brother, Fr. Gustavo Gutiérrez. The cultural, spiritual, and intellectual richness of these experiences pulled me in.

Lured by the promise of ongoing formation in Christian discipleship, I was drawn to religious life like a merchant to a pearl of great price. So, after completing my doctoral dissertation, I let go of my apartment and the independence it symbolized to move across the country, relinquishing my social location in a prestigious graduate program and opting not to pursue a research fellowship or faculty position so that I could enter the congregation as a candidate for admission. The venture felt risky, veering from the academic-career path to become a novice once again. Yet, as Christians, are we are not always beginning again on the path of discipleship? The need for adult faith formation remains lifelong. Vowed life embodies a theological education by way of friendship as sisters teach one another through faith-sharing and example. We learn together by reflecting on the Spirit's movements within and among us. Moreover, formal theological studies are desirable to deepen our relationship with God and prepare us to give public witness when we profess vows of self-dedication to God and God's people.

Study—another word for ongoing formation—is central to the charism of the Dominican family, that is, the Order of Preachers founded by Saint Dominic in the thirteenth century. Dominicans study Scripture, theology, and creation to seek truth, trusting Jesus's promise that the truth will set us free. During the renewal of religious life after the Second Vatican Council, Dominicans in Bolivia likened the order's charism to an oil lamp, an ancient symbol of wisdom and knowledge of God.[4] As oil keeps a lamp aflame, so the study of God's self-revelation fuels the fire of love. No one lights a lamp to hide it under a bushel basket; rather, they set it on a lampstand. In a similar way, we want the love of Christ to shine through our preaching—by which we mean more broadly our ministry and way of life. Theological studies help to keep our lamps trimmed and burning, though the night be long and dark. We do not keep vigil alone. As the beautiful mission statement of our common novitiate program puts it, "Becoming

Dominican is a lifelong, communal venture." The same might be said of Christian discipleship.

Asking to enter a congregation—ritually knocking at the door—begins a process of initial formation that lasts six to twelve years. There is a paradox at the heart of this process. On the one hand, those who enter arrive fully formed in an adult faith and self-understanding. This adult model of formation matters especially for women coming from cultural formations different from the dominant culture of their congregation. To paraphrase Sr. Thea Bowman, FSPA, candidates bring their whole selves—their history, traditions, and experiences—as gifts to the church.[5] It is incumbent upon formation directors to cherish each candidate and respect her complex identity, which is why this ministerial role demands training in cultural competence and frank discussions of power as well as regular peer supervision. On the other hand, entering a religious community and professing vows is meant to be transformative. Becoming a sister means taking on a new identity. In communion, persons committed to lifelong practice of the vows embrace a life-form grounded in contemplative listening that expands their bonds of kinship and enfleshes an economic model of interdependence, equity, and reciprocity.

This adult model remains essential to forming women religious with the capacity for living in healthy, intercultural communities oriented toward mission. As our congregations become smaller and redesign programs for initial and ongoing formation, I would invite us to lean into what Ted Smith describes as "the affordances of the present."[6] Religious life's emphasis on human development attracts people in this age to religious life, in part because it resonates with the cultural value placed on authenticity. Fashioning an "authentic self" involves disciples of Jesus in another paradoxical endeavor. On the one hand, discerning one's vocation and saying yes to the call is about fulfilling one's deepest desire. On the other hand, the Christian tradition distinguishes between the true self, identified with the Christ-self, and the false self of the ego. It uses the language, not of self-making, but of self-surrender, of losing oneself to take on the mind and heart of Christ. In a kind of transfigured authenticity, the goal of the Christian life is the discovery of who I am in God. Religious formation draws us deeper into this mystery that each sister is unique—in Dominican circles we like to say, when you've met one Dominican . . . you've met one Dominican—yet desire for union with the divine lures us toward self-transcendence.

One affordance of the present that may spark trepidation is the reality of changing demographics. Religious life is undergoing an epochal change as our population ages rapidly. The generation of sisters who entered right before the Second Vatican Council, now in their eighties, represent the largest cohort.[7] In ten to twenty years, sisters' lived reality will look drastically different. Navigating that demographic shift entails divesting the congregation of institutions and land—in other words, rightsizing to suit the smaller population of sisters who will journey into the future as a faithful remnant. The sisters who led the renewal after Vatican II took risks, responded creatively to the signs of the times, and transformed governance structures to be horizontal and democratic. Studying the centuries-old history of religious life teaches that different generations have likewise adapted to the concrete circumstances of their day. By naming the present reality and taking a long view, sisters charged with passing on the charism of vowed life today can proceed with boldness and ingenuity.

Finally, the present affords us the opportunity to live the public dimension of our vows in settings outside the institutional church. Women entering religious life today are often already professionals, though in fields other than theology or ministry. Moreover, they are not necessarily going to become professional ministers after they become sisters. Many do become chaplains, campus ministers, pastoral associates, religious educators, and spiritual directors, but others serve as social workers, therapists, health-care providers, scientists, and more. We need theological education—not to enter professional ministry but to preach the gospel with our lives, whatever our ministry may be. We want to give credible, attractive witness to the inbreaking reign of God through who we are and how we show up in the world.

In the crucible of changing realities, formative study and practice of the vows remain essential to the charism of religious life.[8] Formation for mission prepares mature and faithful women to step into the public identity that religious life entails. Being a member of a self-governing congregation involves participation, mutual responsibility, and collective discernment of the mission to which God is calling us. Coming to know God in and through the communal life, sisters engage in a mode of theological education that roots them in practices of contemplative listening, truth seeking, and collective care. In contexts beyond that of vowed life, Christian theological education may benefit from experimenting with these practices in the recognition that all the faithful, whatever their form of life, are called to follow Jesus's evangelical counsels.[9]

CONTEMPLATIVE LISTENING IN A WORLD OF NOISE

Amid a culture that demands constant production and availability, the contemplative grounding of religious life attracts by way of contrast. Vowed life witnesses to the flourishing future that God dreams for us, one in which we consecrate time for rest, recreation, and relationship. Jesus invites each of his disciples to "come away by yourselves to a deserted place and rest a while" (Mark 6:31 NABR). To grow in friendship with God, we must come to know and accept ourselves, just as we are, which may mean resisting the cultural imperative to work on bettering ourselves (or our bank accounts). Rather than striving to optimize individual productivity, we disciples of Jesus seek self-knowledge to loosen bonds of fear and bind up wounds that keep us from living freely and fully. Introspection often leads to personal growth, but prayer is more about listening and letting the Spirit work in us so that the light of Christ within shines more brightly.

Christian spiritual formation differs, in this respect, from the neoliberal project of self-improvement because it fosters acceptance of one's limitations—the cross to be taken up in order to find life. Over the course of my initial formation, I've engaged in intensive inner work, supported by spiritual directors and counselors, with ample opportunity for human development and self-reflection. In each year's self-evaluation written for my formation director, I perceive small but steady movement toward greater freedom to love and trust God's providence. Nevertheless, in the ordinary routine of daily life, I wrestle with the same issues that have always been a struggle, which for me boil down to the will to control and the impulse to criticize both myself and the world. When I find my thoughts running in the same old circles, it can seem like I haven't matured at all!

The inner work of Christian spiritual life involves accepting uncomfortable truths about our self, like our capacity to harm the people we love or to neglect their needs. As fallible humans, we inevitably participate in social and economic systems that do violence to our most vulnerable neighbors, and we often remain indifferent to their suffering. In short, we sin, and no efforts toward self-improvement will prevent that inevitability. This is an unsettling realization, one that is hard to face. The practice of contemplative prayer invites us to sit with the discomfort and to bring difficult emotions—shame, pain, anger, self-hatred, despair—before our loving and merciful God.

The Christian tradition holds profound wisdom on this kind of prayer. Julian of Norwich writes in *A Revelation of Love* about her vision of Christ's passion and resurrection and what it taught her about the reality of sin and the efficacy of prayer. While Julian is contemplating the face of the risen Christ and delighting in him, God disrupts this scene of beatific joy to reveal that Julian will again suffer pain and woe. Yet God immediately assures her, "I protect you very safely." Julian interprets these words to mean the following: "This passing life does not require us to live wholly without sin. [God] loves us endlessly, and we sin customarily, and he reveals it to us most gently. And then we sorrow and moan discreetly, turning to contemplate his mercy, cleaving to his love and his goodness."[10] As limited creatures, humans cause harm and fail to love fully, yet these sins do not constrain divine mercy or obstruct the goodness of God, which is working throughout the universe to bring forth life. God's love tenderly enfolds us.

In contemplative prayer, we become aware of that truth. During times of struggle, we listen for the divine promise: "I am with you to deliver you" (Jer. 1:8 NABR).

The saints and founders of religious orders taught embodied practices of contemplative listening. One of the treasures of the Dominican tradition is a thirteenth-century illustration of Saint Dominic's Nine Ways of Prayer (see figure 1). The sequence of images shows Dominic praying while walking, lying prostrate, standing with arms raised up or stretched out, kneeling, and sitting with a book in his lap. Accompanying captions report that sometimes Dominic "lifted his hands to his shoulders" in the *orans* posture, "as if he wanted to fix his ears more attentively. . . . If you had seen his devotion as he stood there erect in prayer, you would have thought you saw a prophet conversing with an angel or with God."[11]

Full-bodied prayer readies the whole person to listen intently and become receptive to sacred presence. We prepare our bodies, hearts, and minds to be still and open to contemplative awareness. Dominic was said to be always "talking to or about God." Following his example—and imitating Jesus—Dominicans converse with God in prayer as one talks to a friend. As in a friendship, good conversation involves active listening as much as self-disclosure. Different ways of prayer help to open our ears that we may hear. Contemplative sitting, meditative reading, chanting the hours, *visio divina*, labyrinth walking, and drawing mandalas—all such practices invite us to set aside time, clear some space, go offline, and quiet the noise of daily routine so that we can be attuned to bodily sensations, emotions, thoughts, and dreams. Spirit communicates through these experiences—the still, small voice within.

Every way of prayer disposes us to listen and to behold the world—and ourselves—from God's perspective, with a gaze of loving attention and tender care. Learning just to *be*, in silence and stillness, requires discipline as we let go of the impulse to *do*. *Being* without *doing* challenges us to wait and receive while forgoing the immediate gratification of our desires as well as the cultural demand for productive activity. The invitation to pray in community as well as in solitude is a powerful attractor to reli-

Figure 1. Saint Dominic's Nine Ways of Prayer. First half of the thirteenth century, Italy. Vatican Library, MS Ross. 3, fol. 9r. © 2025 Biblioteca Apostolica Vaticana. Reproduced by permission of Biblioteca Apostolica Vaticana, with all rights reserved.

gious life. When we sit contemplatively together, we experience a different kind of focus and spiritual energy vibrating in the space between. Emerging from that vibrant silence, community members speak about God's movement in our lives and world. Dominicans understand this God-talk to be one mode of preaching by which we impart words of grace and challenge to one another. A theological education that exposes women religious to diverse ways of prayer prepares them to model contemplative living for their burnt-out, stressed, overextended sisters and neighbors. For myself, as a person brought up to be hardworking and high-achieving, such a theological education invites me to unlearn the anxious drive to produce and consume so that I can offer the gift of presence in community and ministry.

The wisdom of this tradition is not limited to the formation of vowed religious. It's a gift that can be extended to all people. For instance, I have come to understand that teaching first-year college students is, in large part, a ministry of presence. When studying the Gospel of Matthew as part of the university's core curriculum, I call their attention to passages in which Jesus goes off by himself to a deserted place to pray. "Imagine how Jesus enjoys that time!" For two weeks, I ask them to keep at least five minutes each day quiet and device-free. They may want to experiment with Dominic's Nine Ways of Prayer by meditating on some spiritual reading, sitting in silence and letting go of their thoughts, or taking a walk and observing the natural environment around them. Theological education bears fruit when students can find beauty in solitude. They may encounter God in the silence.

Seeking and Speaking Truth in Community

Facing the truth of one's limitations opens the way to knowing God who is love. Speaking the truth before others is essential to building trust and creating a culture of inclusion in place of isolation and division.[12] Practices of self-disclosure foster connection and nurture relationships grounded in truth. At the ecclesial and institutional levels, naming and confronting legacies of harm is a form of confession that's essential to life together. Theological education can prepare students to engage their faith communities in truthfully acknowledging sinful histories and making amends. Such an education testifies to belief in an intrinsically relational, Trinitarian God. The challenge lies in navigating interpersonal and intergroup differences.

Programs for religious formation intentionally place sisters in living situations and ministerial contexts where they will interact with people of diverse backgrounds and perspectives. These experiences require skills for understanding group dynamics and the cultural histories that shape social identity. Against "us versus them" thinking, religious life witnesses to the open table of Eucharist, where all are welcome, their hunger satisfied.[13] Taking on the name of "Sister" calls us to extend the bonds of kinship beyond our family of birth, and even beyond our chosen family of friends. It affirms the value of solidarity and the truth of our interdependence, which Pope Francis emphasizes in *Laudato Si'*.[14] In a pluralistic society, we want the quality of our communal life to testify that people can live and flourish together across differences, in reciprocity with Earth, by the help of God's grace. Women entering religious life today come from diverse cultures and countries of origin. This reality holds out the promise and challenge of creating communities that are truly intercultural, nondominating, and inclusive. If we want religious communities to be sacraments of the unity-in-diversity of our triune God, we need a theological education that fosters humility, cultural sensitivity, nonviolence, and antiracist commitment.

One obstacle to this dream is the colonial history and predominantly white culture of religious congregations in the United States. These histories contain a mix of grace and sin. On the one hand, religious institutes have provided women a room of their own, a place from which to hold land, educate girls, lead organizations, and exercise self-determination. On the other, US-based congregations have participated in slaveholding, benefited from stolen land and labor, denied admission to women of color, enforced segregation in schools and hospitals, expected sisters of color to conform to the norms of whiteness, and helped legitimate an oppressive dominant culture.[15] These sinful injustices demand confession and repentance. The sisters of my congregation began the work of repair in the year 2000. The Dominican

Sisters of St. Catharine, Kentucky, along with the Sisters of Charity of Nazareth and the Sisters of Loretto, made a public apology for their founders' owning enslaved persons. Last year, during the 200th anniversary of the founding of St. Catharine's, the congregation created a memorial in honor of the enslaved and co-commissioned an art project entitled "I Was Here" to recognize their legacy.[16] These small yet concrete steps signal a desire to take responsibility for the past and examine its ongoing power over the present.

Women religious inhabit broken, wounded institutions and must face these painful histories of domination and exclusion. Yet religious community also holds the radical potential to become a sacrament of inclusive belonging. Vowed life can reshape one's desires through the kind of theological education that Keri Day envisions: "this gospel is about the joining together of lives, of bodies, of desires to live and love and be transformed in and through each other."[17] In a particular way, communal religious life embodies what Day calls "the power of unlikely people being drawn together by deep yearnings to experience radical moments of intimacy and belonging."[18] By fostering mutual dependence and shared decision making, the life-form rejects the illusion of autonomy and self-sufficiency. I pray and share meals daily with adult women to whom I am not related. Across differences of class, culture, and generation, we make a home together. Community draws me out of self-absorption to care for my sisters in daily, concrete action. But that's not all: the point is to exercise this care for people who are different than I am, whom I did not choose. Rather, it was God who chose each of us to build a common life together.

I want to emphasize how important difference is to religious community: it is both the abundant gift and the daunting challenge. While growing up in a predominantly white and wealthy neighborhood, I attended schools that were predominantly white; so was our parish church. As I entered young adulthood, I longed for encounter, a theme Pope Francis develops in *Evangelii Gaudium* on the joy of the gospel.[19] Religious life has answered that longing. I've lived with sisters Black, brown, and white; some grew up poor, others are immigrants and first-generation Americans. The common life can create a space for intimacy that enlarges the soul—if we learn to relate healthfully. Intimate relationality can expand and transform members of a community when no one seeks to dominate the group or impose their cultural norms. I once spoke with a white American sister who lived in a house of three, each of them representing a different nationality, language, and culture. She said that creating a truly intercultural community required that she check her spontaneous reactions. Spontaneity often reveals implicit biases and, for white people, an assumption of racial superiority. Pausing before speaking, reflecting on how we instinctively react, trains us to recognize the harmful cultural conditioning that white women bring into community so that we can unlearn those ideas or behaviors that may hurt our sisters. Daily, intimate encounters with interpersonal difference demand that we grow in self-awareness.

By engaging in courageous truth telling, humble repentance, and good-faith efforts to make amends, communities of vowed religious may yet bear authentic witness to the truth that all are welcome in the reign of God, all are kin, and healing from historical wounds is possible. Modeling an ethic of care and inclusion will help us earn the trust of the many young people who do not feel at home in church spaces. Shaped by these communal values, in my ministry as an educator I aim to make the classroom an inclusive space where all know that they are loved. I enact that love by valuing the voice and experience of each student. Practically, that means attending to group dynamics. In the Dominican tradition, we say that each person holds a piece of the truth, and each piece needs to be heard if we are to arrive at the fullness of Truth. I bring these methods into the classroom by incorporating regular small-group discussion on topics both personal and curricular. Students have much to learn from each other, yet many need guidance and encouragement to help them move through social anxiety and find the courage to speak. Theological education serves students by offering ample opportunity to participate in soulful conversations that honor each participant's sacred dignity.

Collective Care for the Whole of Life

Perhaps the most urgent question facing Christian disciples today is an ecological one: How do we live responsibly before our loving Creator at this moment in Earth's history when humanity is perpetrating such great harm against our common home—and inequitably suffering the consequences? I am convinced that practicing the vows with integrity and living in community can witness to a more flourishing future for all of God's creation because religious life demands the praxis of economic equity. In the wider context of Christian discipleship, theological education must make the connection between worship of the living God and the integrity of creation. Confessing the truth that humanity is wreaking destruction upon Earth, churches and seminaries might commit to collective practices of caring for the lands they hold in trust. All Christian disciples are called to adopt material lifestyles that embody a spirit of poverty.

The commitment to a shared household as modeled in religious community ensures equity among members and supports the flourishing of Earth by prioritizing needs and honoring restraint. Pope Francis in *Laudato Si'* calls for conversion toward an integral ecology and away from the technocratic paradigm of finance capitalism. This paradigm acknowledges no limits to human abilities or economic growth; it belies the need for checks upon the use of technology by states and corporations for surveillance, social control, political domination, and exploitation of the poor. The religious vow of poverty contests this paradigm by valuing humility, the root of which (*humus*) speaks to our close dependence on and love for Earth. Vowed life fosters "a culture and spirituality genuinely capable of setting limits and teaching clear-minded self-restraint."[20] Every sister and each local house commit to a financial budget that will provide enough funds to meet their needs while reducing needless consumption. In local houses, members might ask how they can decrease plastic waste, meet the goal of carbon neutrality, and support local agriculture, for example.

The vow of poverty calls religious congregations to responsible use of their collective buying power and financial investments.[21] Such initiatives build on decades of sisters' labor for the integrity of creation through ministries like farms and ecology centers. Divesting of lands that our congregations have stewarded is both prudent governance during this time of rightsizing and a form of reparations. When making corporate decisions around stewardship, congregations can refrain from selling for profit.[22] Some have channeled the need for divestment toward the movement for land return to Black and indigenous groups through collaboration with the Land Justice Futures initiative.[23] These choices signal recognition of our own limits—we no longer have the capacity to use these facilities—yet the choices are costly. Letting go of cherished places stirs up grief along with gratitude—as we see also in Angela Sims's essay on Colgate Rochester Crozer Divinity School moving to a new site after ninety years in its former location, and after more than two hundred years as a seminary. Out of love for Earth, religious congregations can make corporate decisions that repair the world for future generations.

Actions can be powerful teachers, but theological education is needed to articulate the *why* that motivates faith-based actors to turn toward Earth. Decades before the publication of *Laudato Si'*, Dominican sister-educators were preaching through their writing and advocacy about the religious obligation to reverence and care for creation.[24] Studying their work during my initial formation introduced me to eco-spirituality and creation theology. Retreats on cosmology awakened my consciousness of dwelling within an interconnected universe. The witness of sisters who had themselves undergone an ecological conversion sparked my own longing to share the Creator's delight in the evolving beauty of life.

When I teach *Laudato Si'* to first-year students, many say that they've never heard anyone connect Christianity to the environment. They perceived climate change to be a "secular" topic, or they thought science conflicted with biblical faith. Reading Pope Francis's passionate and accessible message, they respond positively because they worry about Earth's future. I ask them, while reading the text, to commit to one action they will take to care for creation. But I want them also to think about the communities to which they belong and imagine what collective actions might mitigate human harm and allow Earth to rest and regenerate. The Sabbath practices that are part of contemplative living should be extended to our fellow creatures and common home.

CONCLUSION

Religious vows express the deep longing in every person for contemplative depth, communion with Holy Mystery, and participation in realizing God's dream for a flourishing world. In the context of vowed life, the gifts of initial and ongoing formation ground sisters for the lifelong work of creating equitable, intercultural communities with awakening ecological consciousness. Yet practices of contemplation, truth seeking, and collective care offer every Christian a way of coming to know the living God. Approaching theological education as ongoing formation for lifelong discipleship invites teachers and students to prioritize time for solitude as well as experiences of sitting in silence together. Silence clears the ground for listening with one's whole body and speaking truth from the heart. In the stillness of the present moment, we become aware of the deep-down longing for God and one another that motivates all our studies. At this time, our world needs the witness of disciples who live simply in imitation of Jesus.

Dialogue

Ann Killian, OP, Janette H. Ok, David Nacho

Janette: By sharing about your experience and your envisioned future for vowed religious life in your community, you make a connection to every Christian's life. Throughout the essay, I see you weave together your calling, your background, and what compelled you to embrace the order with how that attraction to mission was redirected to a deeper sense of vocation and desire. It's not just about what you do but also about being part of this certain quality of communal life together, and becoming like Jesus through love, the love that you share toward one another. In doing that, you're showing your outward care for the world, but it stems from that deep place of desire for connection to Jesus Christ and community.

You're careful not to proselytize, and I appreciate that. What you are saying is that what drew *you* and continues to compel *you* about religious life, and with this community specifically, is actually in *all of us*. We may not choose that exact same way to fullness. But everything you're describing—for example, the neoliberal project of self-improvement, or the pervasive and pressing cultural demands for productivity, or how disconnected we are from community—left me convicted, and it connected with what I'm trying to say in my essay about that throughline of desire and how it connects us to our desire for God.

David: Continuing from that thought, it made me pause when I read that the naming of desire is at the core of vowed life. To learn to name it in that initial stage—it's a task that most of us don't engage, but it's quite a privilege to have the space, to have the community, to do that.

Perhaps because you mentioned the sisters in Bolivia, reading your piece reminded me of a journal by Henri Nouwen called *¡Gracias!*[1] It's about his time in Bolivia and Peru as he's studying languages. He finds meaning in the now—not what's going to happen after, but what is happening *now*. I was very inspired by the way a community of discipleship can create a learning experience that is valuable in the moment that it's happening. Of course, it will be valuable for certain tasks or for the rest of your life. But even right as it's happening, it's valuable, it's shaping you.

Ann: I love that idea that it's valuable while you're doing it. It's so true, and I also felt the tension during that time of formation. For the canonical novitiate year, you don't work. You're just in this time of intensive reflection and study. It can feel like waiting for real life to begin. I had to be mindful that, no, I am already a sister, now. I'm living the life now. You're not waiting until you make vows or waiting until you're in ministry. Initial formation is a time for grounding me. I need to hold this experience and carry it with me for the inevitable struggles that will come. Initial formation is an incredible gift. The community supports you for a year of not doing anything productive, just doing this inner work. It was both wonderful and uncomfortable because we're so conditioned to be productive and always moving on to the next thing. It was a real lesson in being present and cherishing the gifts of that time.

David: Since we're talking about the present, in the piece you quoted Ted Smith's "affordances of the present," and you name some of the things that are hard about the present. It made me imagine what sisters of the Vatican II generation would write of that time, in a sort of parallel, as I was hearing your voice as a sister writing for this time. I was grateful for your piece because, although it named the goodness of the past, it wasn't longing for the past. You fully give credit to what the sisters in that time did and how they did it. But I don't read your piece as nostalgic—"If only we could go back to that time!"—but rather as a very committed quest for engaging today's realities.

Ann: Hearing the sisters' stories about the renewal after Vatican II, it does sound like such an exciting time—this outpouring of the Spirit when doors were opening, especially for women to be in ministry and have occasions to preach. Now the church is in a very different moment. I can appreciate the stories without feeling nostalgic. As the prioress of my congregation likes to say, "We were made for *these* times." *This* is the time in which I'm entering, and God is going to give us the grace to meet the challenges.

Janette: What you incorporated brings insight to what theological education can be. It both affirms and names what you're doing, and why and how that can challenge this idea of "education to prepare" versus education to help us discover who we are in God. To prepare ministers and equip leaders, that's all good, but it's lacking the whole desire and deep formation and Christ-likeness—the communal venture part. Rejecting "the illusion of autonomy and self-sufficiency" makes me think of what Willie Jennings wrote about the self-sufficient man.[2] We think we're self-sufficient. The way we deal with money reveals this idol, I guess you could say, and it's an illusion. You're saying we need one another to become like Christ. It's not just life together because it's a beautiful life. That we are interdependent is the most truthful reality, and our finances are the blockage to that true depth of interdependence. Your life-form is a counternarrative to the idea of self-sufficiency, which we've just imbibed without much repentance, much analysis, much reflection.

Ann: Yes, and it critiques the cultural emphasis on self-care, and the late-capitalist underpinnings to that idea of self, and instead emphasizes collective care. In a motherhouse with sixty or seventy women, you're sharing meals and praying together with those sisters and accompanying them through their aging and their dying. That accompaniment is so often lost in our society where self-care is the more dominant framework.

Janette: In the Asian American women's circles in which I am involved, we've also pushed against the idea of self-care. Not that there's no merit to it, but collective care is much more resonant. You're not knocking it, but you're also showing the limits of neo-liberal self-help or self-improvement.

A growth mind-set is a great thing. You can say it's a work of the spirit, like a redemptive framework. But it can be very self-oriented—growth for the sake of greater production—because such worth ultimately is defined by what we do, not by who we are. Whereas ultimately everything *you're* doing is countering that narrative, while serving the world, while stewarding the earth.

David: Can I ask you something? Silence is not really a thing among Latin American evangelicals, so I don't know much about it. But I was really intrigued by what you wrote about "vibrant silence." I'm wondering if you have more to say about the role of silence in theological education.

Ann: Part of contemplative prayer is letting go of thoughts or whatever comes up during that time—not to hold on to them or engage with them, but to sink into the silence, that place of being embraced by God's love. Relating to theological education, I usually experience writing or preaching as something that I receive, and that reception happens during the time of silence, of sitting and waiting to receive the word, which doesn't come from me.

Janette: There is a passivity to learning, too. The self-sufficient learner hates the language of passivity.

Ann: But it's a kind of active passivity—or, better yet, a receptivity. The monastic word for meditating on Scripture—"rumination"—

typically refers to a cow chewing on its cud. You take in the word, and then you assimilate it so that it energizes you. Your body and soul absorb it. But it's not a conscious process. It's a bodily and spiritual process.

David: I have never before understood silence in those terms. I've tended to understand it as nothingness, right? But there's something there. It's vibrant.

Ann: It can actually sometimes feel like nothingness! You can sit there, and it feels like nothing's happening. So practicing silence entails trusting that if I've consented to God's work in me, then God is working, even if I don't feel it, or even if I'm not aware of it.

Janette: Okay, so this makes me think of the connection we can possibly make between prayer and silence and theological education. It seems obvious that we would incorporate these practices, but we don't always do it, and particularly not necessarily from the deeper aspect of it, which is so vital to formation as a learner. If we can't listen in that silence, how do we listen to others in conversations like in the dialogues in this book? We're not able to hear people in fullness because we're prepping for the next reaction or response. That's a real shortcoming in the way we do dialogue.

Ann: Even holding space for silence in the classroom may be a way to open students to encountering God or a moment of transcendence.

4

Disruptive Encounter and Ecclesial Discernment in the Vineyard Movement

Caleb Maskell

This essay sketches a paradigm within which to imagine a framework for theological education in the Vineyard movement of churches. I argue that the Vineyard movement has, from its origins, been rooted in a practical spirituality of *encounter* with God, mainly based in John Wimber's commitment to a modality of training drawn from the admonition in Ephesians 4:12 that the job of Christian leaders is to "equip the saints for the work of ministry." Over the years, key leaders of the Vineyard came to recognize that a communion rooted in a spirituality of encounter must also develop a deep facility for *discernment* of the work of the Spirit in the context of the historic church. In particular, this discernment looks for ways that encounters with the Spirit "rhyme" with the witness of Holy Scripture and Christian tradition. A robust dialectical relationship between the encounter and discernment has proven necessary to avoid drifting into theological incoherence and infidelity. Faithfully practicing this dialectic of encounter and discernment does not happen by accident: it requires leaders to ground themselves self-consciously and intentionally in knowledge of Scripture and tradition, while at the same time continuing to pursue disruptive encounters with God.

It is this process that will allow wisdom and experience born of a maturing theological identity to be transmitted to future generations of Christian disciples in the Vineyard movement.

THE VINEYARD MOVEMENT AT FIFTY

In the summer of 2024, the Vineyard churches in the United States celebrated their fifty-year anniversary. Over the course of two weeklong conferences held in Denver and Cincinnati, some three thousand Vineyard pastors and leaders from all over the United States and beyond gathered to remember, rejoice over, and renew commitment to the foundational charisms that inspired the Vineyard at its origins, and continue to breathe life into it today.[1]

There were many things to celebrate, but for the purpose of this introduction I will describe three primary ones: First, over fifty years, the Vineyard movement has emerged from small beginnings as a handful of house churches in Southern California into a communion of some five hundred or so churches all over the United States, and thousands more around the world. As a general rule, Vineyard churches are focused on inviting anyone who comes through the door to become an apprentice of Jesus. Through practical Bible teaching centered on the kingdom of God, through worship rooted in the affections of the heart, and—crucially—through simple, shared practices of prayer and service to others, Vineyard churches focus on inviting people to experience the life of Jesus by obediently trying to do the things that Jesus taught his disciples to do.

Second, over five decades many Vineyard churches have fostered environments of liturgical creativity that have had a deep impact on contemporary worship culture in the Anglophone world. Vineyard songwriters have written a number of now-canonical songs in the genre of contemporary worship music, and in the process helped to develop the genre itself.[2] Consequently, Vineyard churches have developed new liturgical paradigms intended to invite people from all backgrounds to experience the presence of Jesus and, in turn, to learn to follow him.

Third, especially since the early 1980s under the leadership of John Wimber, the preeminent "founding father" of the Vineyard movement, the Vineyard has paid particular attention to equipping regular Christians—the so-called laity—to attempt the work of Spirit-empowered supernatural ministry as part of their discipleship. In short, this means that Vineyard churches encourage regular folks to try to heal the sick, share prophetic words, set oppressed people free, and so on.[3] Vineyard's rubric for Christian discipleship is irreducibly rooted in spiritual practices designed to inculcate the imitation of Christ in "naturally supernatural" ways.

These three eminently practical characteristics—churches focused on apprenticeship to Jesus, liturgical innovation, and equipping of everyday people in charismatic prayer ministry—are core elements of the irreducible center of a recognizable "Vineyard identity," finding perhaps a distinctive position on the wider map of American Christianity.[4]

JOHN WIMBER, THE VINEYARD, AND THEOLOGICAL EDUCATION

With this brief characterization of the practical life of the Vineyard in view, I turn to the central theme of this volume of essays: to ask how theological education intersects with the emergence of these characteristic charisms. Of course, they did not appear spontaneously and fully formed at the Vineyard's founding but rather were discovered, developed, and taught by Vineyard leaders as part of a new paradigm for doing and being church.[5] Establishing a new paradigm required the leaders of the Vineyard movement—chief among them John Wimber, who led the Vineyard from 1982 to his early death in 1997—to adopt a mode of practical theological education at the center of all he did. John Wimber constantly said that the role of Vineyard leaders was "the equipping of the saints for the work of ministry" (Eph. 4:12 NASB) or, in his aw-shucks colloquialism, "doing the stuff" that Jesus told his disciples to do when he called *them* to heal the sick, deliver the oppressed, preach the gospel, suffer persecution, and so on, in his name. The foundation of this spirituality of imitation was commitment to what Wimber called "orthodox/evangelical theology and practice," rooted in his favored theological paradigm: the kingdom of God.[6] Self-conscious about his own lack of advanced theological training, Wimber was happy to let others work to define the boundaries of this "orthodox/evangelical" perspective. However, he certainly understood it as a consensus-based "open evangelicalism" of the sort then being taught at Fuller Theological Seminary, his former employer.[7] While Wimber never deviated from this baseline of theological commitment, he remained above all a practitioner, judging himself primarily by his effectiveness at equipping the saints.[8] In this spirit, alongside calling Vineyard leaders to embrace an "orthodox/evangelical gospel," Wimber also counseled them to maintain enough theological latitude to avoid the divisive sectarianism and arid intellectualism that hamstrung many internecine evangelical theological debates. Much more important than being accomplished theologians was maintaining commitment to the humble, courageous, sometimes risky practices of imitating the life of Jesus that characterized discipleship in the Vineyard mode.

Wimber's primary message to the Vineyard movement about theological education was: Have good theology, but don't overdo it—and definitely don't confuse it with good practice.[9] Fair enough. There are good pastoral instincts that underwrite this perspective. However, fifty years into the life of the Vineyard, a couple of major areas beg for attention.

First, the language of "orthodox/evangelical" that John Wimber used in the 1980s and 1990s to describe a theological consensus on which to build the Vineyard now needs significant clarification as to its meaning and application in the mid-2020s. Surely whatever consensus there was around these terms in his usage has become much more murky in the intervening years. While this essay is not the place to undertake that clarification, it is important to recognize that this work must be done.

The second area is the question of theological education itself. As noted above, by emphasizing the importance to the life of the Vineyard of "equipping the saints," John Wimber located an imitative training modality for theological education firmly at the center of the Vineyard's practical identity. While there are important distinctions between a training modality and a more expansive vision of theological education, it is the place we must start.

ENCOUNTER

The starting point for Vineyard theological education—the base of its training modality—must be *encounter* with God, born out of obedient discipleship. In a 1993 pastoral letter, Wimber argued that "the essential nature of equipping . . . is to repair and prepare a people to do kingdom ministry,"[10] that is, to live for the kinds of encounters that Jesus described as "the kingdom of God coming near."[11] What Wimber meant in speaking of these "encounters" becomes clear with attention to a paradigmatic early healing in his church.[12]

On a Monday morning in February of 1978, Wimber got a call from one of his members asking him to come and pray for his wife, who had a debilitating fever.[13] In theory, this was a great opportunity. Since planting his church ten months earlier, Wimber had preached exclusively about the life and ministry of Jesus as described in the Gospel of Luke. He had intended to establish a foundational conviction in his growing, young congregation that Christian discipleship was fundamentally about three things: worshiping Jesus as God, learning Jesus's word through studying the Bible, and, above all, imitating Jesus's works. Wimber thought that Christians who highly valued the Bible should understand themselves as apprentices of Jesus, people who chose obediently and joyfully to try to do the things that Jesus taught his disciples to do in the New Testament accounts. Christians should aim not merely to *know* the stories of the Bible but also to *enact* them in the contemporary world. And that meant trying to heal the sick.

The problem was that Wimber had been praying for the sick in his church every week for the past ten months, but no one had been healed. He had tried everything. He had preached about Jesus's methods of healing. He had offered examples of healing events from the history of the church. He had taught an encouraging practical biblical theology of healing prayer that placed the burden of outcomes on God's sovereignty rather than on any weakness in the person praying or the person receiving prayer. He had given altar calls at which he had personally prayed for scores of sick people, as well as inviting his congregants to pray for the sick alongside him. Over hours and weeks together, they had prayed lengthy, Bible-soaked petitions for God's merciful intervention, as well as short, commanding prayers in Jesus's authoritative style—"Be healed!," "Stretch forth your hand!," and so on. But absolutely nothing had worked.

For Wimber, as the months of failure to heal people ground on, it became an existentially desperate situation—a point of embarrassment and frustration to him. The only reason he continued to pray for the sick around him was his conviction that imitative obedience to the commands of Jesus was the foundation of Christian discipleship. But it was painful. And so, when he received that call from his church member, asking him to pray again, he was anything but excited about it.

Well, Wimber went to pray, and his account of what happened when he did is as simple as it is astonishing. Laying his hand on the feverish, miserable woman, he "mumbled a faithless prayer, then . . . turned around and began explaining to her husband why some people do not get healed." In the middle of Wimber's explanation, the husband began to stare at something over Wimber's shoulder. "I turned around to see his wife out of bed, looking like a new person," Wimber wrote. "I'm well," she said. "You healed me."[14]

At this point, I want to step outside the story to recognize that for some readers, steeped as we all are in the assumptions of Enlightenment modernity and the undeniable anguish endemic to the trajectories of human existence, this story may strain the bounds of credulity.[15] It may even cause some cognitive distress. If that is so, it is as it must be. There are many important conversations that should follow from any claim of a miracle, and they must not be passed over quickly.

However, what must also be contended with is what happened to Wimber's church in the months after this event. Emboldened by Wimber's testimony, parishioners sought to integrate this practical supernaturalism into their discipleship. At his encouragement, they started praying for the sick as well—remember that Wimber's primary emphasis was "equipping the saints"—and in turn, they began to heal people. More and more stories of physical and emotional healing began to emerge from the congregation, such that, in 1982, Wimber publicly stated that the church was reporting more than fifty healings per week.[16] The church also grew exponentially, baptizing many hundreds of people and gathering more than three thousand people weekly for worship after being in existence only five years.[17]

Let us return, then, to the concept of encounter with God, rooted in obedience, as the foundation of theological education in the Vineyard. What underlies Wimber's healing story is not a commitment to successfully healing people but rather a commitment to being obedient to the way that Jesus taught his disciples to live. Wimber later put it this way: "Obedience to God's word is the fundamental reason that I pray for the sick and receive prayer personally, even when I do not see healing as a result of those prayers . . . none of the instruction [in the practice of healing] will be of benefit if you neglect the fundamental principles of obedience to God's word and reliance on his compassion and mercy."[18]

Thus, the heart of the Vineyard's training modality that constitutes its first opening to theological education is not the teaching of *techniques* for healing people. Rather, it is teaching people to risk practicing obedience to Jesus in matters in which they have no control over the outcomes. In doing so they hold space, with the kind of human vulnerability described in Matthew 10 and Luke 10, for the triune God to establish a moment of encounter, a "naturally supernatural" experience. The disciple brings neither expertise nor certainty of outcomes, but rather obedience and dependence. As Wimber put it, "My job [is] to obey, pray, and rely on his sovereign mercy; [God's] part [is] to heal."[19] Any vision of theological education in the Vineyard movement must never be divorced from this attunement to obedient encounter.

Pedagogy of Encounter: Wimber, Wagner, and MC510

Of course, what followed this posture, according to Wimber and those who were learning from him, was a flood of evidence of God's desire to heal and restore. The people of the Vineyard in those days found that God often met their obedience and dependence with moments of arresting, remarkable power. This connection of obedience and encounter caught the attention of C. Peter Wagner, a friend of Wimber's who taught missiology in what was then called the Fuller School of World Mission. Equal parts evangelical futurist and puckish impresario, Wagner had for some time contended, based on global trends of church growth, that "Pentecostalization" was the future of the American evangelical church. The churches around the world that were growing, mostly in the global south, were practicing Pentecostal miracles. However, Wagner intuited that the style of such churches—not to mention the theology—was hard for American evangelicals to embrace. With the flowering of equipping for healing in Wimber's local church, Wagner found an example he could sell. Here was a church that integrated Pentecostal "signs and wonders" with a nondispensational evangelical theology of the kingdom of God (drawn from the work of Fuller professor George Eldon Ladd) and a winsome come-as-you-are fallibilism that made such ministry seem within reach of any Christian.

With great enthusiasm, Wagner proposed that he and Wimber team-teach an "experimental" course, "MC510: Signs, Wonders, and Church Growth," beginning in January 1982 at Fuller's School of World Mission. There they would demonstrate the training modality Wimber had discovered in a practical "clinic" environment, while also teaching the theology that undergirded it and describing its outcomes, specifically regarding church growth. Wagner believed that this would allow him to advocate for what he named "the Third Wave of the Holy Spirit" in the twentieth century, in which evangelical pastors—who were theologically and stylistically at odds with classical Pentecostals (Wagner's "First Wave") and mainline charismatics (Wagner's "Second Wave")—could embrace supernatural power in their ministries, and in turn begin to experience dynamic church growth again.

The course succeeded beyond Wagner's wildest imagination. Controversial and oversubscribed from the first, every session involved an explanation of theological foundations, followed by a Wimber-led clinic in which students practiced praying for healing. Most sessions involved testimonies of healings that had taken place in a prior session. Wagner himself professed healing of high blood pressure during the first class meeting. By the end of 1982, there was enough national buzz about the course that *Christian Life*, a widely circulated magazine for pastors, published an entire issue on it, declaring on the cover: "MC510: This Number May Change Your Life."[20] Robert P. Meye, dean of the School of Theology at Fuller, said of the phenomenon, "I know only two seminary courses which have become famous. One was the course on dogmatics taught at Basel by Karl Barth and the other is MC510 taught by John Wimber here at Fuller."[21] There is no question that MC510 propelled John Wimber into the public eye as perhaps the exemplary leader in the "pentecostalization of North American evangelicalism," and the face of C. Peter Wagner's "Third Wave."[22]

There is far more to say about MC510 than can be said here—not least concerning its cancellation by Fuller Seminary in 1986 on the astonishing grounds that signs and wonders could be acceptable in churches but were not appropriate in an academic setting.[23] For now, though, it is enough to observe that MC510 was essentially an attempt to practice, in a seminary context, the foundational conviction that animates the Vineyard to this day, namely, that obeying the instructions Jesus gave to his disciples will lead to powerful encounters with the triune God.

DISCERNMENT

The second key element of a paradigm for theological education in the Vineyard is ecclesial discernment—cultivating a capacity to think theologically with the whole church, while also wholly embracing a spirituality of encounter. The two must go hand in hand.

This was one of the key emphases that developed over the course of John Wimber's life as a leader. While Fuller's unceremonious cancellation of MC510 in 1986 seemed to give credence to John Wimber's initial wariness about the value of theological education as an end in itself, by 1997 Wimber had begun to speak in a different register about the practical aims of theological education. Specifically, he began to emphasize how crucial it is for a movement committed to practicing encounter with God also to cultivate a robust capacity for theological and ecclesial discernment, or else be "blown about by every wind of doctrine" (Eph. 4:14 NRSV).

Wimber stated his position on this most clearly in his final pastoral letter, entitled "The Five-Fold Ministry," written to Vineyard leaders just a few months before he died. He described this letter as the most difficult he'd ever written, commenting, "If I didn't believe this topic was so important to the continuing health of the Vineyard, I would have abandoned it long ago."[24] The force of the letter comes early on, with what would be his last statement to his pastors about the defining identity of the Vineyard movement in the context of the wider body of Christ. He wrote:

> Vineyard is a church planting movement that actively seeks to discern what God is currently doing wherever we find His working in the Body of Christ. This philosophy of ministry exposes Vineyard churches to many different beliefs from various streams of thought within the church.
>
> On the one hand, this keeps us honed because we are continually driven back to the Word of God as interpreted by the Spirit of God and to the historic church to ask: "Is this consistent with God's written Word, and with its historical expression through the centuries?" On the other hand, this openness can lead to a temporary drifting from the anchor of our historical beliefs and practices, and even a short-term distortion while the "fresh wind" [of the Holy Spirit] is sorted through.[25]

In this charge, Wimber asserts the need for the Vineyard to be two things at once: on the one hand, a community of spiritual seekers who look for the new things that God is doing, and on the other hand, a community of discerning Christians whose assessment of new spiritual phenomena is constrained by Holy Scripture and the historic expressions of Christian faith and practice. To be clear, this is not at all *divergent* from what Wimber affirmed about the witness of Scripture and church throughout his ministry. However, in this statement, Wimber does offer a much thicker description of the biblical and church-historical manner of discernment he sees as necessary for the stability of a movement in pursuit of a spirituality of encounter.

Sadly, John Wimber came to his understanding of the crucial importance of ecclesial discernment through the painful collapse of his working relationship with C. Peter Wagner in the years after MC510. To the average observer of American evangelical culture, John Wimber and Peter Wagner were inextricably connected throughout the 1980s, working together as they did at Fuller, as well as at conferences about church growth. However, by 1991, their working relationship had begun to fracture over what Wimber called "serious disagreements" about their theological commitments.[26]

Between 1991 and Wimber's death in 1997, the two men engaged in two major theological disputes.[27] The first dispute concerned Wagner's growing enthusiasm for a prayer technique called "strategic-level spiritual warfare" (SLSW), which he believed was a new "spiritual technology" being revealed by God to elite groups of prophetic intercessors. These intercessors, Wagner contended, were able both to discern the presence of demonic principalities oppressing whole people groups (cities, nations, etc.) and also to tear down those principalities through the unique God-given authority of their prayers.[28]

The second dispute was about Wagner's conviction that the church was in the midst of a world-historically significant ecclesiological transformation that he called the New Apostolic Reformation (NAR).[29] Through this "most radical change in the way of 'doing church' since the Protestant Reformation," Wagner argued that God was replacing the "old wineskin" of traditional church forms by restoring the "recognition of the *gift* and *office* of apostle" to the church.[30] "Traditional Christianity starts with the present situation and focuses on the past," Wagner claimed, while "New apostolic Christianity starts with the present situation and focuses on the future," empowering apostles to lead their churches in the power of the Holy Spirit, without the controlling restraints of bureaucracy, legality, and rationality.[31]

The ardency of Wagner's desire to involve Wimber in these theological innovations was perhaps matched only by Wimber's absolute refusal to participate in his friend's post-MC510 emphases. On both matters they engaged in fierce theological argument, and found no common ground. While the specific theological content of these arguments warrants further study, for our purposes we need look only at some formal commonalities between the two concepts of strategic-level spiritual warfare and the New Apostolic Reformation to get at the center of Wimber's distaste for them.

First, both concepts were rooted purely in the metaphysical architecture of contemporary revelation. Each relied on the conviction that God was revealing some new structure in the church that could only be described in esoteric categories, visible to a select group of especially discerning people: prophetic intercessors discerning invisible principalities, apostles discerning other apostles, and so on.

Second, both concepts produced, in short order, an elite class of relatively unaccountable people—people whose spiritual vocations seemed so world-historically significant (though invisible to most "traditional" Christians) that they could only be accountable to one another, not to normal Christians. (In light of this, such mundane things as whether, for example, their ethics were surrendered to the way of Christ were, by definition, of secondary importance.)

Third, both concepts relied on highly speculative and strained interpretations of Scripture for their self-articulation, while looking askance at the "old wineskins" of traditional, "nonapostolic" churches that had no category for the meaning of prophetic intercession.

John Wimber had all this in mind when he wrote "The Five-Fold Ministry" in 1997, essentially as a rebuttal to his old friend Peter Wagner. When Wimber considered the way in which Wagner had, in his view, been deceived by these theories concerning spiritual warfare and the restoration of apostles, he could see how Wagner became susceptible to it. Wimber recognized that Wagner—as indeed the Vineyard movement—could, in attempting to remain rooted in openness to a spirituality of encounter, end up succumbing to such esoterica that have little to do with the Scripture and the historic church.

Throughout "The Five-Fold Ministry," Wimber rejects the claim that God is, in the late 1990s, "restoring" the New Testament office of apostle to the church, as a combination of speculative, spurious, and sinful. For Wimber, the claim that one is an apostle or a prophet is pure human speculation; for Wimber, only Jesus can make that designation. In turn, the claim that the New Testament church was the apex church and everything since has been decline, or similarly, the claim that the New Testament gifts need to be restored through a new apostolic reformation in the contemporary church, was, he said, spurious. What is needed, in Wimber's view, is not that New Testament Christianity should be "*recovered*," resulting in the erasure and replacement of current ecclesial systems, but rather "*exercised*, under the power and direction of the Spirit of God with humility and with a love and respect for the whole Body of Christ."[32] Finally and relatedly, the thought that anyone but Jesus Christ could judge a church to be dead was, in Wimber's view, dangerous and sinful. "If it's the church, it's alive because it belongs to Christ and is in Christ," he wrote. "For us to judge a church as dead because it is in a low ebb spiritually seems to me to verge on sin. Jesus reserved for himself the right to judge the church."[33]

Alongside all this refutation, Wimber also takes great pains to sound two additional themes. First, he underscores that he intends to be "neither polemical nor argumentative." Rather, he says, he is writing as an "under-shepherd, desiring to protect and refocus [the church], not as a critic looking for argument which can be used to hurt . . . others."[34] Second, he reminds his reader that he is fully in support of the renewal of the church—and particularly the mode of renewal that leads to richer expressions of the work of the Holy Spirit in any and all churches. The concern he has is not with renewal but with the self-evaluation of present-day experiences of church renewal by those participating in it. He asserts that there is no meaningful way for churches currently experiencing renewal to adequately assess themselves; "the church," he writes, is a "work-in-progress," always lacking sufficient data for accurate historical self-interpretation.[35]

As such, what is necessary for movement in pursuit of encounter with God is discernment—the kind of ecclesial discernment, rooted in the Holy Spirit and the historic tradition of the Christian interpretation, that safeguards a God-chasing movement against going "too far wrong for too long."[36] Framing the pursuit of ecclesial discernment in the manner that Wimber does appeals neither to dogmatic theological propositions nor to structures of ecclesial authority, but rather to questions about the range and limits of human knowledge before God, in primary relation to Scripture and church history. Thus Wimber offers an applied example of the mode of discernment to which he exhorted the Vineyard at the beginning of his article—the kind of discernment on which he asserted that the Vineyard movement's practical identity rested.

All of this is to say that to the extent that framing a paradigm for theological education in the Vineyard remains—as it must—committed to a spirituality of encounter with God through obedience to Jesus, it must in the same movement remain committed to rhyming with the historical Christian past. Vineyard theological education must root down in ecclesial discernment, attending in humility, obedience, and faith to the quality of its relationship to the norms of what Wimber called "the Word of God as interpreted by the Spirit of God and . . . the historic church." This kind of orientation toward the Christian past enables one to continue to take risks in Christian discipleship and leadership in the present. Conversely, doing as Wagner did and naming one's own potential future theological significance—assigning oneself or one's movement even a speculative place in the future trajectory of salvation history—was, to Wimber, a huge mistake. "I don't believe it is valid for us to write our own history," Wimber wrote. "Ultimately, an era of the church must be evaluated by ensuing generations. A better question to ask is 'What will they be saying a hundred years from today?' Or better still, 'What will Jesus say?'"[37]

Conclusion

In this essay, I have described the complex and dynamic tensions that have emerged at some moments in the history of the Vineyard's attempt to navigate the relationship between a practical spirituality of encounter with God and the attendant need for the constraints of ecclesial discernment. As we have seen from the earliest days of the Vineyard movement, John Wimber led people to pursue interruptive spiritual experiences—encounters with God emerging from obedient discipleship. The structures and forms of collective church life in the Vineyard are intended to adjust to make space for the potentially disruptive behavior of Christian disciples being obedient to the Holy Spirit, and not the other way around. In turn, it is precisely this disruptive intention that requires the kind of backward-looking, ecclesial groundedness that only the pursuit of a historically conscious theological education can afford. The very possibility of the Vineyard taking innovative, risky steps in encounter-driven discipleship as a movement of churches is predicated on being radically connected—rooted and grounded—in a practice of "rhyming" with the testimony of Scripture and the witness of the historic church about what obedience to Jesus looks like. Developing the infrastructure to invite Vineyard leaders into such a process *as* Vineyard leaders is the work to which we must turn our hand.

Dialogue

Caleb Maskell, Grace Y. Kao, Ann Killian, OP

Ann: In the 1970s, some of the sisters in my order became involved in the Catholic charismatic prayer movement. Because the movement was never mainstreamed in Catholic circles, I didn't really know much about it until talking with some of them about their remarkable experiences with healing prayer. Learning about these untold stories stirred questions for me about theological education and the ways we often separate biblical studies from church history, and sometimes both of those from practical ministry training—which, especially in my context, has a significant gender component to it.

As you describe John Wimber's philosophy of ministry, all those things are absolutely tied together and essential—which I love. My question, then, is about the process of discerning *how* to hold those things together. How, as we're reading New Testament stories about practices of Christian ministry, should we be thinking about how the cultural context informed and normed those practices? And then, how should we relate that to our current cultural context? For example, there are both theological reasons for and historical examples of women fully participating in ministry, but, in the Roman Catholic Church, pontifical studies have concluded that women were never ordained as

Catholics understand ordination, and so women should not be ordained today.

How does a Vineyard person think about what it means to rhyme with the witness of the historic Christian past—and what do we do about dissonances?

Caleb: For me, these are perhaps the most crucial questions to consider regarding the future of theological education. The future of the Vineyard demands that we learn to operate in continuity with the witness of the historic and the global church. The triune God has established the church and has promised to continue to work, fundamentally and eschatologically, through the church that bears witness to God's reality. The church is a work of the Holy Spirit, and thus its existence makes a claim on us.

To learn to rhyme with our immediate forebears in the faith as well as with the church across time and space, we must develop a very robust practice of *ecclesial* discernment. Let me give an example of what I'm talking about. In evangelical communions you have people who call themselves "complementarians," and others "egalitarians." Complementarians believe that the Bible says women should not be in senior leadership in churches, whereas egalitarians believe that the Bible says that women should be able to be in leadership at every level in the church. Both sides can marshal what is called a "biblical" argument for their position—and that's a very important thing to do. But a robust practice of ecclesial discernment must take the next step in the conversation, going beyond simply asking, "What do we think the Bible says?" to the further question: "In light of the witness of Scripture and church, what has our communion discerned that the triune God is asking us to bear witness to in this moment?" This is what Wimber meant, and what I mean by ecclesial discernment. It is very sobering work to lead in this way. The stakes are high.

Ann: A lot of this makes me think of the ongoing Synod on Synodality that Pope Francis has initiated. Pope Francis says that the

Holy Spirit is the protagonist of the Synod on Synodality, and that to begin to listen to the Holy Spirit, a faithful leader must create conditions for each person to speak truly about how God is moving in their life. At the end of all this, the leader's final move is to synthesize what is being heard, in a way that, as you've written elsewhere, "introduces people to the things they already know God is doing among them, but perhaps struggled to say."

Caleb: I have been closely tracking the Synod, as well as the fractious debate it has produced, especially in the USA. I think the reaction to the Synod exposes a sense of crisis in the churches concerning things like the nature of leadership, the manner and mode of revelation available to the church, how we relate to canons of authority, and so on. The problem is that each of these matters is a tension to manage, not to solve. My sense is that we're going to have to get a lot more comfortable as leaders in holding the tensions that Scriptures say *must* characterize the lives of the followers of Jesus, in spite of the desire for political resolution for which those most formed by the politics of left and right constantly call. A truly discerned account of the work of the Spirit among the people of God will be an account of tensions held, in light of the church's global, historic witness.

Bottom line: our moment calls for a long-needed renovation of evangelical ecclesiology, rooted in the cultivation of historical memory and awareness of the global dimensions of our family of faith. This requires epistemic humility and honesty about our shortcomings—especially our capitulations to what the book of Revelation images as the powers of Babylon. We're not meant to win a culture war! I often think of imprisoned house church pastors in China and Iran. We must learn to never speak or act as leaders in ways that would be embarrassing or bewildering to people like them.

Grace: On quite a different tack: the Vineyard's story begins with an institutional break. Vineyard separates from Calvary Chapel in 1982—that's an institutional separation. John Wimber's original Calvary Chapel began out of an institutional break from the Yorba Linda Friends Church in 1977. And, as the story of the Vineyard has unfolded, there have been a number of other institutional breaks. So, in the midst of the story you're telling about the dissolution of the working relationship between C. Peter Wagner and John Wimber, how should we be thinking about the institutional side of things?

Caleb: It is so important to consider the place of schism in narratives of the emergence of new works of the Holy Spirit in the church. In a very real sense, the Vineyard has schism in its origins. Its originary leaders realized that they could work with their forebears up to a point, but eventually, at the end of the day, they wanted to do something ostensibly distinct. And the standard narrative is that "God is doing something different with us than God is doing with those who came before us." Which may be true. The trouble is that such rhetoric can easily provide a veneer of justification over the same kind of parricidal progressivism that characterizes so many of the obsessions of American capitalism—lionizing the ability to create spectacle by a commitment to "move fast and break stuff."

To be honest, I think it is a both/and. There's a sociological reality to the fact that when leaders find momentum behind their ideas, they want space, time, and freedom to experiment. Great. But then, as Jesus says, the fruit has to be tested over time. The problem is that we don't know the crop cycle of a new entity! The technocratic metrics of capitalistic success mustn't be the way we assess the life of a church.

So, in this question about schism we find that we have yet another tension to manage—a tension that can only really be managed in communities of discernment, seeking the presence of God and committed to obedience to Jesus. What are the implications of recognizing that we are always already a people connected not just by our choice but by God's free choice in the world? How should our awareness of our connection make a claim on our freedom? What does it mean to be constrained by commitment to a community? These are profound questions for reflection.

Grace: One final question. How would you describe the type of malformation that John Wimber is afraid will happen to people who adopt C. Peter Wagner's innovative frameworks regarding spiritual warfare and the New Apostolic Reformation?

Caleb: In a nutshell, the main harm that Wimber is concerned about is that Wagner's theology invites people to understand themselves as a class of spiritual elites who think that God is giving them a particular metaphysical insight—what we might call gnostic "special knowledge" about what God is or isn't doing in the world. Under Wagner's promise that regular Christians can become the vanguard of a revolutionary new kind of Christianity, Wimber is convinced that such Christians will be malformed into people who understand themselves as something other than imitators of Christ and humble disciples. For Wimber, everything in discipleship should be rooted in humility and imitation, not in innovation and the amplification of one's own significance.

Grace: I appreciate the response, but now I have more questions. I mean, if you believe that your powerful and fervent prayers can cure cancer, why can't you believe that your powerful and fervent prayers can tear down unseen principalities? It doesn't seem to me like a bridge too far—and so I don't fully understand Wimber's point about harm.

Caleb: I hear what you're saying. To me, the key issue lies in the adjectives "powerful and fervent," not in the noun "prayers." Wimber would say—and I agree—that nobody's prayers are especially powerful in themselves. Your prayers are your prayers. It is God who is powerful. Wimber's concern with Wagner is that he's teaching that there's an emerging elite class of Christians with special insight and gifts who have been given power by God to do things that other Christians can't see—thus making them the vanguard of a new apostolic age.

Wimber argued that this was fanciful beyond imagination, in fact bordering on delusion and hysteria. He argued instead that prayer is prayer, God is powerful, and we live in the time between the times. When we pray, God in God's sovereignty can choose to act in a miraculous way, or not. None of that is the responsibility of the disciple. What is the disciple's responsibility is to be faithful in imitating Jesus, not as an elite but as a servant of all.

5

Liminality as a Way to See the Heart of God's People

Juan J. Molina Flores

Whereas other books tell about grand things, says the author of Ecclesiastes, his book offers wisdom for ordinary and daily living (Eccles. 12:9–14). In theological education, there is likewise wisdom to be gleaned from ordinary experiences and institutions. In this essay, I invite you to "see what is already there" in what God has already given us to form God's people for their journey. Certainly, there are grand gifts in theological education. But I particularly invite us to recognize the gifts of liminal spaces and institutions—what they can teach us about how to embrace a "new era" of theological education. For while the content (the what) of theological education has typically been the focus of attention, the actual form (the how and where) of education is also important.

Is your theological institution building up the body of Christ with the kind of education it offers? An institution that builds up the body of Christ is a gift from God (1 Cor. 12:4–11). The Mexican American Catholic College (MACC), where I serve as president, can claim space in this great orchestra of instruments God has given the church.[1] But any goodness attributed to the institution must be defined primarily by its goodness for the people it serves.

That is, the institution's goal is to help those whom it serves find their own place in this glorious orchestra. In a way, MACC helps its students find out what instrument they, in turn, can be, as God uses them alongside others to make God's music. These students can claim their space as believers or as ministers of some kind. Carlos, whom you will meet below, found his place serving those in need using his skills as a lawyer while also serving as a lay minister. But he is just one example. There are many other MACC graduates that do not have any degree beyond their certificate from MACC that are likewise serving the church in various ways attuned to God's melodies.

MACC graduates tend to serve in liminal ways, ways that are between cultures or professions or nations or other realities that define life in this age. One reason MACC graduates can serve in these ways is that the institution itself occupies a liminal space. In this essay, I want to give some examples of people who were formed theologically in this liminal institution and for whom this formation was a gift for their ministries. These examples begin to show what liminality looks like in life and in the world (and certainly in an institution like MACC). In light of these stories of faithful leadership in liminal spaces, I want to consider the question of accreditation for this in-between institution that is MACC. I conclude with some reflections on theological education and formation in this liminal institution—and by implication other liminal institutions.

THEOLOGICAL EDUCATION FROM THE MARGINS: MACC YESTERDAY AND TODAY

Previously called the Mexican American Cultural Center, MACC was founded in 1972 to serve as a bridge connecting Mexican Americans with the larger church and society. It sought to give this community a voice in wider conversations. This meant being a bridge between a minority looking for affirmation and acceptance and a society that itself was evolving. Mexican Americans suffered by being considered neither "fully American" nor "fully Mexican." Many of them spoke English with a different accent, and many of them did not speak Spanish at all. While fully American citizens, they were not considered worthy of government positions or other "status" professions. They were, as we say in Spanish, *ni di aquí ni de allá* (neither from here nor there). Yet, they became an integral part of many movements in the late 1950s and 1960s that worked to integrate US society, and would eventually become part of what US society now calls "Hispanics." In the church they were likewise not fully accepted. Neither the church leadership nor the rest of society considered much of what they had learned at home (and even in their "ethnic parishes") regarding the faith as the "proper" way of living the faith. While Mexican Americans had learned much of the faith through popular devotion, processions, and imagery, the predominant US religious culture was based on learning the catechism (among Catholics) and on reading the Bible (among Protestants). While most Anglo-American Catholics learned the faith by memorizing the catechism, most Mexican American Catholics learned the faith by participating in the traditional Our Lady of Guadalupe celebrations, the traditional "posadas" during Advent, and other devotional events like the passion plays of Holy Week. And so, MACC was founded to bring to greater consciousness the faith as lived by Hispanics and to help Anglo-Americans (as well as some Mexican Americans) learn Spanish.[2] Now reimagined as the Mexican American Catholic College (still MACC!), it has not yet moved toward regional accreditation but has a strong connection with an accredited university and continues this two-part mission and tradition. There is a good reason for this.

The constituency that MACC serves is different from the one that can be found at an established, accredited, academic institution or school of theology. While MACC, like other schools, is forming ministers to serve in multicultural settings, it is doing so from a (liminal) Hispanic background or space, and this enables it to see and do what "establishment" groups and spaces do not see or cannot do in terms of responding to the needs and learning that minoritized populations have.[3] Who are those minoritized populations? Let me introduce you to some of MACC's graduates.

MEET MACC'S GRADUATES!

When she came to MACC, Sr. Rose[4] was already a consecrated woman in a Catholic religious congregation that had a variety of ministries in the United States and around the world. As part of a program at MACC, she went on a US-Mexico border-immersion experience to see the situation in the region and to spend time with people living there. Sr. Rose met many people who were living in poverty in migrant shelters while waiting either to move north or to find a home and work in the vicinity. Sr. Rose returned from this journey so transformed that she decided to ask her congregation to let her begin a new ministry in one of the *colonias* in a border town. She lived and ministered there for many years until she passed. She also founded a community organization there that still exists, and with which MACC collaborates, and to this day she is remembered as a giant of that community.

Carlos, whom I mentioned earlier, is a native of Nicaragua. He was a well-established and influential lawyer in a South Texas town when he came to MACC as part of a process of discerning a calling to offer his gifts in service to the community. He started working with Catholic Charities by offering pro bono services to those who needed them. After a few months, however, Carlos realized that his desire to do more to serve his neighbors was deepening his hunger for knowledge of God. He wanted, he said, "to take a few theology and ministry courses that were well-grounded, but that were not so heavily theoretical, and that included a rather practical component." Carlos added: "I don't need a PhD—or to be an expert—in theology to offer accompaniment and service to someone in need." This is how Carlos entered a formation program at MACC designed for lay pastoral ministers in the church who work both in a professional field and in the church. Once he graduated, Carlos started working full time with Catholic Charities but also became a eucharistic minister in his parish. He also serves on several boards of community organizations.

Tom completed his bachelor degree in pastoral ministry at MACC before going on to graduate studies in theology. At MACC, Tom took several pastoral ministry courses that prepared him to do theology and theological reflection in more contextual settings and to engage in biblical exegesis with the eyes and minds of ordinary people. Tom was ordained a priest in May of 2020 and was one of the priests who responded to the aftermath of the Robb Elementary School shooting in Uvalde, Texas, in May 2022. He served in a nearby parish in a community where families of victims as well as police personnel lived. And so, given the intense tragedy and moral complexity of the situation, Fr. Tom found himself ministering not only to student and staff survivors of the assault, and to the families of those killed, but also to traumatized members of the police—all while simultaneously supporting fellow ministers in Uvalde. This was challenging on multiple levels. Fr. Tom had to help the families and the victims process many feelings of anger, while also helping his ministerial colleagues process feelings of inadequacy. Not only that, but he also had to help members of the police force process their own feelings of helplessness and despair—amid urgent media interest and huge public outcry. Many police personnel were so ashamed of how their response unfolded—and so fearful of facing members of the community—that they were afraid of even staying in town or coming out of their homes to go to work. In the wake of the catastrophe, police personnel arrived from all over Texas to help an overwhelmed Uvalde police department. In the midst of this complex crisis, Fr. Tom was one of the leaders supporting the local priest and ensuring that other priests came to help provide much-needed pastoral care to all the various constituencies.

These three stories only begin to show the ways in which MACC alumni serve. Across many different contexts, they share a common formation. During their studies at MACC, our graduates have learned to live and minister in "liminal" or "in-between" spaces, to be in the middle of what is and what can be, to hold some things that are naturally in tension, and not to give a quick answer to try to resolve that tension. They have learned that sometimes they need to stay with the pain, not disregarding it even as they know that something can eventually come out of a situation. This is not easy and requires a certain capacity to know that not everything has to be confronted all at once and that God is present amid pain that sometimes feels interminable (Matt. 28:20; Ps. 23:1). Of course, evil must be confronted when necessary and pain must eventually be named. Yet, most of the time our society prefers to move too quickly to try to end uncertainty, to solve a problem before it can be solved, or to move too rapidly to a more stable environment or situation. Contrary to these impulses of the dominant culture, MACC forms students who can linger in the difficult in-between times and spaces and see what God works there.

Facing Change and the Need for Stability: The Challenge of Liminality

During the COVID-19 pandemic, we all wanted things to be more stable and predictable, but that was not an option back then. Other changes and situations also appeared at that time and continue to appear, such as the Black Lives Matter movement; levels of immigration now seen in the United States as overwhelming and many times unwanted; the war in Ukraine; and the conflict in Israel-Palestine. Yet many of us have realized that all these situations simply accelerated what was there in many aspects of our lives and of history: that we are not in an "epoch of changes" but in "a change of epoch."[5]

When one experiences a crisis, change, or transition, one often wants to return quickly to how life was before, or to create something that will be grounding and will help one attain a new status quo, or equilibrium. Institutions tend to do this as well. Yet "what was" is sometimes not the best there can be, and what we want to do or create quickly is likewise often not the best option and may not serve us well in the future.

This can also be the case in theology and theological education. What was taught in the past cannot be taught in the same way today. Sometimes even revelation must be seen and interpreted in a new way, and new paradigms of teaching the faith must be developed to make sense of the current situation, which includes both changing congregations and a changing society. Consider how many different interests drive a student to study theology—be it a desire to teach in the academy, teach in more popular settings, or use what they are learning in a diverse array of settings where experience and reflection may be more useful than abstract knowledge.[6] In chapter 10 of the Acts of the Apostles, for example, Peter experiences revelation in a new way as he interacts with Cornelius and his household. As a result, Peter reinterprets what he once understood as divine teaching and revelation in a more inclusive way. The Second Vatican Council was this kind of historic moment for the Roman Catholic Church in the twentieth century—a moment in which the church opened itself in different ways to an evolving world.

A Surprising Gift: In-Betweenness as a Liminal Way of Life

At MACC, our institutional experience has taught us that the period (or space) of "in-betweenness"—when one doesn't exactly know what is normal and what may come next—is more normal than people typically expect. And this has taught me that oftentimes it benefits us to learn to live with or accept ambiguity (and thus uncertainty). Things don't have to be clear and simple all the time. We can find life in liminality, and that can be a gift. Our MACC graduates, like Sr. Rose, Carlos, and Fr. Tom, seem to have internalized this understanding of the benefits of liminality during their studies. The liminal life of the institution served as a deep part of the curriculum for them, forming them for their own ministries in in-between spaces. As I described earlier, MACC's liminality goes back to its founding, and it remains in its mission.

Although liminality can be difficult, it is inevitable. As inevitable, perhaps we can learn to see it as a gift, as a space or span of time in which some creativity may emerge and lead to new things. In short, the benefit of liminality is that it may eventually bring us to a new and better recognition. On the other hand, liminality certainly isn't always a gift, especially if it doesn't lead to a better situation or status quo. For example, forced marginalization, migration, or displacement does not look like a gift to displaced or disadvantaged people. We mustn't overlook this reality.

Change takes time. Even the Bible tells us that God didn't create everything in one day. God took some time in creation (Gen. 1:1–2:3) and is still doing so in many aspects of it! The Gospels also tell us that God didn't raise Jesus from the dead overnight. There were many hours—an eternity, in some sense—between when his disciples laid him in the tomb and when they arrived and found him gone. Nature also has a period of gestation in most of what it does. And human activities like cooking, wine making, and distilling all take time. Since uncertainty is a feature of liminality, many writers agree that uncertainty isn't a human flaw but rather a feature of the world.[7] Faithful theological education for this kind of uncertain world will help form students able to dwell in liminal times and spaces.

Other areas of life also fit this "in between" description. Many of us are immigrants with relationships in at least two countries, and some of us go back and forth in between these countries. Many of us are bilingual and bicultural, and we understand how people think and behave differently in different languages and cultural contexts. Many ministers nowadays also have bivocational careers or jobs. For example, many students went to seminary as young adults and later realized that they also needed to know about law or accounting to do their ministry better. To gain that additional knowledge, perhaps they enroll in lifelong-learning workshops and courses. Others have done the opposite—started in a professional career and later realized that going to seminary and becoming ministers, even part time, would be meaningful for them. Like Carlos, many ministers may want to minister in the church but need an additional job to sustain their families. And so, they divide their time between their job and their ministry (which may be their true calling). This in-betweenness gives each aspect of their lives a different perspective and helps them work and minister in richer and more varied ways.[8]

The process of education also reflects this in-betweenness. We know, for example, that a master's or doctoral degree invites one into more desire for knowing and researching—that is, knowing invites one to seek more knowledge. And surely our spiritual lives are like that, too: when we know God somewhat, we desire to know God more.[9] As Saint Augustine of Hippo wrote, "For you made us for yourself, and our hearts are restless until they find their rest in you."[10]

At MACC, I have learned that in-betweenness can be the "normal" in one's status of "bifocal" (and sometimes multifocal) living. One can have an experience in which one is both here and there,[11] where one is living both now and in the future. In the church, we call this eschatological hope and living, the "now and not-yet" of the coming of the kingdom of God. There are both present and future aspects of the kingdom: God is here with us and yet still to fully come. The MACC alumni I have introduced to you seem to know they are living here and there (in the kingdom of God). But for MACC as an institution, this in-betweenness has evolved because of MACC's own history and desire to bring about God's kingdom to people who were marginalized and did not have (and still may not have) a voice in the church and society in the United States.

Institutional In-Betweenness

As I have learned at MACC, some organizations are "in between." That can be life-giving. It can also be painful and destabilizing.

To have a mission to serve those in need, or those without a voice, or those who are systematically marginalized, is not easy for an institution or for an individual. But the founders of such institutions and those working in them may find that goal important, as they address poverty, homelessness, discrimination, access to affordable education, and so on.

These kinds of institutions exist in between the academy and pastoral life, in between levels of government and the daily lives of people, and in between a church movement and the church's structures.[12] These in-between groups or entities tend to do a lot of good as they mediate between "the structure" and "the Spirit." And this, many times in history, is what has given birth to new moments and ways of life. Unfortunately, our culture encourages us only to see the status quo or the more stable status. That status is typically regarded as the "higher" and "better" one and, of course, the more comfortable one than the one that is actually being lived, and thus as the only one that is acceptable.

I think of MACC as an organization whose DNA determines it to be "in between." This was relevant when MACC was founded, and it continues to be relevant today during this change of epoch. In the church, the needs for learning theology have changed due to the array of different kinds of ministries available to serve the faithful in modern times. The academy, in its most scholastic sense, seems to be essential for some ministries but not others, leaving a gap. From the scholarly side of this divide, practical and pastoral theology stretch to fill the space between academic theology and pastoral practice.[13] People in these fields link sacramentality and mystery in human life and experience to some aspects of what feels like "liminality." We look to these fields for something that is enlightened by reason but animated by faith in all its expressions—culture, art, devotion, the psyche, and so on. That is, we are looking for what reason cannot fully explain or guide, things that may not fit easily into the traditional educational system for giving "academic credit." Many people want to serve the church from their own fields of knowledge, yet also want to increase their theological knowledge to hone that service.

From the practical side of this divide, some leaders are creating "communities of practice" in which practitioners from different fields come together to advance a common cause, such as eradicating poverty and illiteracy, or undertaking community development. While this has been more prevalent in Protestant circles with the idea of *misión integral* (holistic mission), many Catholic organizations are now working in the same style.[14] The focus on practice enables these communities to value not only the wisdom of practitioners but also that of academics from many different disciplines around issues of common concern. In short, we are understanding that theology has a place in a much larger ecosystem of change, and that theology doesn't do this alone but in collaboration with other disciplines. This is an example of a *pastoral de conjunto* (collaborative ministry) approach.

This is why MACC serves as a bridge between the academy and those who desire to serve the church in ministry in traditional as well as new ways and who come with different backgrounds and for different purposes to learn pastoral theology at MACC. Perhaps the academy has too long forgotten or failed to include marginalized communities, cultural aspects, and practical ministry, or has done so only reticently and recently.[15] This is why places like MACC are recasting theological education for people of different needs and levels of knowledge.

Much research in the last few years has taught us that humans have different ways of knowing beyond just the intellectual way of knowing.[16] Arts like music, dance, and certainly painting have a lot to do with the ways people learn and come to the knowledge of God. At MACC we know that popular devotions, for example, help the faithful come to "know" God in very particular ways.[17]

But how does one set standards for such art forms and spiritual experiences? They certainly must be different from just a question and an answer presented in a logical way. Finding ways to account for this in the academy can be a challenge. However, at MACC we see this as an opportunity to help future and current ministers learn and engage in different ways, and develop new ways of ministering to different people. I can think here, for example, of those ministering to persons with disabilities. The theological academy still does not have the practices and beliefs it needs to engage these communities in meaningful ways, and thus ministers in these fields find themselves short of resources to brainstorm on how to engage those they serve.

The academy can collaborate with institutions like MACC to provide excellent and relevant pastoral formation to individuals who will minister in different kinds of environments. There is a great need among Catholics, for example, to form leaders who can serve the growing Hispanic community in both rural and urban settings—and many times with only a few priests as the sacramental ministers. Many seminaries and schools of theology have addressed this need by increasing the number of master of divinity programs with a concentration on Hispanic ministry, and by developing specific initiatives to support Hispanic students (such as the Hispanic Theological Initiative and the Hispanic Scholars Program). We at MACC offer certificates at the undergraduate level that help people with little academic background to be formed so they can serve in different capacities, both in urban and in rural settings. Other people come to MACC to be formed with more academic rigor (including seminarians, religious men and women in formation, and master's-degree-seeking students) because they prefer a learning context in which culture and language are prioritized. Sr. Rose learned to live and minister in in-between times and spaces of a community experiencing poverty. She didn't need to do that, but, thanks to being immersed in our in-between institution offering a different kind of theological education, she felt God was calling her to do so.

Here at MACC, we are increasingly aware of the great urban and rural differences in Catholic dioceses, and the ways in which our students are called to serve differently in them. In response, we have begun to do more contextual and pastoral theology to help our students develop tools for learning and doing theology in either a rural or an urban setting—or perhaps in both—for our students are likely to have to minister in each at some point.[18] While the academy prepares students for doing theology "with the books," we also prepare students to do theology and ministry "with the people" or "of the people"—wherever the people are living.[19]

Called to Be Comfortable, Patient, Persistent, and Hopeful

In a "liminal" situation, responding to a call entails not only dealing with the pain that the uncertainty may bring but also trying to be patient with it, and to be persistent in learning and knowing how to live in this situation while still working toward a different, better one. It requires hope that things can get better or that God will bring some good out of what may currently be causing pain (cf. Gen. 50:20; Rom. 8:28). A disadvantaged family or group, however, may want to change the situation as soon as possible, feeling it lacks the luxury of time. And that kind of liminal situation also needs to be discerned to find the best ways to address it for the better.

Our alumni have learned to do such discernment in liminal situations, not just here at MACC, but in their own ministries. Several of our programs introduce our students to pastoral methods for doing theology and ministry by praxis and experience by taking them to places where this "in-betweenness" is lived every day, such as the US-Mexico border and rural communities experiencing poverty. As it did for Sr. Rose, this kind of immersion experience gives our students a sense that some situations are not merely to be studied and written about from a distance but are to be experienced in person so that one can imagine alternatives and work to bring those alternatives about. One encounters many stories of suffering, abandonment, and despair while ministering—let alone living—in these situations. Such contextual education therefore helps our graduates in their own ministries, at that time or later, when they must also practice the virtues of patience and persistence, as well as be comfortable with ambivalent and at times painful situations, and situations that are slow in shifting.

For Fr. Tom, this call to become somewhat "comfortable" with the pain of the people (and his own) and be patient in dealing with it became a reality in the aftermath of the Uvalde school shooting in 2022. Understandably, that community was still dealing with the pain a couple of years later when the records of the police response were published. At that time, the police were roundly blamed for the way their slow response unfolded and allegedly allowed more children to be killed. The community and its ministers had to find new ways of dealing with it. This presented Fr. Tom with an opportunity to embrace a kind of comfort and patience that can only be experienced and sustained when one is somewhat at ease with in-betweenness. In more everyday terms, Fr. Tom had to learn to be patient doing "band aid" ministry (dealing with the present pain of the community) before jumping to doing justice ministry (asking: Who is responsible for such an incompetent and irresponsible response to the shooting?). Fr. Tom's education and experience at MACC made him resourceful.

While our students learn by experience to deal with this in-betweenness, MACC itself also lives in this kind of in-betweenness, modeling for our students that easy and quick answers may at times be neither available nor the best option.

MACC as an Instrument in God's Orchestra

MACC participates as a member of God's orchestra as God creates music through it for the world. In his first letter, Peter reminds us that God has given each of us different gifts (1 Pet. 4:10–11). And Paul, in his first letter to the Corinthians, states that there are different gifts in the community but the same spirit who grants them to the believers for the forming of the body of Christ (1 Cor. 12:4–11). In short, gifts are given for the common good, for the mission of the church.

We also know that God speaks to us in different ways and through different means (Heb. 1:1–2). Some of those means come to us as and through the gifts that God distributes to God's people. In the last thousand years or so, God has spoken to us through a logical body of knowledge kept in trust by the academy. But the true "keeper of the faith and of knowledge of God" has always been the people of God. Intellectual knowledge and teaching have their place; they are instruments (means) in God's orchestra. But there are often other instruments besides these.[20] Institutions that are "in between" are another kind of instrument God uses to accompany the people of God. I have described to you how MACC is one such in-between institution—not fully in the academy, not only a Bible institute, but certainly informed by the academy and reaching out to those who need a more "understandable" and practical theology and pastoral ministry.

That MACC is an instrument God uses to play God's music for me means that for MACC to be where it is, it occupies the space God has wanted it to occupy. It may not be following the usual route of "success"—that of seeking accreditation as soon as possible, becoming well known, and enrolling a lot of students. But I am confident that it is where it needs to be, fulfilling the mission God has entrusted to it. Certainly, MACC is developing important relationships and forming effective ministers.

Making God's Music Together: The Way Forward

Teasing out this metaphor of the instruments God uses to play God's music, I wonder: How can we make music together? For MACC as an institution, the answers to this question invite discernment about our future.

Networking and collaboration with other institutions are important aspects of the future of MACC. We have long collaborated with a select group of other institutions; now we are collaborating even more intentionally. These collaborations have proven beneficial to all the institutions involved; we literally complement each other in areas in which we ourselves have not developed expertise, such as rural ministry or intercultural competencies.

An easy way to answer the question about a way forward is to suggest that MACC seek accreditation either with the Association of Theological Schools (ATS) (for MACC's MA program) or with the Southern Association of Colleges and Schools Commission on Colleges (SACSCOC), either through MACC's collaboration with the University of the Incarnate Word (UIW) or on its own (for MACC's AA, BA, and MA programs). But perhaps a more thoughtful, even if more difficult, path forward entails considering a few questions that bear upon the future of MACC's mission—questions about MACC's constituency (the ministers MACC forms) and about those whom this constituency serves (the people served by those ministers).

The college already has accredited collaborative AA, BA, and MA programs in pastoral ministry in association with UIW. Our programs and courses have the rigor of any accredited institution. They are overseen by UIW, and both institutions keep records of compliance. In mutual dialogue, we ensure that there is sufficient staffing and other resources to serve the student population in these programs, that standards are upheld, and that we have the facilities and equipment to offer quality programs. In short, MACC is considered a noncontiguous teaching site of the University for those programs. In the last few years, these programs have been excellent tools to support Hispanic students who initially needed help and then a "push" to obtain their degrees. Yet not all of MACC's students are eager to go on for further studies. Whether a lay student has decided to enter the AA, the BA, or the MA program usually depends more on finances than on a desire to do ministry with an accredited degree. All the seminarians that come to MACC are required to study for the BA (like Fr. Tom) or the Certificate in Pre-Theology. Our certificate programs—even at the undergraduate level—have seemed sufficient for most of our lay students to be empowered to do ministry in their respective dioceses (like Carlos). In short, some of our students claim their space as ministers with a certificate, while others find their space by continuing on to further theological studies. Whichever journey these students decide to take, MACC's mission of claiming a space for them and with them has been fulfilled.

This experience of being empowered for ministry is what is important. That empowerment has many dimensions: knowing and loving the people and the way of life of the community; having the appropriate background, disposition, and training to be effective; and having particular expertise in using practical theology to inform their particular contextual practices of ministry.

This in-between freedom of having both accredited and non-accredited undergraduate programs for ministry gives MACC the flexibility to create programs that can respond to immediate needs or that are tailored to a specific diocese or religious congregation or ministry situation. Later on, in dialogue with the University, MACC can gauge whether those new programs can actually be of service at the accredited level. An example of such flexibility is a program we created specifically for religious sisters coming from Latin America to minister in the United States. These sisters needed formation to help them get to know the US culture and context, and to become more comfortable doing theology from an academic perspective.

CONCLUSION: KEEPING THE ESSENTIALS AND INCLUDING THE BEAUTY OF GOD

The in-betweenness that is part of MACC's DNA continues today and exists for a reason: to give nontraditional students a nimble and in-between place to be formed, one that is able to respond quickly and creatively to events and challenges. Even if MACC were to be more fully accredited, being liminal would continue to be a strength at MACC. It will likely continue to offer nonaccredited courses and certificates, and ironically, they might continue to be the ones that attract the most students.

Thanks to being an inherently nimble and in-between institution, MACC can claim a vocation as an eschatological institution—a "here and there" institution that encounters and forms people where they are but helps them move to another place where they can be affirmed and more effective with their gifts.

In short, MACC helps students find their calling as disciples. This echoes Vatican II's concept of the priesthood of all believers grounded in our baptismal call, as MACC seeks to form lay ministers who can serve alongside ordained and consecrated persons. Whereas theological education used to be focused on training and producing ordained ministers and professors, MACC embraces our current reality that there can be several ways of forming ministers because there are several objectives for that formation. Moreover, such formation helps people who are disenfranchised and marginalized because they don't have the requisite training or the credentials. But perhaps being trained for liminal ministry practice is itself a pressing goal, especially in liminal places like South Texas, and in Hispanic or multicultural parishes and congregations. It takes an in-between institution to prepare people for these in-between ministries.

I imagine that it will remain an essential part of MACC's educational ministry to help students who want to do ministry achieve the agency to see themselves as disciples and ministers in the church without necessarily having to study at a fully accredited institution and be ordained. Their time at MACC helps those who do want to be ordained to develop the "eyes" to see beyond the academy and into the hearts of the people of God. That is MACC's mission: to empower disciples, and to enable them to grow sufficiently to be able either to enter the academy or to become effective ministers. This is what Sr. Rose, Carlos, and Fr. Tom did on their respective journeys. The role MACC plays is to be a bridge, an instrument. While the content of their formation at MACC is important, how MACC forms them enables them to be disciples and accompany others on their journeys in in-between places.

Dialogue

Juan J. Molina Flores, Angela Sims, David Nacho

Angela: Juan, there is richness in the essay, and I think it comes from your focus on the people of MACC. I would suggest expanding this with studies of current students, alumni, and current and past administrators. This would give us a glimpse of who MACC and its people are. It would be a compilation that broadens the understanding of theological education in an always-changing world.

David: These portraits show how theological education at MACC goes beyond academic matters. The characters involved in the education and learning are real people. Through their stories, you guide the reader into a reflection on the nature of theological education. I feel personally enriched, as I had a similar experience in South America. I like how you introduce the different people and how they are somewhat comfortable in liminality. Their lives have shown us how a MACC education really embraces both spirituality and the institution's way of being. The richness of people's experiences and the reflective nature of the essay come together.

Angela: I particularly appreciated the paragraph introducing Sr. Rose's experience because it shows that one way to get to the depth of theological dialogue is through attention to language. "Sr. Rose met many people who were living in poverty" is how you describe it, instead of saying, "She met poor people." To me, this gets to the heart of theological anthropology, to the essence of who these characters really are. First and foremost, they are children of God. Juan, you also present some ways in which theology is always "crisscrossing" these types of artificially constructed boundaries. Having students who have come to MACC from multiple contexts around the globe, and yet find themselves at a particular place and moment in time, points to the vastness of what it means to begin to think about God's presence in and among us.

Juan: Yes, this is what I was trying to say in this essay. People are realizing that theological education goes beyond just "head" knowledge, beyond learning a set of principles and norms. Theological education also needs to incorporate your "heart" knowledge. That is, you also need to grow in your heart, in your affections, and incorporate that knowledge into both the "academy" and the practice of ministry. However, the academy has focused on a particular kind of knowledge and has done so in a particular kind of way. That sometimes creates a big distinction between the theologians (that is, those who "know") and the rest of the church, instead of simply referring to everyone as faithful people who do theology from the experience of the church, as it used to be in the early times of Christianity.

Angela: And yet, you are graduating practical theologians!

Juan: Absolutely! People who know theology from the heart and the head!

Angela: People from MACC know God through their heart, but they also have a deep appreciation for the cultivation of the intellect as a spiritual and academic discipline. And MACC students are taking your message back to their countries of origin and to their ministry contexts! So, another question that could be asked is this: What does it mean for MACC to be a geographically dispersed institution? Because the institution's mission leaves San Antonio and goes around the globe with its graduates.

David: On this issue of liminality, I am personally very encouraged by the way people from diverse countries and backgrounds are welcomed at MACC. And in that welcoming, the students are given space to shape the narrative of MACC. To me, that is very reflective of the culture of today's practices—and so it is very different from most theological institutions. The institutions tend to be at the center of that exchange, and they manage the narrative. Here the narrative is more flexible [because it depends on the conversation partners]. That is why I don't see the accreditation issue you mention in the essay as being at the center of MACC's narrative. It seems to be an addition but not something that would add much more meaning for MACC and its ministry. So, liminality is what the gift is in this case.

Juan: Right! We know people come to MACC because this is a place where the liminality of life will not only be accepted. . . .

David: . . . But they'll also learn "to be patient with it," as you phrase it in the essay. So, the students may or may not obtain some kind of accredited degree or certificate. But what is certain is that they will get that profound experience of being shaped in terms of the liminality of life. And in that process, MACC's own narrative is being deepened and expanded.

Juan: That's one main point I am trying to make. Although accreditation is the end for which most schools strive, we at MACC have been exploring that option much more slowly for historical reasons. And I have come to realize that, given our relationships and our mission, it may not be the end of our journey or even a stop. I am not excluding accreditation, but I do not think it is the most important part of our mission at this time.

I remember that when I first came into this writing group, Angela was concentrating on her school's own restructuring, the move to a new location, and what it meant for her to be the first Black female president in a historically white school. And that seemed to be very important in her story. I knew we had some issues in common.

So, as I began focusing on what accreditation might mean for MACC, I thought, "What will it do for us? What will it do for our students if our mission has always been to minister from the margins?" And when you minister from the margins, you don't have that center stage. And sometimes you don't have that privilege of being accredited. From the beginning we have been mainly about the mission, without focusing so much on the institution and its status. The center of our mission has always been people-focused, church-focused, and accreditation is not at the center for us. I understand this is not exclusive nor definitive, but rather a matter of priorities at a specific time.

Angela: So, Juan, what would you say about accreditation if you had only five minutes to speak to Frank Yamada, the executive director of the Association of Theological Schools, about it? What would you say about accreditation as a limitation to an expansiveness to theological education?

Juan: I would say that my impression is that accreditation in most schools serves to focus them on educating ministers for specific tracks, to get them employed in particular positions, generally ordained ministries or to teach. At MACC, we go beyond that vision. Therefore, accreditation is not at the center. It's more of an addition, rather than a reason why we do what we do. There's a greater breadth of theological education at MACC than a track that leads to ordination or to a teaching position. There is formation for all kinds of ministries, which the accredited schools have done as well but have not taken as seriously as we do at MACC. Think of Bible institutes and even popular movements. The ATS only supports part of that formation (the part connected to ordination or teaching) and helps schools in maintaining excellent standards for the approved tracks. But nowadays, "where the action is"—or rather the tracks that many new aspiring ministers want to enter—are the ones that are "not for credit" but are also more than just adult faith formation. They focus on the heart, not just on head knowledge. . . .

This conversation helps us agree that the fourfold model of theological education that has been traditionally taught as the necessary tools for being ordained doesn't do the trick of forming most people in the church. That kind of preparation helps for ordained ministry, but not for many other people who want to minister in the church yet not necessarily be ordained. It seems, then, that theological education now should not be thought of as needing to be designed for the exclusive purpose of ordaining students to parish-based or congregationally based ministry. When we look at the teaching that has taken place over the centuries, it's usually layfolk without formal theological education that are teaching catechism, for instance. Clearly, MACC has not missed this point.

David: I agree. I think MACC is enriching the broader ecology of theological education. This also shows the in-betweenness that MACC inhabits, between the church movements and church structures.

Juan: I initially wondered why I, representing MACC, had been invited to be part of this group, and eventually got the point that our in-betweenness is how we belong. And so, we need to own it! Unless we understand that theological education is not just preparation for ordination or for teaching but the work of the entire people of God as we get to know and experience God, we miss the point.

Angela: Yes, perhaps accreditation may seem equal to some kind of elitism that can lead to a misunderstanding. Your essay shows that it takes different kinds of institutions to help the people of God be formed theologically. And so, for MACC, accreditation may not be the goal and may not need to be given so much regard. After all, MACC is already doing quality theological education.

6

Identity, Desire, and Non-Self-Sufficiency

David Nacho

The following passage from the Gospel of John had a profound effect on my ministry as a theological educator in Latin America:

> Now Jesus learned that the Pharisees had heard that he was gaining and baptizing more disciples than John—although in fact it was not Jesus who baptized, but his disciples. So he left Judea and went back once more to Galilee.
>
> Now he had to go through Samaria. So he came to a town in Samaria called Sychar, near the plot of ground Jacob had given to his son Joseph. Jacob's well was there, and Jesus, tired as he was from the journey, sat down by the well. It was about noon.
>
> When a Samaritan woman came to draw water, Jesus said to her, "Will you give me a drink?" (His disciples had gone into the town to buy food.)
>
> The Samaritan woman said to him, "You are a Jew and I am a Samaritan woman. How can you ask me for a drink?" (For Jews do not associate with Samaritans.)
>
> Jesus answered her, "If you knew the gift of God and who it is that asks you for a drink, you would have asked him and he would have given you living water."

"Sir," the woman said, "you have nothing to draw with and the well is deep. Where can you get this living water? Are you greater than our father Jacob, who gave us the well and drank from it himself, as did also his sons and his livestock?"

Jesus answered, "Everyone who drinks this water will be thirsty again, but whoever drinks the water I give them will never thirst. Indeed, the water I give them will become in them a spring of water welling up to eternal life."

The woman said to him, "Sir, give me this water so that I won't get thirsty and have to keep coming here to draw water."

He told her, "Go, call your husband and come back."

"I have no husband," she replied.

Jesus said to her, "You are right when you say you have no husband. The fact is, you have had five husbands, and the man you now have is not your husband. What you have just said is quite true."

"Sir," the woman said, "I can see that you are a prophet. Our ancestors worshiped on this mountain, but you Jews claim that the place where we must worship is in Jerusalem."

"Woman," Jesus replied, "believe me, a time is coming when you will worship the Father neither on this mountain nor in Jerusalem. You Samaritans worship what you do not know; we worship what we do know, for salvation is from the Jews. Yet a time is coming and has now come when the true worshipers will worship the Father in the Spirit and in truth, for they are the kind of worshipers the Father seeks. God is spirit, and his worshipers must worship in the Spirit and in truth."

The woman said, "I know that Messiah" (called Christ) "is coming. When he comes, he will explain everything to us."

Then Jesus declared, "I, the one speaking to you—I am he."

Just then his disciples returned and were surprised to find him talking with a woman. But no one asked, "What do you want?" or "Why are you talking with her?"

Then, leaving her water jar, the woman went back to the town. (John 4:1–28 NIV)

As I said, participatory studies of this passage did much to shape my understanding of my ministry in Bolivia and my work as academic dean of the Community for Interdisciplinary Theological Education (CETI, for its acronym in Spanish), a transnational community that gathers participants from across Latin America.[1] Reading the passage together with instructors and facilitators shaped not only my own ministry but also the ethos of our community. By retelling the story in John 4, we rediscovered Jesus's dialogical approach to theological reflection. We also explored challenging aspects of Christology, soteriology, and our own identity as theological educators. Here, I offer you a taste of that process of community formation.

"*Give me a drink*," the weary theological educator asked of a surprised woman coming his way. The teacher was weary not only because of the scorching midday heat. He had also just finished a fruitful teaching season, and he had stopped at that well in search of a safe place where he could restore his energies. His success had drawn the attention of his critics,[2] who realized that more students had enrolled with him than with one of the most iconic teachers of the time, the Baptizer.

Noon is not the usual time of day for women to gather at wells to draw water. Why did this woman come at such an unusual hour? Was she trying to hide from the community? Perhaps! What we know with more certainty is that Jesus, the theological educator, needed a space of safety and comfort, was exhausted, and didn't have the means (a jar or bucket) with which to draw water to satisfy his thirst.

The characters of our story find themselves at this place because of a common need (water), but the exchange begins because the teacher is at a disadvantage. He is the one who does not have the means to draw water from the well. What kind of theological learning can happen out of a situation like this? That is, what kind of learning can happen when the exchange begins not with an offer from the teacher but with his recognition that he needs help?

Recognizing our common need does not automatically create solidarity between people, as the teacher learns from the woman's perplexed and perhaps curt response: "You are a Jew and I am a Samaritan woman. How can you ask me for a drink?" We are no different today. Even when we meet, we can remain divided by the norms and expectations of the communities to which we belong. It is tempting to say that this is the woman's problem, not the teacher's: the woman was bound by cultural norms while the teacher transcends them. But this would not do justice to the fact that the teacher could not afford to abide by the expectations. He was thirsty! Not in a docetic way, in which he only appeared thirsty, but in a deeply embodied way. The teacher *needs* to transgress dividing lines to get water. The kind of learning that the teacher is cultivating begins not with the high-minded crossing of boundaries that always includes a kind of condescension, but with a recognition of the teacher's own needs for the other.

Theological reflection that begins out of the need for life-giving water does not ignore the differences between the teacher and the woman; it needs to untangle them. The teacher must keep creating space to ask and receive questions. So, he continues the conversation with an evocative "If you only knew . . ." The teacher's awareness of his own need does not keep him from offering what he has to his conversation partner. The teacher sparks the woman's imagination by offering her water that isn't stagnant but that bursts forth, water that's alive.

The woman has so far brought to this exchange her cultural expectations. Now, as an astute and practical observer, she reminds the teacher that he has no means to satiate his own need for water: "You have nothing to draw water with and the well is deep." After her practical assessment, she articulates a life-changing question laden with theology: "Are you greater than our father Jacob?"

The conversation moves forward because of the kindling of desire. The meaning of water becomes richer and more interesting, and so do the identities of the teacher and the woman. With her question, the woman creates space for the teacher to reveal a bit more about himself: "I can make you into a spring of living water," he promises. Once he creates this space, she becomes the one who asks for water. Into that space she brings once again her orientation to practical matters; she is already thinking about putting this water to good use.

As we get to know this woman, it is easy to fall into the mistake of being condescending toward her. It is easy to assume that this "poor woman" couldn't understand that Jesus was wanting to have a theological conversation with her, and that she couldn't think beyond H_2O and the practical needs of both parties. Such an assumption would only reveal how little we understand or appreciate the form of knowledge that she brings to the theological conversation. As we saw above, she was already asking theologically nuanced questions not just about the water but about the identity of the teacher who was offering her water. Her boundaries between the categories of material and spiritual needs are not ours; because of that, perhaps she understands the teacher not only better than we assume, but maybe even better than we understand him.

Does the teacher understand her? If he does, why does he say, "Go, call your husband and come back"? When I posed this question to a group of CETI students in a *favela* in the outskirts of São Paulo, Brazil, one of them raised her hand timidly and said, "If he is going to reveal himself, perhaps he wanted to make space for the woman to reveal herself as well . . . but I am no theologian." This Brazilian woman was reading with deep insight, but she did not feel as if she belonged among the theologians. However, the fact that she spoke up during our meeting means that she felt as if she belonged in the faith community that had begun to study ecclesiology through a CETI module. Perhaps neither the Samaritan woman nor this Brazilian student might see themselves as belonging among the theologians. What kind of belonging should theological studies lead to, then? The conversation between the teacher and the woman proves fruitful again.

The life story of the woman at the well had been rough. So it is no surprise that when asked about marriage (which at least promises a life-defining experience of belonging), she doesn't tell her whole story. She simply says that she has no husband. Most likely, her "not having a husband" had turned her into an outcast. Likewise, we do not know why she had had five husbands, as the teacher says, but we do know that it was much easier for men to divorce and abandon their wives than the other way around. Whatever the details, her life has surely been difficult.

The teacher reveals more of her story, but his words are respectful: "You are right. . . . You have spoken truth," he says, before telling her more than she thinks he could possibly know about her life. Living water begins to flow in the exchange between the teacher and the Samaritan woman as both identities are being revealed. And so, the bold woman names the identity of the teacher with a theological category that makes sense to her: "I perceive you are a prophet." Then, she expands her observation while asserting her own belonging: "Our ancestors worshiped on this mountain." Earlier, she had identified herself as a daughter of Jacob. Now, she speaks as a member of a community that has inherited traditions from the ancestors. We learn in these words that it would be reductive on our part to characterize her simply as an outcast. If we pay attention, we recognize her as someone who is ready to assert their belonging.

Asserting her belonging makes space for her questions and her contextual theological concerns as they are. In fact, the question she brings is no trivial theological matter. The correct place for worship was one of the greatest and most polarizing theological debates of those times: "Our ancestors worshiped on this mountain, but you Jews claim that the place where we must worship is in Jerusalem."

The persistent negotiation of differences provides the opportunity for the teacher to reveal more of his intentions. The theological depth of the teacher's response must match the acute perspicacity of the woman's questions. And so he responds to the theological question about the correct place for worship by deepening it and reframing it: "A time is coming and has now come when the true worshipers will worship the Father in the Spirit and in truth, for they are the kind of worshipers the Father seeks. God is spirit, and his worshipers must worship in the Spirit and in truth." In the teacher's answer, God's identity and desire are at stake. Can this conversation get any more theologically profound!? How does one worship God in Spirit and in truth? If we take the teacher's commendation of the woman's truthfulness, we may say that worship includes naming our relationships of belonging. So, the kind of belonging that theological education should foster can include the guild of theologians. However, for the Samaritan woman and the woman from our CETI group in Brazil, the sense of belonging that emboldens them to speak comes from the communities with whom they share life.

Once more the woman asserts her belonging by naming the desire of her people: "I know that Messiah is coming. When he comes, he will tell us all things." Having articulated God's desire and having heard the woman's articulation of her people's desire, the wearied, non-self-sufficient teacher reveals (or claims?) his full identity: I AM.

When the teacher's students arrive, they interpret what they see through the differences between the teacher and the woman but don't know how to negotiate them; accordingly, they choose not to ask questions, neither about her desires nor his motivations. But the woman knows that the I AM teacher desires water and doesn't have the means to get it from the well, so she leaves her jar behind for him and his disciples.

THEOLOGIZING IN COMMUNITY

We shift our attention from the dynamics of the interaction between the teacher and the woman to the woman's process of making sense of her experience. Of course, these two aspects are inseparable, but I originally chose to treat the next part of the story in a separate section to allow me to connect this experience with what we have aimed to do at CETI within our own Latin American context.

> So the woman left her water jar and went away into town and said to the people, "Come, see a man who told me all that I ever did. Can this be the Christ?" They went out of the town and were coming to him. . . .
>
> Many Samaritans from that town believed in him because of the woman's testimony, "He told me all that I ever did." So when the Samaritans came to him, they asked him to stay with them, and he stayed there two days. And many more believed because of his word. They said to the woman, "It is no longer because of what you said that we believe, for we have heard for ourselves, and we know that this is indeed the Savior of the world." (John 4:28–30, 39–42 ESV)

Once she returns to her community, the woman's testimony asserts the value of her own lived experience (both before and at the well): "He told me all that I ever did." The fruit of theological dialogue is not her diminishment but a recognition that her experience is the site in which and through which theological revelation happened. She also names the hope of her people. The community responds, and, as they too take a taste of living water, they come to know for themselves that the wearied teacher is none other than "the Savior of the World."

In the process of revealing himself, the teacher embodied non-self-sufficiency in two ways. First, in this exchange, he shows that being the Messiah is about asking for life-giving water as much as it is about offering living water. In other words, the teacher did not begin with a proclamation of his messianic identity or with his offer to give living water to anyone who would need it. Instead, the profound theological exchange between the teacher and the woman begins and ends highlighting the thirst of the teacher. Second, the teacher chose to engage the woman's observations and questions. In doing this, he allowed the woman's identity and concerns to shape the form of his self-revelation. Through the lens of Latin American contextual theological education, I see the woman's speech as an instance of self-theologizing, which begins with the recognition that different cultures not only raise different theological questions but also create and use different categories based on different principles and different logics.[3] We saw that the exchange between the teacher and the Samaritan woman welcomed the categories that the woman brought to it. Latin American contextual theology resonates with the teacher's approach because it emphasizes that we learn by theologizing from where we are.

So, theological reflection happens as we acknowledge ourselves in need of help and as we struggle to get the things we need. This encounter recalibrated the wearied and thirsty teacher's journey. He found not only water but also the safe place he desired from the beginning, as he was fleeing from the critics. Similarly, the woman and her community were invited to join in the process of Christological revelation, recalibrating their own journeys as they experienced salvation. This raises another crucially important question for theological educators: What if theological education helped us, not only students but also theological educators, make sense of the experience of being saved?

What the woman learned at the well (i.e., the teacher's Christological self-revelation) did not erase her life story. Furthermore, she experienced salvation as the Messiah's solidarity in a joint struggle. As she experienced salvation, theological reflection in solidarity with the teacher emboldened her to name her desires ("give me that water") and the desires of her community. But before that, it made her sensitive to the needs of another.

FURTHER REFLECTIONS OUT OF LATIN AMERICA

My purpose with this essay is to evoke a story that invites theological conversations regarding the posture of the educator, the method by which learning takes place, and the role of the social identities of those involved. Just as the teacher and the Samaritan woman had to untangle the antagonisms, so too theological educators and students must often negotiate conflicted identities to create new shared spaces. In the final section of this essay, I offer an account of how this imagination shaped the institutional life of CETI before and during my time as academic dean. I begin with some observations coming from Latin American theological educators because they show how necessary *and* how challenging it is to imagine and strive for new spaces.

In Latin America, theological education institutions operate within the system of the free market that has permeated the continent since the 1980s and that has affected every area of public life, including education at all levels.[4] Because of this, the number of options for theological education in Latin America has also spiraled rapidly upward.[5] Meanwhile, traditional theological education has remained problematically stagnant in a number of ways: it takes place primarily at the seminary or faculty of theology, where the content of this education is transmitted (with an almost exclusively cognitivist emphasis) as a systematic reflection on faith divided into disciplinary silos, such as Bible, history, systematic theology, practical or pastoral theology and ethics, etc.[6] The instructors are mostly male, and the purpose of the theological education they give is to consolidate and reproduce a denominationally defined church. The degrees offered are copied from the secular academic nomenclature (e.g., bachelor's, master's, etc.) but are not always accredited by official educational bodies.

Nevertheless, despite the heavily commodified nature of education in general and the stagnation in theological education in particular, many Latin American theological educators still embrace high ideals about their craft and vocation. At CETI, one of those high ideals has been providing access to a wide variety of students because we understood that the quality and pertinence of the theological education we wanted to offer was intrinsically tied to the plurality of voices engaging in our theological reflection. In this, CETI's vocation for theological education deeply resonates with the words of Cecilia González-Andrieu, a leading scholar in theological aesthetics and educational justice, who highlights the humanizing mandate of education and raises the issue of access to theological education: "[Without] a sufficiently diverse group in the conversation, we are just reinforcing what we already know, and thus, the efficacy of education itself is lost. What is more, as a Christian theologian I understand there to be a nonnegotiable requirement presented by biblical faith—the imperative to embody the true universality of God's love. . . . To paraphrase theologian Roberto Goizueta, we cannot speak of theological education as in some way having a real connection to the search for God without speaking of such education as available to all. Anything else is a contradiction."[7]

For reasons like those González-Andrieu names, CETI has sought to honor the need for access—which leads to true diversity—as part of its commitment to quality and depth in theological education. To do this during the decade I served as academic dean, we pursued three courses of action. First, we offered both accredited graduate programs and church-based informal programs. Second, several of our faculty and students from the graduate program were involved as either facilitators or students in the informal programs in order to bring mutual enrichment to both programs. Third, we hosted regional and national gatherings at which we created spaces for the exchange of stories and experiences between participants of both programs.

I want to make clear that our accredited program was not the "quality" program. For the fact is that CETI's quest for quality predates the process of formal accreditation. One of the key markers in the history of CETI is the participation of one of the former directors, Guillermo Steinfeld, in a group of some of Latin America's most influential theologians, educators, and institutional leaders, who all signed a manifesto called "Toward quality theological education," which outlines a shared understanding of the purpose of theological education in Latin America:

> We understand theological education to be part of the Church's mission of announcing and anticipating the Reign of God in history. [Theological education or TE] deals with a particular kind of education connected to the creative, organized, and critical learning of those who reflect on their faith—that is, those who do theology—from the diversity of their gifts and ministries. . . . We

> propose a TE that is open to all believers, women and men, that is continued throughout their lives, and with an incidence in different spheres and degrees of specialization. To accomplish this, TE will dialogue with political practices, cultural expressions, and the sciences committed to the defense of all aspects of life.[8]

It would have been simpler to limit quality to accreditation; instead, by adding our voice to this manifesto, we allowed our desire (that is, our hopes and aspirations for our communities) to inform the meaning of "quality" in theological education. During my years as academic dean, I learned that it is important to name our desires and to see whether they are serving us and others well. Otherwise, it would be tempting to think that non-self-sufficiency for theological institutions is simply a fruit of the perennial lack of funding. Instead, non-self-sufficiency has to do with a pedagogical and ethical stance toward the subject of our studies and toward the communities that embrace us. It is a stance we have learned from our teacher.

Dialogue

David Nacho, Janette H. Ok, John Kartje

David: Friends, thank you for taking the time to witness with me the encounter between Jesus and the Samaritan woman. I always enjoy hearing what other people see in the story. I hope my essay was evocative and inspiring.

Janette: The thing that intrigues me most about your essay is the idea of Jesus as non-self-sufficient. What would that mean for the theological educator? How would a theological educator need to reframe how she sees her task, her posture, her *self*, vis-à-vis her students, if she understood herself as non-self-sufficient? That is no small pedagogical question! But then you also talk about the non-self-sufficiency of God's self in Jesus—and that is even more profound. It's about who God is in Christ. And the implications of that for the teacher are mind-blowing. This is not how we usually think about ourselves as theological educators; we tend not to think of ourselves as self-sufficient. In fact, we go beyond that: we impart, we deposit, and then we leave. You are really messing with that model. You are interrogating the model by unfolding the story.

John: You give insight into who and what God is like. Your piece resonates with Julian's; you both give insight into what we, as theological educators, are invited into. As I was reading your piece, it was the story that grabbed me. I am glad that CETI has been a welcoming space in which to take those questions seriously.

David: A big emphasis of my work as academic dean at CETI was to build a pedagogical approach together with others. I used this story with my faculty to show that Jesus himself used a dialogical approach along with a stance of non-self-sufficiency to reveal something as deep as his identity. And if he can do that, then surely we also can adopt this stance in whatever subject we are teaching.

Janette: We need to be reminded of that, for sure. But the question of what this means for salvation is no small footnote.

John: Yes! I want to know about the connection between the experience of being saved and the experience of non-self-sufficiency. I could see in your piece that those two are connected in your heart.

David: Thank you for articulating it that way! You are right: the amazing paradox is that the experience of being saved includes both an embrace of non-self-sufficiency and a kind of empowerment. Both Jesus and the woman are modeling this.

Janette: The woman accepts and names who she was, which I find remarkable. Often, theological education diminishes the noneducated other, even if that other is part of ourselves, or some past version of ourselves. Such a stance leaves us with the impression that we have to set aside who we are to embody this new knowledge, but the woman models a different view. There is new revelation, but it is not at the expense of who she is. Being emboldened is one of the effects of being saved: being seen, being heard, being challenged, and being able to challenge. We don't erase our identities as we are being saved.

David: I appreciate your point about the woman being emboldened to name herself, to be who she is. It is an important thing to recognize. You don't have to be less Korean American to be the amazing New Testament scholar that you are. I don't have to stop being Bolivian to be an effective Bible teacher.

John: One can still be a Samaritan and be saved.

Janette: This conversation has revealed to me that, as writers, we are not self-sufficient. We need one another. We see things differently because of our different experiences. So, in a sense, this experience points to a different kind of pedagogy. . . . Talk about collaboration! It helps us think about how to coteach or even how to participate in a collaborative sermon series. We don't really *talk* about how to do that, but this process is *showing* us the way.

[David's note: When Janette and John met to talk with me about my essay, they had read a version of it that had somewhat buried the flow of the story about Jesus and the Samaritan woman. After their responses, I went back and edited my piece to lean more on the story. So, Janette is absolutely right: we need each other.]

John: In terms of inviting the story to frame subsequent discussion on what needs to happen in theological education, questions like, "Does there need to be a reform of existing institutions? Or can something new come out of nontraditional venues?" got my heart thinking: Is there a whole new way of thinking about or approaching theological education?

Janette: Yes, the story provides a new pedagogical lens. We may never have used the story as a way to think about theological education or about the formation of the teacher.

At the same time, I want to go back to the question about the experience of being saved. I remember you were already asking that question when we met as a group in San Antonio: "What does it mean to be saved?"

John: Yes, I wanted to draw attention to that too: "What if theological education helps us makes sense of the experience of being saved?" I love that question!

Janette: To me that is the most unique question you are asking, and it is so fundamental! Strangely, that isn't really a question that comes up in class or in the way we structure our courses or think about theological education. What is the role of knowing our need in being saved—our need for God and one another? When we are in need, we can't be self-sufficient.

John: Yeah, that's what I was thinking! I would put that in the preface of our book. I love how you talk about "the experience of being saved." In theological education contexts, we often talk about soteriology theoretically, without asking, "What does that actually feel like?" But the story is so evocative of experience. It's one thing to say "need," but it is quite another thing to say "non-self-sufficiency." I find that awkwardness helpful, promising.

David: To me, non-self-sufficiency is more than a recognition that I may need something; it has to do with the posture with which I am called to relate to others. Incredibly, the one that is recognized as "the Savior of the World" in the biblical story is actually modeling non-self-sufficiency. If I embrace this posture, I am not only a better teacher, I am a better person. I experience salvation as I experience non-self-sufficiency toward God and toward the neighbor.

John, I loved your expression "got my heart thinking" because to me it hints at the possibility that it was Jesus's non-self-sufficiency at the well that got the woman's heart thinking as they made space for each other to reveal their identities.

John: I would like to learn more about how CETI has tried to put all of this into practice. You don't mince words when you talk about the non-self-sufficiency of Jesus. You say that goes along with the incarnation, and therefore it's part of being human. So, I wonder how that idea expresses itself in the pedagogy of CETI?

David: One example that comes to mind concerns how we discussed issues of family. In our graduate program, we began by reviewing literature that talked about "new models" of family versus the "traditional model." We did this because legislation about marriage in several Latin American countries was changing. The language of "new" and "traditional" seemed like the norm, so we also began to use those terms in the new material for our church-based nonaccredited program.

That all changed once our teaching met the lives of our students—and ourselves! In CETI's program, the participatory approach particularly emphasizes the importance of starting any study with people's experience of any given reality (church experiences, vocational journeys, family relationships, etc.). So, we began discussing the topic by asking people to describe their experiences of family configurations. It was incredible to see how many people did not live in a "traditional model" of family. For instance, the experience of migration over the last few decades has reshaped the family configurations in several Latin American countries. Many families have one or both parents living somewhere else. Consequently, grandparents take on a much more prominent role in raising their grandchildren. Also, it is much more common to have aunts and uncles living under the same roof. All these are tightly connected families that are "traditional" in many ways. But the households don't look like the way the politicians were using that word.

And so we had to change how we spoke about family configurations and leave behind the binary of "new" versus "traditional." We brought this insight back to our graduate program. Understanding the lived experience of families in Latin America made us more competent readers of the narratives about families in the Bible. Think, for instance, about Samuel's family configuration (as described in 1 Samuel 1–2). The experience of family for a lot of children in Latin America is similar to Samuel's: they end up being raised by someone other than their biological parents.

Janette: David, I have two questions for you: What would you like your readers to get out of the story about Jesus and the Samaritan woman? And what would you like your readers to get out of your essay as a whole?

David: I want readers to witness the wonderful transformation that happens as this mutual revelation between Jesus and the woman unfolds. For as they make space for each other, that creates more space for the rest of the community to ask their own questions, and to start their own conversations with Jesus. That was always my intention as I used this material with the CETI faculty and facilitators.

And I would like readers to get the idea that the retelling of biblical stories is a crucial skill in theological education. It honors the subject of our discipline, and it can open space for a wider range of interlocutors in theological education.

7

Wisdom and the Pedagogy of Desire

Janette H. Ok

In Min Jin Lee's novel *Pachinko*, which follows a Korean immigrant family living in twentieth-century Japan, a wealthy man named Koh Hansu provides young Noa with a well-appointed apartment, a generous allowance, and everything he needs to get the best university education. Not knowing that Hansu is his biological father, Noa feels grateful for his benefactor's generous investment and interest in his learning. He remembers Hansu instructing him, "Learn everything. Fill your mind with knowledge—it's the only kind of power no one can take away from you," and he recalls that "Hansu never told him to study, but rather to learn, and it occurred to [him] that there was a marked difference. Learning was like playing, not labor."[1]

Hansu's advice assumes that knowledge is a form of power and that studying does not necessarily result in learning. Noa's response reveals that learning is less about striving and more about enjoyment, even desperation, as he consumes books "like a man starved."[2] This voracious hunger on Noa's part speaks to the driving force that makes education so potentially transformative and meaningful, but also to its potential to fuel desire without guiding it.

Desire motivates Noa's insatiable and disciplined drive to learn everything, but he is not aware of what he desires and why.

Hansu recognizes the importance of keeping Noa rooted in purpose, so he reminds him regularly of the need to have "some higher purpose in the world," though neither knew what this could be.[3] Noa's unspoken desires drive his intellectual appetite, which is to "be a European from a long time ago" or to "be himself, whatever that meant" and "forget himself sometimes."[4] But his ultimate aim in excelling at his studies is to become virtuous and well educated like the man he knew as his late father, Baek Isak, whom he loved and admired, and to disprove the Japanese stereotype that Koreans have dirty, criminal blood. This is why Noa shifts his attention from his education to the brilliant, beautiful, sensual, and nonconformist Akiko, his Japanese girlfriend, with whom he thinks he can be himself. This is also why he subsequently hates and rejects not only Akiko but also his mother and himself when he discovers that Hansu, the *yakuza*, is his real father, not Isak, the respectable minister, and why he withdraws from university and hides from his family. All of his life, Noa has tried to be a "good Korean." What was the point of trying to be a good Korean like your biological father, Noa thinks, when you are cursed with filthy *yakuza* blood? What Noa fails to recognize is that being himself does not mean forgetting himself. It rather means embracing Isak, the man who raised and loved him as his true father, even as he accepts that Hansu's blood does not defile him. Instead of accepting and exploring this past as he fashions a new self, Noa wants to escape from his past and become someone else entirely. He views education as a means to that end, and so he loses all desire for education when he realizes that escape is impossible. His objective for learning is fundamentally flawed and his desires misguided.

"The task of the humanities teacher," according to literary theorist Gayatri Spivak, "is to provide a non-coercive rearrangement of desire in the classroom."[5] The same could be said of the task of the theological educator. A noncoercive rearrangement of desire in theological education differs fundamentally from an instrumentalist approach to education because it does not guarantee outcomes, such as making students ready for ministry.

Theological education should certainly equip students to take up certain roles and succeed in ministry, but its strength lies in redirecting vocation to its source and end, as Christians' vocation emerges from their relationship with and groundedness in the "One who *calls*."[6] In seminaries, students often seek professional and practical skills that help them become more effective ministers and leaders. But what if the task of theological education went further and aimed to cultivate and instill in students a deeper love for God, themselves, and others? What if theological education could be understood and experienced as an act of worship? Through my analysis of the characterization of wisdom in Proverbs, I attempt to make a closer connection between wisdom and desire. The desire for wisdom is at its core a desire for God, and the cultivation of wisdom should be a pedagogical priority. Becoming wise people who love God is the telos of theological education. A pedagogy of wisdom connects students more deeply with their desire for communion with God and others.

DESIRE AS TELOS

The most effective theological educators attend to their students' desires rather than try to change them, and they redirect those desires toward greater ends. Philosopher James K. A. Smith makes the compelling case that education is first and foremost not about what we know but about what we love.[7] Basing his ideas on an Augustinian anthropological model, he underscores how humans are not primarily thinking and believing beings, but desiring and doing beings—beings with bodies, histories, and temporality who have a sense of unfolding and development over time.[8] Human beings are loving beings and are defined by whom they—we—love. Smith extends this vision by arguing that we are by nature oriented toward primal and ultimate love. As affective creatures motivated by primal love, by default we navigate the world with our gut, in a noncognitive and prereflective manner. As teleological creatures motivated by ultimate love, we cannot help but point our desires at some longing for the good life, some picture of human flourishing and living well. The objects of our desire differentiate individuals from one another. We can direct our love toward different objects or point those objects in different trajectories. We can be compelled by different visions of what constitutes the good life, but we are inevitably shaped by and drawn to what we desire. Theological education, Smith contends, is about aiming our hearts toward God and shaping our desire toward the kingdom of God.[9]

I propose that desire, specifically the desire for God, is the telos of theological education. Theological education not only rearranges our desires but reframes what is desirable. We desire a God who longs to know us and be known by us. The One whom we desire also desires us.

THE DESIRABILITY OF WISDOM

The book of Proverbs recognizes that desire is fundamental to the human condition. Through a teacher, it depicts desire as a powerful, complex, paradoxical force that brings pleasure and pain, life and death, and compels people to pursue various ends.[10] Because the teacher[11] knows that desire will either thwart or serve his larger pedagogical aim of inculcating wisdom through discipline, he spends a significant portion of the book we call Proverbs "discussing, invoking, and shaping desire" with his students.[12] Proverbs 4:7 associates the beginning of wisdom with acquiring it:

> The beginning of wisdom is this: Get wisdom,
> and whatever else you get, get insight. (NRSV)

Here, the lack of wisdom serves as the impetus for attaining it. But in order for this lack to enter the right kind of chain of motivations, it must first be experienced as a lack. One must know and experience the absence of wisdom as a need for wisdom in order to begin becoming wise. And the best way to get wisdom is to desire it. Lack gives rise to longing, even as rightful longing teaches lack.

Thus, rather than suppress his students' longings, the teacher in Proverbs seeks to direct them toward God by appealing to their senses: "My child, eat honey, for it is good—the dripping of the honeycomb sweet to your taste. Know that wisdom is like that for your whole being; if you find it, there is a future, and your hope will not be cut off" (24:13–14).[13] Here, Proverbs depicts desire as bodily appetite, encouraging students to savor wisdom's nourishing and satisfying sweetness. As they crave the drippings of honey, they should crave wisdom because it is delicious. Even more, it benefits their whole being (*nefesh*). Students must be discriminating about what they put in their mouths and attentive to the sources of their food, for the delicacies of the ruler lead astray (23:3) and the delicacies of the stingy induce vomiting (23:6–8). The teacher's pedagogical strategy here is to tantalize, temper, and direct his students' cravings.

Old Testament scholar Anne W. Stewart explains that the characterization of desire as bodily appetite in Proverbs points to "the magnetic pull of desire to influence human behavior, drawing a person toward the desirable object that is found to be lacking."[14] Smith similarly attributes this "magnetic power" to the "resonance between the *telos* to which we are oriented and the longings and desires that propel us in that direction."[15] Desire operates in a dynamic state of lack between the bounds of the lover and the lover's desired object. The introduction to Woman Wisdom and Woman Folly in Proverbs 8–9 illustrates how the lack of wisdom brims with pedagogical possibilities and dangers.[16] As desirable women who long to be desired, Wisdom and Folly vie to capture the hearts and minds of the simple and naïve. They offer, however, starkly different paths and ends. Wisdom wants to make herself known and feels no shame in raising her voice to be heard (8:1–4). Wisdom feels at ease in the public square, where the community gathers and conducts business. The strange woman in chapter 7, on the other hand, does her bidding at nighttime and in dark corners (7:9, 12).[17] In broad daylight, Wisdom stands in crowded intersections, high places, and beside the city gate, crying out, "To you, O people, I call, and my voice goes out to all humanity. O simple ones, learn prudence; O fools, develop discernment" (8:4–5; see 1:20–23). Although Wisdom wants to be heard by all, she specifically exhorts the gullible and stupid to get educated in wisdom. Wisdom offers herself as their teacher and lists her teaching credentials and characteristics: Every word that comes from her mouth is righteous and true. She speaks ethically and justly, never twisting words or saying what she does not mean (8:6–8). She not only teaches but is a learner herself as one who dwells (*shakhan*) in prudence (8:12a) and finds (*matza'*) knowledge and discretion (8:12b). In other words, Wisdom embodies, inhabits, and grows in wisdom.

Most astonishing about Wisdom is her unparalleled identity as God's primordial creature and creative partner (8:22–31). In 8:1–4, Proverbs depicts her involvement in everyday human affairs as she stands at the center of human activity, beckoning anyone who will listen to her. However, in 8:22–31, Wisdom recounts her involvement in God's work of creation as one who not only witnessed God bring the world into existence but also worked alongside him in the making of the heavens and the earth:

> I was beside him, like a master worker;
>   and I was daily his delight, rejoicing before him always,
> rejoicing in his inhabited world
>   and delighting in the human race. (8:30–31 NRSV)

The language of joy and delight conveys Wisdom's intimate knowledge and relationship with God. God delights in Wisdom, and she rejoices in God and humanity. Her unique liminal identity as creature and cocreator "enables her to mediate between heaven and earth," as she "ardently tries to bequeath wisdom from above" to all who desire God from below.[18]

With her divine authority firmly established, Wisdom addresses her audience with stern motherly affection: "And now my children, listen (*shama'*) to me: blessed are those who listen to me. Accept discipline (*musar*) to become wise; and don't avoid it" (8:32–33). Old Testament scholar Alice Ogden Bellis points out how translations that render *musar* "instruction" (e.g., NRSV, CEB, ESV) fail to convey the "discipline, chastening, and correction" implied in the word (8:33; cf. 1:2, 7). Talk of "discipline" better captures these dimensions of *musar.*[19] From a pedagogical standpoint, Proverbs aims to teach students that they must undergo the "difficult, life-changing process" to experience moral and ethical change.[20] It also seeks to encourage sustained attention to Wisdom through the use of temporal ("watching daily" and "waiting") and geographical details ("at my gates" and "beside my doors").[21] Like desperate suitors, those who seek Wisdom must be on the prowl, waiting patiently to pounce on any opportunity to find her. This imagery reiterates Wisdom's desire to be pursued and loved, as expressed in 8:17:

> I love those who love me,
> and those who seek me diligently find me. (NRSV)

The image of watching and waiting with vigilant diligence also points to the high stakes involved. Those who find Wisdom find life and obtain divine favor (8:35). Those who fail to find Wisdom harm themselves and prove that they hate her and love death (8:36). Wisdom sees no neutral stance toward her: one either wants her or rejects her, loves her or hates her. Yet she does not coerce or ensnare but attempts to win the hearts and minds of the uncommitted and uneducated with her hospitality.

THE HOSPITALITY OF WISDOM

Wisdom has made her broad appeal to anyone and everyone who will listen (8:1–21). Proverbs 9:1–6 marks a transition from Wisdom's activity in the public square to her activity in the domestic sphere. Wisdom has already referred to the gates and doors of her home (8:34) as the places where her devotees watch and wait for her. Her attention now focuses on engaging the simple and senseless who are inclined to enter her home. The details offered about Wisdom's craftsmanship/handiwork reveal her great skill, industry, and intentionality. With the same creativity she used to help God establish the heavens and the earth, Wisdom has built her house with seven columns (9:1). The home's seven pillars signal the architectural grandeur of the house and its perfection (cf. 6:16; 24:16; 26:16, 25). Wisdom's home is perfectly suitable for entertaining a large number of guests (cf. John 14:2). The sequence of actions—building her house, hewing her seven pillars, slaughtering her animals, mixing her wine, setting her table, calling her servant girls (Prov. 9:1–3)—suggests that Wisdom has personally made all these labor-intensive preparations to invite the gullible to feast at her home and get an education.[22]

Thus, Woman Wisdom broadcasts an invitation to those ignorant of their need for her. Because such simpletons lack sense and understanding, Wisdom appeals to their hunger and thirst to compel them to come to her house (9:4). The exhortation to "turn in here" implies that even the aimless, despite lacking intention, remain in motion and on a path. Proverbs associates life with progress along a path. To walk in the right direction, one must receive the right guidance.[23] Wisdom does not require that they bring her anything, but she does demand that they get rid of their immature, brainless, life-diminishing habits:

> Abandon your simplistic ways and live;
> walk in the way of understanding. (9:6 CEB)

The imperatives "abandon," "live," and "walk" suggest that the mentally and emotionally naïve, and the gullible, have at least some moral agency to resist the pull of deadly desires and deceitful invitations. However, they do need to change direction along the way, which is another way of saying "repent." The urgency of Wisdom's call for the ignorant and gullible to turn into her home makes sense in light of Woman Folly's nearly verbatim invitation (9:16; cf. 9:4).

Funlola Olojede, a scholar whose research focuses on feminist interpretations of the Old Testament from an African perspective, describes Woman Wisdom as "indiscriminately charitable," welcoming to her home and table anyone who cares to come and eat, especially those who lack. As a person of social prominence, she desires to share her abundance.[24] She sees wisdom in sharing and demonstrates real wealth through her generosity to those who lack. Beyond providing abundant food and drink to her guests, Woman Wisdom offers life born out of wisdom, reiterating the close connection between wisdom and life (3:16, 18; 8:35).[25] Olojede's emphasis on those who are physically hungry points to Wisdom's role in alleviating economic and material poverty. Wisdom provides not only intellectual and spiritual nourishment but also material and physical nourishment, all of which are needed for a thriving life. Wisdom concerns herself with all dimensions of life, including socioeconomic realities. Wise people do not close their ears to the cries of the poor, for they too know what it means to call out to Wisdom and receive an answer (21:13; see also 3:27–28).

Wisdom's generosity is certainly unsolicited, but it is not undiscriminating. She does not invite the scoffer (*letz*) or the wicked (*rasha'*) into her home (9:7–8). Unlike the mentally and emotionally naïve, who are ignorant of the ways of Wisdom and have some prospects for moral formation, however dim, the scoffer and wicked outright reject Wisdom and oppose her ways. Proverbs depicts sinners (e.g., 1:10–14) and the wicked (e.g., 21:10) as having purely negative and distorted desires, but does not attempt to direct these desires toward Wisdom.[26] Rather, the teacher uses these perverted desires as a cautionary tale for his students (see 21:11–12).[27] Chapter 9 implicitly wrestles with the question of who is educable and who is not.[28] The teacher who attempts to correct the scoffer and the wicked will effect no change and suffer harm. Their lack of wisdom does not compel them to desire it or some version of it. Rather, the wicked are tormented by the absence of wickedness in wisdom, revealing their moral and psychological confusion.[29] Their delight in wickedness reveals their moral perversion.[30] Their addiction to evil means that they cannot help but devise and do evil, even when it does not profit them.[31] The wicked have no regard for God and thus cannot enter Wisdom's home, receive her hospitality, or accept her instruction.

Unlike the strange woman in chapter 7, who seeks to seduce the simple away from ethical and moral practices, and Woman Folly in chapter 9, who hosts a feast of stolen foods, Woman Wisdom brings people into her home to make more just, discerning, and loving people. Wisdom has the pedagogical aim of forming people in her likeness.[32] To love Wisdom is to be changed by her virtues and become more like her (8:12–21). Wisdom as the object of desire wants to be desired in a certain way. She does not want to be objectified by the lustful male gaze and belong to the realm of fantasy. Rather, she wants her lovers to become so intimately acquainted with her thoughts and ways that they begin to take on her virtues. Those who love Wisdom become wiser and experience ethical and moral transformation.

THE DESIRE OF WISDOM

As previously mentioned, desire operates in a dynamic state between the lover and the desired thing, "each separated by a condition of lack."[33] Does this mean that Wisdom lacks something that the lover has? How can something so transcendent be mutually desirous of human beings and oriented toward us? Proverbs portrays Wisdom as both "the ultimate embodiment of positive desire" and one with desires of her own, all of which are entirely honorable.[34] What the teacher attributes to a lack of wisdom on the part of the student, he attributes to the abundance of love on the part of Wisdom to impart and inculcate wisdom through discipline (8:17, 20–21). It is out of the abundance of love, not the lack of it, that God desires to make himself known: "The Lord gives wisdom; from his mouth come knowledge and understanding" (2:6). It is out of love, compassion, and hope for their moral and ethical transformation that Wisdom focuses her attention on capturing the attention and affection of those with an openness to God to bring them into fuller communion with God.

THE THEOLOGICAL CLASSROOM AS A PLACE OF DELIGHT AND LOVE

In *Teaching to Transgress: Education as the Practice of Freedom*, educator, cultural critic, and activist bell hooks explores the role of pleasure in the higher-education classroom. Although many of her pedagogical paradigms were shaped by the ideas of educator, philosopher, and theorist Paulo Freire and feminist thinkers about radical pedagogy, she notes that none of them adequately examined the role of pleasure in the classroom. Instead, she takes her cues from educators writing about the importance of "fun" in grade-school education.[35] She begins with the premise that the classroom should be an exciting place, not a boring one, pushing against the widely held assumption that serious intellectual work does not need to be exciting in order to be engaging (7). She recalls the Black women grade-school teachers who were wholeheartedly and single-mindedly "committed to nurturing intellect so that we could become scholars, thinkers, cultural workers—black folks who use our 'minds'" (2). These teachers helped students contextualize themselves within an intergenerational framework, in relation to how they lived and the communities in which they lived, and connected them to antiracist struggle (3). Her teachers called her and her classmates not to be passive consumers of knowledge but to resist the knowledge that promoted white racist colonization and discover instead wisdom that served the life of their community (2). Learning taught students to love knowledge, love themselves, and love justice. Thus, in stark contrast to her high school, undergraduate, and graduate education, hooks remembers her childhood education as "sheer joy" and school as "a place of ecstasy" (3).

hooks recognizes that ideas alone cannot generate and sustain this kind of excitement in the classroom; it takes the collective effort of a learning community to create dynamic synergy (8). The classroom serves as a communal place where "our capacity to generate excitement is deeply affected by our interest in one another, in hearing one another's voices, in recognizing one another's presence" (8). In theological parlance, the classroom serves as a place of encounter, where the teacher helps students recognize the *imago Dei* in each individual and their respective communities. The mutuality between the persons of the Trinity reflects divine wisdom and invites us into divine fellowship that has profound and practical implications for how we see the dignity of other human beings and why community stands at the heart of wisdom.[36]

Wisdom is needed for imperfect relationships to flourish. Those who live wisely learn to navigate between narcissism and self-neglect, care for the self and care for one another, and what to carry and what not to carry for our sake and the sake of others.[37] Wisdom helps us nurture healthy relationships and mend broken ones. The theological classroom can acknowledge the collective wisdom brimming from within the learning community itself and the ancestral wisdom individual students bring with them to the learning community. But it can also be a place where the need and lack of wisdom can be embraced as the opportunity to grow in the desire for wisdom and to undergo moral and ethical formation with and for others.

The classroom should not serve as a platform for either the teacher or students, but should be a place of passionate teaching and passionate learning. Bringing passion to the classroom means that the teacher also has to be on the dynamic journey of loving and being loved by wisdom. If educators approach the classroom with a lack of zeal, passion, and desire, how can they expect to make their classroom a place of delight and love for their students? hooks offers this corrective: "To restore passion to the classroom or to excite it in classrooms where it has never been, professors must find again the place of eros within ourselves and together allow the mind and body to feel and know desire."[38] That place of eros for theological educators is that dynamic state where longing for God, ecstasy in God, and humility before God remind them that they are learners and lovers. It is the open space where they teach students for purposes beyond professional training.[39] It is the convergence of worship and communion with God. It is, to borrow Theological Education between the Times author Mark D. Jordan's sonic metaphor, the "deep bass" of Christian Scripture that undergirds their instruction, conversation, prayers, and worship, and the "scriptural notes" amplified by their self-actualized, embodied presence.[40]

The seminary or theological classroom, particularly the biblical studies classroom, has the potential to be a radical space of pleasure where our desire for God and delight in God converge in the pursuit of wisdom. Wisdom generates delight:

> Wisdom will enter your mind,
> and knowledge will fill you with delight.
> (Prov. 2:10 CEB)

Augustine expresses this awe-filled, ecstatic pleasure when describing Scripture: "The wondrous depth of your utterances, whose surface may indeed be flattering to the childish, but the wondrous depth, my God, the wondrous depths! It gives one a shudder to peer into it—a shudder of awe, and a tremor of love."[41] The theological classroom can also be an unresolved, open space of possibility, discomfort, and pleasure.

How can I teach the Bible in ways that entice and direct my students' desires toward wisdom? How might my intro course leave students shuddering with awe and trembling with love for God, as they gain a basic knowledge of the literature, history, and theology of the New Testament? How can I introduce students to a diversity of critical methodologies and a multiplicity of conversation partners in ways that awaken wonder and deepen love and humility in them? How can learning various histories of interpretation promote justice and warn against the weaponization of the Bible? How can learning to read the Bible in Hebrew and Greek evoke joy? How might students experience pleasure through the discoveries they make by engaging the interpretive process? How might they also experience the transformative pain of having their presuppositions about what the Bible means challenged, their ideas nuanced and expanded? How can I help them recognize Christ through every aspect of their lives and not just seek Scripture to speak to limited aspects of their lives? How can I help them kindle the desires to live "scriptural lives"?[42]

CONCLUSION

One of the distinctive things about theological education is that the Wisdom we desire also desires—even seeks—*us*. Wisdom's desire for us means that our telos seeks us out of an unceasing abundance of love. In our pursuit of God, we are pursued by God. God longs to be known. Theological education is only possible because the incarnate God has already sought believers.[43] Thus, while learning outcomes and course objectives are necessary to ensure that students have measurable and attainable goals for learning, they are insufficient indicators of a course's success in directing and deepening the students' desire and love for God and a teacher's effectiveness in hosting spaces for delight, communion, and encounter.

Theological education begins and ends with the assurance that we can know and be known by God.[44] By his grace, love, and desire, God makes himself known to us in his Son, Jesus Christ, by the power of the Spirit. At this time, we know God in Christ but only "in part," which means the need for theological education in its many traditions, shapes, and contexts will not cease until "the perfect comes" and "what is partial will come to an end" (1 Cor. 13:9–10). It means that theological education is less about knowing God and more about coming to know God, and in the process becoming more fully ourselves.[45]

This is the paradox that Noa could not make sense of in *Pachinko*: that education makes us more deeply ourselves, even as it leads us beyond ourselves. Theological education, in particular, reconnects us with the selves God has created, loved, and redeemed, even as it cultivates our desire for the God who transcends us. And so it is not just studying; it is *learning*.

The desire for God—not a degree to serve God—is the telos of theological education. This end enlarges the scope and normalizes the need for theological education as being for anyone who seeks to know and be known by God. Seminary mission statements often include the aim to train, educate, or prepare Christian leaders for faithful service to the church and the world, yet such aims presume a professional model of education. Wisdom, by contrast, calls out to anyone who might seek her, which means that theological institutions must do more to entice every adult Christian, not only leaders and pastors, to pursue theological education and to make it as affordable and accessible as possible.

The pedagogy of wisdom that I seek to offer directs students' desires toward a vision of wisdom incarnate in Jesus Christ. It is a wisdom shaped by ethical practices, rooted in community, and oriented toward justice. In becoming wiser, students can become better thinkers, readers, and lovers, as well as leaders. They become thinkers who are not afraid of complexity, uncertainty, and contextualities, nor lured by easy answers. They become readers who commit themselves to rigorous and humble engagement with the Bible in diverse learning and ecclesial communities in thick communion with others. They become lovers who understand wisdom's value and who find theological education not only invaluable but desirable. And they become leaders who are so intimately acquainted with Wisdom that they walk in her ways, take on her character, and compel others without coercion to desire the God who desires them.

Dialogue

Janette H. Ok, Caleb Maskell, Julian Davis Reid

Julian: I loved your opening. That distinction between studying and learning was so fascinating; it never left me throughout the essay. I find it a very generative frame for thinking about theological education.

For the biblical exposition, I also really liked how the wisdom components went deep into understanding how a student relates to wisdom, particularly Woman Wisdom versus Folly. I really liked how you attended carefully both to the Scripture and then also to what bell hooks was doing by looking at excitement in theology and what Gayatri Spivak was doing by raising the notion of rearranging desire. You note that desire was present with Woman Folly, but also that it differed from the desire present with Woman Wisdom, and that this presence of desire was what bell hooks was trying to arouse with students in the classroom. This connected to your conversation about pleasure. But I really dug the idea of the rearrangement of desire in the classroom.

I'm interested in *your* story. Can you describe what enticed *you* to wisdom? Can you entice us with a story? Is there a story from your life at Fuller or your life in the academy or elsewhere that you can use to draw us into the architecture of wisdom that can make us want to move not toward the street but rather toward Woman Wisdom?

Caleb: I was very struck by Spivak's framework of a noncoercive rearrangement of desire as being the task of the humanities teacher. And then I was also very struck by the journey that we go on in the essay to get to the idea that the theological classroom is meant to be a place of delight, desire, and love for God.

Janette: Exegesis is often viewed as "gaining mastery" of the biblical text's meaning, which can be a form of folly and be dangerous when there is no connection to God—who God is, and how God wants us to live and engage this world. There's no love in that. And to your point, Julian, I really do think there are big ramifications to being foolish in our study of the Bible, which I didn't flesh out in the essay. I do think we are fools when we coercively try to rearrange desire through the use of the Bible, and that is not what I want seminary education to be about.

Julian: That last line right there. Yeah, that feels so pithy for a thesis.

Caleb: Well, I just wanted to say that when you said, "there's no love in that," I wanted to hear you talk more about that. Like, I want to hear what is underneath that framing for you. . . . What is it about the love for God that produces the right kind of desire for the moment that we're in right now?

Janette: So, I was thinking about bell hooks and the classroom as a site of delight and love, and how that doesn't mean the classroom is all rosy, easy, and chummy. Love fights, love disagrees, love accepts, and love also challenges and helps people grow. Love creates space. It is spacious. I was thinking about, "How can I talk about the biblical studies classroom as a site of delight and love rather than as a place to claim authority or possession and then to extrapolate from that in ways that extend that authority to claim more of life as possession?" Paulo Freire talks about the banking model of education. I think the Bible for many is the ultimate site of the bankers. Like, let me take a little of this and take a little of that to build, to justify the things I want to build and do.

When we imagine or describe theological education in terms of equipping leaders, we rob Christian education of its soul and make its purpose too shallow. But what if we took the task of theological education deeper and further? What if we reframed the task not as the equipping of leaders but as the cultivating of lovers? Don't get me wrong, I am very committed to leadership formation. But if the aim of theological education is primarily to equip leaders for ministry, then seminary cannot become a place of thick communion. Students won't need one another to know and experience the presence of God. Their peers will only be like fellow pilgrims along the seminary journey, only good friends or colleagues in ministry. But if theological education aims to connect students more deeply with their desire for communion with God and others, then classmates are vital partners to the process of knowing and being known.

Julian: Yeah. I think this gets at what I was saying earlier about studying versus learning. I'd love to hear more from you about the danger of study and also what that looks like. What are the symptoms of studying without learning?

Caleb: One thing I'd love to hear you talk about is how important you think the study of the humanities is in general for becoming able to think in these kinds of ways. Like, can a person love God if they don't love art?

Janette: You know, your connection between a humanities education and theological education is interesting. I agree that there are resonances. Like a humanities education, theological education helps rearrange our desires. The humanities teacher teaches close reading in which readers are to suspend judgment for as long as possible and show a reoccurring commitment to imagine the other in the text, as Spivak has talked about. However, I see a fundamental difference between the two, and that difference makes all the difference. What is unique to theological education is that what (or Who) we desire also desires us. We desire a God who longs to know us and be known by us, and that theological truth is the basis for theological education.

Julian: Have you read Mark Jordan's *Transforming Fire?* The reason I'm bringing it up is he writes there about how he does *not* regard theological education as part of the humanities. Because we are addressing God and are addressed by God, theological education will always be different from English or philosophy or anything else because those subjects do not presume this divine address. He argues that theological education should be different, maybe adjacent, but still distinct. This could be a really interesting claim for you to play with; Caleb is connecting the humanities, which don't need to be theological, with wisdom, which for you is entirely theological.

You hint at the ways this is theological when you say near the end of your essay that wisdom is embodied in the incarnation of Jesus Christ. And I was like, "Where did that come from? It's tight." I want to hear more because Christology is not really taken up at all in this essay. And that's fine. There's not necessarily space for it, but there are these doctrinal claims that you're making, particularly around Wisdom helping cocreate the world with God in the beginning and that claim briefly at the end about the incarnation.

Janette: I need to spend more time with Jordan's Theological Education between the Times book, so thanks for reminding me of that connection. I'm not equating the humanities with the study of the Bible and theological education. While Spivak and hooks talk about desire, I am offering a Christian way of understanding the object of our desire. Jesus is our ultimate desire. But Spivak and hooks help to frame the role of desire in education in ways that can loosen us theologians up because we tend to be disconnected from the fiery heat of desire. The association of seduction with theological education seems weird and inappropriate at first, but when you think about it more, it makes sense, especially when you read Proverbs, and the idea that theological teachers seduce or entice students by way of desire.

Caleb: Going back to whether you should see leadership formation as a part of theological education: I think Wisdom by definition has the momentum of leadership in it. I don't think there's a distinction between cultivating one's love and desire for God and developing one's ability to lead well. You know the best Christian leaders are the ones who lead out of their lives with God and from all the humility and courage that that brings.

Janette: I agree. The desire for wisdom is at its core a desire for God, and cultivating wise leaders who love God will be an outcome of a pedagogy of wisdom. My point at the end of the essay is that theological education is for any Christian who seeks to mature in faith, hope, and love. Some will come as leaders and leave as wiser, more Christlike, and impactful leaders. Some will not come in as leaders or with official ministry titles or roles, but in their pursuit of wisdom they will become leaders and find themselves placed in official roles. Why? Because wise people positively impact the vitality of people, communities, organizations, and institutions in their orbit. Wisdom first leads people and then people can lead out of wisdom, but first, we must acknowledge our lack and need for wisdom.

Caleb: I see you writing as a worshiper, which means you're writing from the position of someone who knows that desire and wisdom are fundamentally connected in worship. A Christian worshiper, especially one who loves the humanities, understands that all wisdom is God's and that all desire culminates in the worship of God in Jesus Christ. I mean, that's a fundamental claim, which doesn't imply anonymous Christianity and the inability to live in a pluralist society. It simply implies that the point of view of a Christian worshiper is inclusive and totalizing in the context of also acknowledging wisdom in all of these places of particularity.

To me, the entirety of what you're doing is fundamentally Christian and fundamentally worshipful. It strikes me that there's something about the encounter with the Spirit of the living God in the context of community that enables a person to become a humanist. It enables a person actually to see and receive wisdom from all corners because it's all an act of worship. This is what your essay on teaching drew out of me.

Janette: Wow. This has all been super helpful. I am full of thoughts and grateful that we were put together. I'm all the wiser for our conversation. Thank you.

8

Notes of Rest as Theological Education

Julian Davis Reid

During the first year of my MDiv studies at Candler School of Theology, I was a chaplain at Atlanta's Metro Regional Youth Detention Center. Along with my colleagues, I served the young male residents, mostly Black boys, by helping them reflect on where they had been and where they were going. For much of the year, conversation felt stifled, in part because I felt my range of topics was limited. Because my colleagues and I were chaplains and not evangelical ministers, I did not have the freedom to talk explicitly about Jesus as I would have preferred. As such, sometimes I thought I was sitting on my hands. But God works in mysterious ways: unbeknownst to me at the time, a singular encounter with two of the Black boys living there would help inspire my experiment in theological education, Notes of Rest.

Toward the end of my internship, one of my chaplain colleagues—knowing that I was a musician and music educator—invited me to teach piano lessons to these teenagers. Initially I was skeptical that teaching piano would be acceptable as part of our chaplaincy curriculum. I figured we were supposed to limit ourselves to discussing their understanding of God and the directions in which they wanted their lives to move after their incarceration ended. But I decided to table my confusion and accept my coworker's invitation, thinking that perhaps she saw something I didn't.

One day I was teaching a resident a common folk song, something along the lines of "Mary Had a Little Lamb" or "Twinkle, Twinkle, Little Star." While the student slowly sounded out the notes on the keys, another Black boy pulled up a chair and exclaimed: "Hey, man, keep playing that! I was angry and wanted to fight, but now I don't want to fight anymore." He then sat and listened to the rest of the lesson.

That moment humbled me. Years later it is still teaching me about theological education. My colleague was a conduit of grace, bringing to me the gift of an invitation for which I had not asked but which in fact I sorely needed. I thought that theological education had to be housed within a formal structure of discourse explicitly about God. But God was expanding my view of what and how we could learn about God by exposing me to the twin powers of rest and creativity. Before teaching piano, I had barely thought about my musical career as relevant to my ministry. My music happened in clubs and churches, but I discussed rigorous matters of God in formal classrooms. However, in that piano lesson, Black music, which has never been a respecter of institutional bounds, graciously tore down the veil. As one teenager learned piano because of the invitation I accepted, the other grew in emotional intelligence and was able to practice stillness amid a place of chaos and dis-ease. And I was learning about the various possibilities for theological education that I could access with my pastoral and musical skills. It was a teaching moment, with all kinds of learning happening on all kinds of levels.

Despite the restlessness and bleakness of that overall situation, rest was breaking out via Black music, which I broadly define to mean either music originally created by Black folk or music that Black folk are interpreting. (This episode with the youth was the latter.) Teaching music as part of my chaplaincy work became a context of pastoral care and theological learning. The boy who had previously wanted to fight could have done real damage in that space. But instead, much like in the *Confessions* when Saint Augustine responds to the child's imperative to take and read about Jesus in Romans,[1] the distressed teenager allowed his restlessness to yield to the gracious gift of music, a sound that he did not request yet happily received. Responding to the grace bestowed upon him, he drew close to his neighbor and rested in his presence. The would-be fighter's honest admission that his emotional attitude was changing for the better challenged my narrow view of where and how theological education can happen. God's rest was landing on us all despite the shackling antiblackness inherent in the United States carceral system. Who was I to get in the way?

In the spirit of carrying forward the fruits of that piano lesson, after seminary I eventually founded Notes of Rest, a contemplative-musical experience that invites participants into the rest of God found in spiritual disciplines laid out in Scripture and in Black music. I started Notes because I wanted to create a container for my interest in Black music, for the generative possibilities of rest, and for vigorous theological discussion. This container would be a space for exploring the kind of transformative dynamic I witnessed in that youth detention center, and it is a dynamic into which I would like to invite us as theological educators and students now.

What follows is a guided experience of Notes of Rest. We will explore seven interlocking spiritual disciplines of rest from Scripture: Sabbath (consecrated rest from usual labor); sleep (rest from consciousness); simplicity (rest from excess and distraction); silence (rest from noise); stillness (rest from movement and control); slowness (rest from speed); and sanctuary (rest from irreverence and danger). We will braid these notes together with my music, which you can access via the provided QR codes. I center Black music because it *can* (though does not always) inspire restfulness and creativity amid those who are defying odds to continue living, hoping, and believing. That is my hope for us today as we sit with these notes. But before turning to them directly, I want to explain how I conceptualize the notes.

PRACTICING THE SCALE

This graphic of simultaneously ascending and descending C major scales depicts how I hold together the notes of rest. First, superimposing the notes onto the scale reminds us that these spiritual disciplines are to be practiced just like musical scales are to be practiced. The lessons God has for us in rest come from the routine practice of each kind. They are disciplines, just like learning the notes to the folk song was a discipline for my student. And like all spiritual disciplines, they are grounded in, and open us up to, grace. That is vital to remember, lest we think that practicing rest is just another means of becoming superior to someone else who does not rest as well as we do. God invites us instead to let the practice of rest conform us to the image of God in us that God has freely bestowed upon us.

Second, I arrange them in this format because when we practice scales, we can solo each note. When I am practicing difficult scales on piano, I must pay attention to what each finger is doing on every key. Striking every key requires care and attention; I cannot blow past the notes that are difficult. Sometimes I must isolate problem notes to ensure that I am approaching them correctly so that the scale can move fluidly. Similarly, I invite us to think intentionally about each note of rest. We might be stronger at some kinds of rest than others. That is okay. Let this unfolding experience give us space to reflect on how our practice can deepen. Third, notice that the scales are stacked on top of each other. This is to denote harmony between the notes. For instance, Sabbath harmonizes with sleep, as does simplicity with stillness.

Even though we practice these notes separately, our disciplines reverberate off one another. Our time walking through the Scripture passages below will show some of these resonances.

Lastly, notice that the note on the far right—middle C—is not labeled with a spiritual discipline. If we were to play from left to right, just the musical scale degrees that have labels underneath, we would stop just shy of that last note, which is supposed to be played in unison (meaning left hand and right hand play it simultaneously). If we leave that note unplayed, the scale does not resolve. This lack of resolution is intentional, as it is inspired by the lack of final resolution in much of Black American music, a harmonic texture that figured prominently from the blues era onward after the failure of Reconstruction. The music critic Amiri Baraka (LeRoi Jones) puts it well in his seminal work *Blues People: Negro Music in White America*: "The Negro [after the failure of Reconstruction] could not ever become white and that was his strength; at some point, always, he could not participate in the dominant tenor of the white man's culture. It was at this juncture that he had to make use of other resources, whether African, subcultural or hermetic. And it was this boundary, this no man's land, that provided the logic and beauty of his music."[2] Black music emerged from refusing—and being refused—the conventions of white music. One common convention in traditional Western tonal harmony from the seventeenth through the nineteenth century is concluding a piece of music with strong tonal stability, which gives the listener a sense of feeling at home at the end of a song. (The cadence typically responsible for this feeling is known in music theory as the authentic cadence. J. S. Bach's preludes and fugues exemplify this pattern.) By contrast, blues music of the late nineteenth and early twentieth century does not provide such resolution. Instead, the convention of that genre is to conclude the song on a penultimate harmonic chord known as the dominant chord. This convention also shows up in descendants of the blues, including gospel blues, jazz, and soul.

Dominant chords are typically the chords that harmonically signal that the home chord (the first scale degree, or the "do" in solfège, as in Rodgers and Hammerstein's "Do Re Mi" from the *Sound of Music*)[3] is coming next. For instance, in the key of F, playing the C7 chord (the fifth scale degree of F) should lead to an F major chord (the first scale degree). But blues music does not follow this convention, instead making the C7 chord the home chord and never resolving to F major. (In fact, F major is rarely, if ever, played in the classic blues pattern.) The blues, with its dominant harmony, created a new home, one that gestured toward another home but never resolved there.

This musical decision reflects the *Sitz im Leben* of the composers. Blues does not reflect a stable return home because its creators did not experience stability in their homes. Though Black folk had fought in the Civil War and had pined for freedom in the North during slavery and the Great Migration, they were met with Jim and Jane Crow and the Ku Klux Klan. Severe social antagonisms persisted throughout the country when white folk sought to reestablish "the chasm" between Black and white that Baraka observes. One place into which Black folk poured their disappointment about their lack of social, political, and economic rest was their music—the blues, and subsequently gospel blues, jazz, and hip-hop, too. Though they could not claim freedom in America's political sphere, through their music, in some measure, they resisted the assault on their humanity.[4]

This use of dominant harmony in the blues grounds the theological framework of Notes of Rest. The people of God since biblical antiquity have relied on classical spiritual disciplines to endure harsh realities, just as Black folk have relied on music, alongside faith, to do the same. Like the dominant chord, disciplines such as Sabbath and sleep point toward the coming ultimate resolution: oneness with God that will suffuse all of creation, where all will be at rest. By pairing classical spiritual practices with the dominant harmony logic in various forms of Black music, I am trying to orient ancient practices toward modern stakes.

James Cone's masterpiece *The Cross and the Lynching Tree* articulates these modern stakes. He argues that awareness of the first-century cross and the twentieth-century lynching tree is needed for a healthy practice of Christianity in America (and, I would argue, a healthy practice of Christian faith throughout the modern world, given how racial terror has been part and parcel of the United States' growth as a superpower). Cone argues that the horrors of the lynching tree cast light on the horror of Jesus's cross, and that the hope for Jesus's cross casts light on the hope for Black people and thus all people.[5]

The mutual need of the cross and lynching tree resonates with my experience of classical spiritual disciplines such as Sabbath and silence. The church (of any racial demographic) can discuss these contemplative practices in ways that ignore the material horrors narrated in the Hebrew Bible and New Testament *and/or* the material horrors of the United States. As a counterpoint to this, Notes of Rest invites the body of Christ to practice these dominant harmony notes not as a means of "abstract, sentimental piety" but as a way of standing in solidarity with the teenagers around the piano (in the case of the correctional center) in their "reality of suffering."[6] We do so by attending to the material challenges in the original context and by attending to how our own practices stand in solidarity with those facing similar burdens now. This means, for instance, that our practice of Sabbath and sleep should be mindful of the ways the most vulnerable among us need routine rest and are often denied it. This denial of rest needs to be redressed, for rest is not only a health and wellness issue, but also a theological issue about an otherworldly vision that demands this-worldly justice. While Notes of Rest extends this call to all of society, for the purposes of this essay, I limit our focus to the theological academy.

Alongside solidarity, the dominant harmony framework that I employ from the blues invites us to reflect on our own confinement. I use the term "confinement" loosely because most of the readership of this essay likely does not live behind bars as the students at that first piano lesson did. Nevertheless, we remain confined within systems of oppression. God is inviting us as theological educators and students to consider what those forms of confinement are. What sins of the world ensnare and exhaust our theological communities, and how can we resist those? (Near the top of this list should be addiction to work, a severe sickness in the academy.)[7]

My hope is that the following meditations on the seven notes and on my musical offerings will help us identify those forms of oppression and to encounter a God who graciously sojourns with us amid our struggles, just as God did with Hagar in the Genesis account,[8] and as God did with the teenage boys in prison. May we hear what rest is teaching us about God and help us imagine new possibilities for the weary institutions to which we belong.

To aid in that discernment, I have clustered the notes into three "chords": Sabbath and simplicity; sleep and sanctuary;

and stillness, slowness and silence. Holding the notes together makes each one richer, just as notes played together resound with new energy.

Each meditation has three segments: "Guiding Scripture," "Analysis," and "Reflection Music and Questions." I invite us to move as slowly through each segment as needed. Re read the Scripture passages; think slowly with the analysis of how the notes apply to your context today; pause the essay to listen to the song; journal on the reflection questions. May God help us hear the music of our lives. Amen.

As we begin, let us sit with this image, "You, Sparrow" by Shin Maeng, which he created as the album artwork for my record Rest Assured. *While viewing it, I invite you to scan the QR code and listen to my version of "His Eye Is on the Sparrow." As God provides for the birds, so will God provide for us.*

Here is a breath prayer to center us before we continue: Inhale: God. Exhale: Give us your rest. (Listen to the rhythm of breath. Give thanks for it. We would die without it.)

THE CHORD OF SABBATH AND SIMPLICITY

Guiding Scripture

"On the seventh day some of the people went out to gather manna, and they found none. The Lord said to Moses, 'How long will you refuse to keep my commandments and instructions? See! The Lord has given you the Sabbath; therefore on the sixth day he gives you food for two days; each of you stay where you are; do not leave your place on the seventh day.' So the people rested on the seventh day" (Exod. 16:27–30 NRSVue).

Analysis

God had just liberated Israel from Egyptian slavery, and now the newly freed people were contending with the costs of life on the other side. Some longed wistfully for Egypt's rule again, for though he was harsh, Pharaoh gave bread. God responded to the spiritual and physical needs of the wayward liberated by giving them food from heaven (manna) and instructing them to practice Sabbath and simplicity. Observing Sabbath, the practice of resting from labor on God's holy seventh day, meant they were not to gather manna on Saturdays. And observing simplicity, the practice of refraining from excess such that no one had too much or too little, meant the Israelites were not to gather extra manna during the week; only on Fridays could they gather double, to account for Saturday's needs. Any extra collected during the week would rot—a lesson they learned the hard way.

The people were stiff-necked and did not listen to God's instruction. For whatever reason—greed, desperation, distrust of God's capacity to provide versus Pharaoh's proven track record—some tried to pick up extra on the Sabbath.[9] Only after God's rebuke did they decide to practice contentment and live simply within the limits God had assigned. God was teaching them to practice the notes. Eventually they listened.

Later, in Exodus 20 and in Deuteronomy 5, the people of God received the Decalogue (or Ten Commandments), in which they were instructed to observe the Sabbath for two reasons. In the Exodus text, we notice that they were to rest because of God's vision of shalom instituted in Genesis 1, where the completion of all things included and culminated in the rest of God (Exod. 20:8–11). In the Deuteronomy text, they were to rest because of God's salvation of the people of Israel from bondage in Egypt (Deut. 5:12–15). In both cases, like in the manna episode of

Exodus 15, they were to rest their bodies because of who God had proven to be to them, namely, a creator of rest, a liberator from bondage, and a provider of sustenance for when they could not work. For this fledgling nation to practice Sabbath was for them to practice memory-work and hope-work amid the precarity of death and scarcity swirling all around them in their wilderness experience.

We are well acquainted with the significant changes in theological education in North America rendering our institutions more vulnerable. Our schools and churches are in various states of numerical decline, and pastors who do go into the ministry are often burning out or are ingloriously and publicly falling from grace. With such change afoot, we can be like the Israelites and find the sacred gift of Sabbath, God's routine gift of pause from work, burdensome or impractical. To compensate for our precarity, we can justify our decision to search for food no matter what day of the week it is. This is Sabbath under threat.

By contrast, the precarity of the current moment can also illuminate the importance of Sabbath for us. Perhaps the stats and the doomsday scrolling increasingly open us up to the gift of rest from God. We realize that we did not conduct our own exodus, and that we cannot sustain ourselves in the arid wilderness. We realize that God's provision for the sparrow is going to lead to provision for us. From this perspective, we can now hear the wisdom of Abraham Joshua Heschel, that Sabbath is "the melody sustained throughout all agitations and vicissitudes which menace our conscience; our awareness of God's presence in the world."[10]

Whether institutional decline is threatening or illuminating Sabbath, I invite us to see Sabbath as a gift of a teacher. The divine injunction to rest taught Israel to learn more about the God who had liberated them from the horrors of slavery and sustained them afterward. The rhythm of Sabbath would remind them of this lesson again and again. So it can be with us too.

Weekly Sabbath feeds into daily simplicity. In the passage, God called the Israelites to be foragers as they moved away from Egypt toward Canaan. But God put limits on what they could take. They were tempted to acquire needlessly, and sometimes they gave in to the temptation, as evinced by their excess gathering of manna. We see God's verdict on this practice when the divinely given bread rots away. And still the people survived, for they did not really need it.

For us in our institutions, it can be easy to give ourselves over to needless ambition, desires to acquire that which we do not actually need for the lives God has called us to live. God invites us to simplify those ambitions. This invitation to rest will look different for each of us. Perhaps there is a project that I think I need to write but that is in fact going to rot because God has not instructed me to do that. Perhaps you are making yourself too available to students and it is wearing you out. Perhaps we feel the need to acquire extra knowledge in extra classes or in extra degree programs, but God is in fact saying that more is not necessary for the work at hand. It is not that we cannot strive for excellence in our teaching or studying. Rather, it is that these agendas need to be subjected to God's instruction and healthy limits.

Practicing simplicity, like Sabbath, flies in the face of the limitlessness that the United States espouses. This Exodus passage invites us to remember that accomplishing more does not necessarily mean that we are witnessing to God with any more fidelity. In fact, gaining the whole world and losing one's soul hampers our witness to the Lord who provides (Mark 8:36 NRSVue). The lie of limitlessness is oppressive and is wearing us out. God, journey with us and free us. Amen.

Reflection Music and Questions

As we sit with this chord of Sabbath and simplicity, I invite us to listen to my version of "Blessed Assurance." It's an old and powerful song, and I pray that you will be inspired by the ways I play with the rests in its familiar refrains. In crafting these unorthodox rests, I am thankful to stand in a legacy of Black folk who often did not have restful Sabbaths and yet found spaces to creatively tend to each other, such as in the hush harbor. There they found space to breathe and say, "I am somebody." They did not let the precarity of their situation keep them from resting, like the boys in the detention center.

Tricia Hersey, an evangelist for rest and a role model for me in theological entrepreneurship, talks about this in reflecting on the iconic abolitionist Harriet Tubman, who subversively found her way to freedom by following God. Tubman exemplified resting that resisted white supremacy and capitalism and that made space for dreaming of an otherwise life, a life grounded in the freedom of God. Hersey suggests: "Harriet Tubman crafted space to listen, to strategize, and to pray while guiding people on the Underground Railroad. . . . This energy of refusal and maroonage grounds [Hersey's] personal experimentation with rest as resistance."[11]

Just as I creatively place the rests in "Blessed Assurance," and just as Tubman creatively sought rest in her own life and in the life of fellow slaves, may we be inspired to protect the gift of Sabbath for ourselves and for others. And may the rests be subversive to the systems that say we must always work to be valuable, perhaps even more so in the North America church's era of decline.

I hope that this version of "Blessed Assurance" also embodies simplicity, particularly in the chorus. Usually when sung in a church service, the chorus is resoundingly triumphant: "This is my story / this is my song!" There is certainly a time for jubilation about the goodness of God's salvation. But in my version, I present it as almost a whisper, to assert quietly—and knowingly—that this is my story, this is my song. Simplicity invites us into the wisdom of living trustfully within the boundaries that God sets, not taking too much, not taking too little. The opening of Psalm 131 sums up this vision of Sabbath and simplicity well:

> O Lord, my heart is not lifted up;
> my eyes are not raised too high;
> I do not occupy myself with things
> too great and too marvelous for me.
> But I have calmed and quieted my soul,
> like a weaned child with its mother;
> my soul is like the weaned child that is with me.
>
> (Ps. 131:1–2 NRSVue)

As you scan the QR code to listen to "Blessed Assurance," I invite you to ponder: How does this time of transition in theological education threaten or illuminate my Sabbath practice? How is God inviting me to simplify my ambition despite the pressing needs of my vocation?

THE CHORD OF SLEEP AND SANCTUARY

Guiding Scripture

"Now at the festival the governor was accustomed to release a prisoner for the crowd, anyone whom they wanted. At that time they had a notorious prisoner, called Jesus Barabbas. So after they had gathered, Pilate said to them, 'Whom do you want me to release for you, Jesus Barabbas or Jesus who is called the Messiah?' For he realized that it was out of jealousy that they had handed him over. While he was sitting on the judgment seat, his wife sent word to him, 'Have nothing to do with that innocent man, for today I have suffered a great deal because of a dream about him'" (Matt. 27:15–19 NRSVue).

Analysis

In Scripture, God reveals God's plans to protect the vulnerable people via the linked practices of sleep and sanctuary. For instance, God taught a sleeping Joseph how to avoid the impending infanticide that an insecure King Herod would bring upon the Jewish people in colonized Bethlehem. And at the end of Jesus's life, God would use the same tactic to teach Pilate's wife about the innocence of the Righteous One who stood condemned.[12]

Sleep did not *have* to lead to sanctuary in this instance. Pilate's wife could have ignored this dream's insight altogether and supported Pilate in sentencing Jesus to death. And even if she had accepted the verdict of Jesus's innocence, she could have conformed to the oppressive confines of patriarchy and not attempted to sway Pilate's decision at all. But instead she chose to be courageously prophetic. Her faithfulness to Jesus led her to intercede on behalf of Jesus, which is especially notable in Matthew's Gospel given the comparatively obvious unfaithfulness of the men surrounding Jesus, including his own disciples.[13] In so doing, her note of sleep opened onto the note of sanctuary.

We in the theological academy can follow the example of Pilate's wife's by practicing this chord of sleep and sanctuary ourselves. Akin to Pilate's wife (and Joseph), we might receive dreams in which God speaks to us about the vulnerable who stand condemned among us (e.g., the woman, the poor, the Black, the less educated, the LGBTQIA community, the earth). If we receive such miraculous messages from God in dreams, I encourage us to follow Pilate's wife's example and speak truth to power about those who stand unfairly condemned by systems of oppression. (And even if we cannot remember our dreams, we can still pay attention to insights we receive from God right before we fall asleep or right as we wake up. These too can be spaces of unique clarity that can yield the same insight that the dream of Pilate's wife did.)

In addition to dreams, the note of sleep resonates with the note of sanctuary in that sleep renders all its practitioners vulnerable and thus in need of divine protection against the condemnation of grind culture. When we in the theological academy choose to get adequate sleep, which itself is not a productive activity, we risk standing wrongly condemned by a culture that says we are what we produce. It is no wonder that getting adequate sleep often eludes people inside and beyond the church alike. We need sanctuary from these accusations of being insufficiently productive so we can get the sleep that God gifts.

Psalm 3 depicts God as providing sanctuary for those who sleep.

> I lie down and sleep;
> I wake again, for the Lord sustains me.
> I am not afraid of ten thousands of people
> who have set themselves against me all around.
>
> (Ps. 3:5–6 NRSVue)

What a gift of a lesson from the psalmist. Sleep is an act of practicing sanctuary, of trusting God to sustain, redeem, and bless the world in ways that exceed our actions. Taken together with Pilate's wife, the psalmist invites us to remember that God created us to sleep, to receive sanctuary, and to extend it to others who stand condemned too.

I pray we can hear the good news reverberating from the chord of sleep and sanctuary. Let us play these two notes so that people do not stand condemned under the insatiable appetite of grind culture that exhausts professors, students, administrators, and churchgoers alike. Tricia Hersey asserts that "[the academy is] one of the main sites of grind culture."[14] We can practice sleep and sanctuary such that it need not be.

At a Notes of Rest session with pastors, I once asked rhetorically: "What if instead of the church being known primarily as punitive or territorial, we instead were known for being well rested?" The clergy literally laughed aloud, as if that vision were outlandish. That made me grieve for the church and the academy that had formed us all. Our manic pace is a kind of oppression that I pray we can see as such and from which we can ask God for freedom. Rest will teach us who God is if we choose to be students. When we choose to do so, we stand in solidarity with the Black teenager who pulled up a chair to listen to the rest of the lesson.

Reflection Music and Questions

The last song that I played on *Rest Assured* was "Give Me Jesus." I played it to declare the inviolable relationship that those enslaved persons who called on the name of Jesus had to God. No matter what this world gives or takes, they could know that God was with them. I now commend that song to us as a sanctuary song. To return to Tubman, her contemporary Elizabeth, a fellow enslaved girl who would also become a Black holy woman in the eighteenth century, learned from her mother that Elizabeth's ultimate help came from God: "'nobody in the wide world to look to but God.'" Her mother told her this because she lived on another plantation and Elizabeth had to steal away at night to meet her.[15]

There were many Black girls who had to develop a keen sense of spiritual life to navigate the horrible world of slavery in which they were placed. Amid the constant threat of death and the perpetual condemnation of antiblackness inherent in chattel slavery, God afforded these Black girls sanctuary. And when Harriet became an adult, she partnered with God to help others find sanctuary, even being aided by visions in her sleep. I am continually inspired by Harriet's embodiment of "Give Me Jesus," one that led to political freedom for her people and for the Union during the Civil War.[16]

As we listen to "Give Me Jesus," may we reflect on our own sleep practices and on our own awareness of who stands condemned and in need of sanctuary. Pilate's wife stands as a guide. Amen.

As you scan the QR code to listen to "Give Me Jesus," I invite you to ponder: Who stands condemned that God is calling you to see anew? Who needs to hear about your insights drawn from rest?

THE CHORD OF STILLNESS, SLOWNESS, AND SILENCE

Guiding Scripture

"Accordingly, though Jesus loved Martha and her sister and Lazarus, after having heard that Lazarus was ill, he stayed two days longer in the place where he was. . . . Then Jesus told them plainly, 'Lazarus is dead. For your sake I am glad I was not there, so that you may believe. But let us go to him.' . . . Martha said to Jesus, 'Lord, if you had been here, my brother would not have died'" (John 11:5–6, 14–16, 21 NRSVue).

Analysis

Jesus interwove stillness, slowness, and silence to teach his disciples about his identity and work in the world. He practiced stillness and slowness in his decision not to move at the pace others expected of him, staying two days seemingly too long before traveling to Bethany to visit Lazarus. When Jesus finally did arrive in Bethany, others criticized him for his practice of notes of rest. First, Martha castigated him for being still and slow, saying that his absence was the reason that Lazarus was dead. Then, after Jesus began to weep at Lazarus's tomb, members of the crowd disparaged him, wondering why Jesus did not keep Lazarus from dying given that he, the miracle worker, had previously opened the eyes of the blind man.

Jesus practiced stillness and slowness not because he was "insensitive to the family's needs, but [because] he [understood] that this family drama belong[ed] to a larger story. Lazarus's illness [was] part of the story of the glory of God."[17] As a result of his intentional movement, the women and men who were studying Jesus learned about his identity as the one sent from God.

The Gospel of John is replete with instances in which Jesus responded directly to critiques of him (e.g., chapters 5, 7, and 8). But in this case, he let the critiques pass, choosing to rest in silence. Instead of spending time responding to his critics, he focused on Martha, saying that if she believed, she would see the glory of God. After that, he raised his friend from the dead, revealing the glorious fruit of practicing this chord of stillness, slowness, and silence. Jesus's model is one we can practice.

In the theological academy we can practice stillness and slowness so that we can see the glory of God in our midst. This might look like moving slowly with texts that we read and arguments that we write so that we can discern the nuanced invitations from God to us emerging in our souls throughout the process. Doing so avoids capitulating to the "strange magic" of constant activity that Howard Thurman cautions us against trusting with "too much confidence."[18]

One of my favorite memories from seminary was pausing my reading of Saint Augustine's *Confessions* somewhere in the last few chapters of the book and asking my wife to pray over me because the power of God was so immense in that moment that I had to sit still. At that moment, I was less concerned with understanding Augustine and more concerned with understanding the glorious God he addressed. I felt a deep rest during that time of prayer, a rest that came from practicing the chord of stillness and slowness.

We can add the third note of silence to this chord by carefully selecting when to respond to critics. To be sure, the academy is all about critique, and that is a healthy feature of the intellectual rigor that typifies theological education. However, I noticed during seminary that some professors, authors, and students responded to every critique that came their way and thus could not find their own voice amid the sea of others to which they felt an obligation to respond. Indeed, this was also a personal struggle for me, as it kept me from writing freely during many seminary courses. I routinely felt that I always needed to read one more book before making a claim, a restless feeling that filled me with a sense of perpetual inadequacy as a thinker. Of course, there is a time to engage criticisms, but sometimes the rest that God has for us comes from choosing to remain silent in the face of certain critiques so that we can focus on glorifying God with our unique contribution to the discourse at hand.

Practicing the chord of stillness, silence, and slowness helps us keep the larger arc of God's glory in mind that transcends the grades of our professors or the assessments of our colleagues in the guild. Despite the chronic threats of insecurity, perfectionism, and anxiety that constantly apply pressure to us, we can practice this chord and thus be conduits of God's gracious presence in the world.

Reflection on Music and Questions

In my rendition of the Negro spiritual "O Freedom," I play the melody slowly and circuitously, like a labyrinth. Reinterpreting it in this way underscores what the lyrics of the spiritual demand of the singer. The lyric "before I'd be a slave I'd be buried in my grave" is not a simple statement to comprehend. It takes otherworldly commitment to a subversive freedom to say that one would rather die than serve as chattel property for the nascent US empire. To sing this song is to therefore resist the glory of this world and the manic logics that drive it, and instead to hold to the larger arc of God's glory.

I invite us to listen to that song slowly and feel the inscrutability of those lyrics wash over us as my playing twists and turns. Notice that as the song fades to silence, there are slow, ominous octaves in the left hand. Though this was not consciously intended, in retrospect I hear in those octaves a funeral bell tolling, the slow ringing of the bell for the one who refused to be a slave in this world. Black music has always been a means by which "Black folk respond to the terror visited on Black life and . . . refuse it."[19] "O Freedom" invites into its restful embrace anybody who dares sing slowly this otherworldly melody of freedom. Remember the hope of the cross even as we contend with the horror of the lynching tree, be we those marked for it, those descended from its makers, or those who are just thankful that the angel of death has passed over our home.

As you scan the QR code to listen, I invite you to ponder: Despite the death that surrounds you in the theological academy, what stillness, silence, and slowness do you need the faith to practice?

REST THAT HOPES FOR RESOLVE (A DOMINANT HARMONY CONCLUSION)

I hope these meditations on Scripture have created space for you to encounter the God who gives deep rest to our souls amid the varied forms of confinement we are experiencing in this life. Even as you think about the systems of capture that oppress you and yours within the theological academy, the Holy Spirit is there, just like in the detention center. The Spirit of the crucified One will equip you with these notes of rest to gesture toward the world to come, a world in which all of creation and God will find home here. Lord, help us play these dominant chords.

To conclude this session of Notes of Rest, I invite us to pray this final prayer together. May we remember the freedom that Jesus is bringing and that we already have, notwithstanding the chronic pains of our lives and this world.

God, I resolve to rest in you.
God, we resolve to rest in you.
God, we resolve that they will rest in you.
We are loved because you made us,
not because of what we make.
Amen.

Dialogue

Julian Davis Reid, John Kartje, Matthew Wesley Williams

Julian: Hi, Matthew and John, thank you for engaging in this dialogue about my Notes of Rest essay. Matthew, I invited you to respond because of your focus on Black theological education, which is where I slot Notes of Rest, given its emphasis on Black music and thus, by extension, Black faith and Black existence. And John, I invited you to respond because of your attention to theological education as formation, given your interest in the moral formation of the priesthood. Similarly, I see Notes of Rest as attending to the spiritual formation of the theological academy. To that end, I'll start with you, John. What were you hearing in my piece?

John: What made this piece so formational to me is the encounter present in the opening narrative. I say to my faculty all the time that without encounter we have nothing. I recall that YHWH encountered God's people, and Jesus encounters us with the glorious Trinity, which chooses to be known.

I'm gathering that a primal vocational lure for you is the music. Even when you were in the detention center as a student chaplain, music is the fire in Jeremiah's bones that you can't keep down forever.

You went not knowing if your music was allowed to be there. But in the encounter with the boys, you encountered yourself and God. You chose to listen to God, and as a result, there was an invitation to recast theological education around this encounter.

I note that the student was learning a song in a structured way. Out of the structure of that educational moment, encounter happened. What a school of theology can do is enforce a certain structure—for instance, I need you to take this class or get this pastoral experience—but if that structure is set up in love, encounter can take over. This means that the only template is the natural encounter itself.

This natural encounter of the moment resists your resistance: "This isn't what my theological assignment was." In this case, because the music is you, it's inevitable that the music would come up in this context, too.

If I were head of formation at Candler and I sent you into the detention center, I would say: "This is glorious, I can't wait for the music to come out."

In the Catholic tradition, spiritual direction is important. But I tell people all the time that the only spiritual director is the Holy Spirit. What we do is help each other be better listeners. And you were listening to what the Spirit was doing inside that guy's mind and heart, and eventually you could name that in your essay. Formation is this glorious feedback loop, and a whole lifetime's formation has made you such that now you can frame this encounter for yourself and invite other people into it. I'm excited for any musician to read this.

Julian: That framing around formation helps me connect this essay in my own vocational journey, which is tied to the boy who calmed himself.

Throughout seminary, before Notes of Rest started, I was negotiating three vocational pulls—calls to the local church, to the theological academy, and to the music industry. I was pastoral but wanted to play at a high level, meaning I couldn't do conventional pastoring, at least in this season. The same issue proved true for the tension between music and traditional academia.

Only after graduating did I see Christian spiritual formation as a lens through which to hold it all together. However, though I loved the world, I noticed how white it was, both in authors discussed and students in the tradition. Henri Nouwen, Thomas Merton, and Teresa of Ávila are all dope, but it was only when I considered Black music as a spiritual discipline that Christian spirituality framing made sense.

John: Ah, I hear all of that.

Matthew: Yes, I do too, but I want to caution you, Julian, not to situate Notes of Rest too comfortably within the theological academy proper. After all, where were Black folk receiving theological education in 1807 when Andover Theological Seminary was founded? We were gathering in the hush harbor in secret, to make sure the white folk couldn't hear us. The Creator and our ancestors met us there, and we learned, channeled, and conjured. Andover and the institutional template it generated was never designed to hold the cauldron of the hush harbor.

Allow Notes of Rest to keep some critical distance from the academy because the subversive logics of the hush harbor that animate your work cannot be subsumed, captured, or fully explained by the academy.

Julian: This is a challenging perspective because theological education proper has been so core to my formation as a thinker. Moreover, it has connected me to cats such as yourself who push me to expand my thinking about theological education. You are helping me see the subversive logic of teaching in the prison, which reminds me of John's idea of encounter. God was unexpectedly forming me through that encounter with the boys, helping me reach back to the hush harbor impulse to find space to reflect on God's sacred presence and capacity to teach in spaces that I was not ready to see as such. I endeavor to heed your word of warning, Brotha Matthew.

John: Julian, your piece also left me with another burning question about rest. You raise a critical point that theological schools are filled with harried people. But you're not just saying that we should rest as a counter to that manic pace lest we lose the mission of our schools. You're saying something deeper: that part of the constitutive quality of God *is* rest. You say, "They [the Israelites] were to rest their bodies because of who God had proven to be to them." Well, God had proven to be the God who rests. Instead of rest being something God performs, rest is core to the being of the Trinity that moves in *perichoresis*. So my question is: Given that we are made in the image of God, is rest part of our anthropology? To the degree we are not living into that rest, it seems we are living less than human lives.

Julian: Yes, yo. That explains why I grow uneasy when people try to reduce Notes to a mere health and wellness offering. That speaks to the dehumanization of enslaved folk in the hush harbor who could not rest, too. Rest is not just a nice-to-have that makes us healthier for the living of these days in this-here world. Rest enables us to participate in the divine life that God has created us to enjoy, a life that lives within the restful life of God. And to your point about lack of rest and dehumanization, enslaved Black folk, and many Black folk since then, have not been allowed to rest properly. That is not just a health concern, though of course it is also that. It is also a theological concern. We are denying ourselves and other created kin (human and nonhuman) the opportunity to participate in the restful divine life.

Matthew: Yes, that resonates with me too. I couldn't agree more that rest is part of who God is. But I want to take the need for rest in the theological academy in a different direction. It ties to the detention center being the site of your story, Julian. Both the prison-industrial complex and the academy are built on similar logics of extraction and separation, which stem from the Western intellectual tradition that undergirds colonial Christianity and the colonial project writ large.

As I was saying earlier with Andover, the predominant intellectual traditions on which our schools are founded reflexively traffic in separation and fragmentation instead of the interrelatedness and holism that represent the philosophical root structure of the Black art, music, and thought that underpins Notes of Rest, as expressed in the Bantu concept of Ubuntu. Ubuntu holds that a person can only become a person through relatedness with other people. Notes of Rest, especially with its emphasis on Black music, is an intervention in our context of fragmented, extractive life; it invites us back to that integration and interrelatedness.

What you're doing with Notes of Rest is an experiment *in* theological education but also an indictment *of* traditional theological education. Theological education over the last seventy years made ministry a competitor with other professions. After WWII, seminarians were being trained to bolster the labor force of the church as a constitutive element of the re-budding US empire. It is therefore unsurprising to me that we Christians are just as exhausted as everybody else; we are oriented toward the same imperial ends.

Julian: Man. I have rarely labeled my work an intervention but appreciate that prod to see it as that. Along with making an intervention into the weariness of the academy, I am also intervening in the traditional ways of thinking about vocation that had me stuck between conventional pastoring and teaching. By blending music, pastoring, *and* academic thinking, I model how the Spirit of God is braiding our vocations in theological education between the times. When I was beginning seminary, I felt I had to leave music out. But as the story from my time in the Metro detention center suggested, God brought all the stories together, and continues to weave them together. The experiment is still unfolding in me, that's for sure.

Matthew: That brings me to a point about Black music. Throughout reading your work I thought about Psalm 137, with its range of complex emotions, including rage, lament, and even hopelessness for the weary, vanquished people of God:

> By the rivers of Babylon—
> there we sat down, and there we wept
> when we remembered Zion.
> On the willows there
> we hung up our harps.
> For there our captors
> asked us for songs,
> and our tormentors asked for mirth, saying,
> "Sing us one of the songs of Zion!"
> (Ps. 137:1–3 NRSVue)

Notes of Rest helps us *all* sing our songs in a strange land, for we have all endured the ramifications of the violence that Europe had perpetrated on itself and its peoples for centuries before spreading it to the rest of the world. To that end, I commend you on the Sankofa work you're doing as you have us pick up our harps again.

9

Naming Realities, Imagining Possibilities

Angela Sims

> But we have this treasure in clay jars, so that it may be made clear that this extraordinary power belongs to God and does not come from us. (2 Cor. 4:7)

Sixty months. Sixty months of service at Colgate Rochester Crozer Divinity School. Sixty months marked by resilience during a time marked by a campus relocation, institutional reorganization, a global pandemic, implementation of a strategic plan, enhanced process efficiencies, and a host of mission-focused, internal, and external collaborative initiatives. Sixty months as a new seminary with a history of over two hundred years, creating a new narrative against the tremendous odds of public perception.

Sixty months of observing and engaging with faculty and staff who invest time, energy, and resources that convey the ways in which Colgate Rochester Crozer's mission is not static but vibrant. Sixty months of stepping into spaces and places where very few persons resemble me. Sixty months of gratitude to Monroe County women executives and other business and community leaders who facilitated introductions on my behalf. Sixty months of walking by faith, taking leaps of faith, listening and questioning, learning and relearning, and understanding more each day why Colgate Rochester Crozer matters.

Sixty months can sometimes seem like a lifetime when measured almost exclusively by *the bottom line*—fluctuating endowment value and percentages of budget to actual performance on financial statements. Sixty months presented me with some valuable lessons. Perhaps chief among them is understanding the perils associated with putting *new wine in old wineskins*.

Sixty months for which to give thanks for the faith-filled persons with whom I journey, individuals who are shaped and formed by specific religious traditions: Episcopalian, African Methodist Episcopal Zion, United Methodist, Baptist (American, National, Progressive), Pentecostal, Christian Methodist Episcopal, Presbyterian Church (U.S.A.), Roman Catholic, Presbyterian Church in America, Mennonite, spiritual but not religious. Sixty months of service in which to give thanks and praise to God for eyes to see what might be and for a capable and willing team with whom to do the necessary work of reestablishing Colgate Rochester Crozer as a vital resource in western New York. So how did it all begin?

INTRODUCTIONS MATTER: WHEN, WHERE, AND HOW BLACK WOMEN ENTER

On April 10, 2019, in the rotunda of city hall in Rochester, New York, the chair of Colgate Rochester Crozer Divinity School's board introduced me as the school's thirteenth president. Hosted by the city's first woman mayor, herself a Black woman, I stated that two hundred years ago Colgate Rochester Crozer appointing a woman as its chief executive officer would have seemed an impossibility. One hundred years later, this moment might have been only a fleeting thought. But on that day, I looked back, while moving forward, ever mindful that in each generation there is indeed a great cloud of witnesses who serve as trailblazers for those who are yet to be. On the day I was introduced as the school's first woman president and the first Black woman to serve as president of any Rochester area institution of higher learning, I gave thanks to the many known and unknown persons who challenged systems of oppression, who were firsts so that others might follow, who asked questions and refused to succumb to the status quo.

As I prepared to join the Colgate Rochester Crozer Divinity School community a few months later on July 1, I took seriously the words of the prophet Micah, "to do justice, to love kindness, and to walk humbly with the divine." This prophetic mandate, reflected in Colgate Rochester Crozer's mission, would serve as a guide as faculty, staff, students, trustees, alumni, friends of the school, and I all together renewed our commitment to honor the school's allegiance to peace and justice. It was a commitment that continues to be reflected in our educational programs and collaborations; cocurricular offerings; church and community partnerships; and engagement with alumni, donors, and friends of the school.

What was certain on April 10, 2019, was that change was abounding at Colgate Rochester Crozer Divinity School! With a foundation upon which to build, a campus relocation would offer opportunities to reimagine living laboratories and experiential learning; the use of technology to build community while simultaneously expanding the school's presence; elimination of deferred maintenance that, with time, would allow the school to gradually increase its investment in students as well as provide increased professional development opportunities for faculty and staff. How did we get to this new place?

Change is not easy. Change is not without risk. Change is a catalyst. Change is an invitation. Change is a constant.

Space and Place Matters: From the Hill to Village Gate

For all but three Colgate Rochester Crozer Divinity School employees and myself, Tuesday, August 20, 2019, marked the culmination of a three-year process to move less than 2.5 miles. It was a journey marked by ongoing internal and external conversations, culling of files and artifacts, designing and redesigning space, and imagining the not-yet but possible.

I am privileged to have spent my initial seven weeks at the location that was the school's home for ninety years. Beginning my presidential tenure on those historic grounds afforded me a glimpse of the school that is not captured fully in publications. My time at 1100 S. Goodman Street enabled me to consider ways in which photos and other memorabilia can be used to blend past, present, and future as we began to reimagine theological education at 320 N. Goodman Street, always mindful that space and place matter!

August 20, 2019, symbolized a continuum in Colgate Rochester Crozer's history characterized by intentionality to position this 205-year-old educational institution to remain a vital member of the Rochester metro area. From a hillside location with spectacular views of the city to the Neighborhood of the Arts in a building that faces an active railroad track, Colgate Rochester Crozer reaffirmed its commitment to prepare, equip, and engage students for service to church and world as we simultaneously discern together how we as administrators, faculty, and staff will live the school's mission. For, as George Washington Carver put it, "Where there is no vision, there is no hope."

HOPEFUL FRAGMENTS

Fragments—pieces, clues, indicators—point to something larger than what was, what is, and what might be. Historical, sociological, and theological fragments invite us to discern the significance of defining moments in an institution's life. For Colgate Rochester Crozer, the birth of a social gospel, a nineteen-day student lockout, the establishment of the first Black Church Studies program in the United States, and an early commitment to women and gender studies are all treasures that emerged within a community as it sought to install listening and hearing as practices to be valued.

People, purpose, and passion beckon one always to be mindful of what matters most. Time, memories, and hopes demand of one a level of accountability that may be disruptive and interruptive while simultaneously requiring a leader to model responsibility in a manner that, per Dr. Stephanie Sauvé, an alumna and former vice president for academic affairs and dean at Colgate Rochester Crozer, communicates always that *we are a people with hope*.

With that hope in mind, I have made it characteristic of my presidency to articulate an annual theme that serves as both guide and reminder that theological education is sacred work. Recalling those themes can be a generative way to reflect on these sixty months twelve months at a time.

Except for the first two years of my tenure, each theme has been informed by a biblical text. As we strive to live our mission, we are cognizant that for more than two centuries, Colgate Rochester Crozer has come this far by faith. With a keen awareness of challenges in higher education, and specifically those with which seminaries contend, for such a time as now, as we focus on stabilizing this institution, we are compelled to ask the Divine to revive us again as we give thanks in all things. Colgate Rochester Crozer is a treasure whose value is still being determined. The school's worth is not calculated based on a campus footprint or location or the size of its endowment. While these are concerns that are my constant companions, the school's annual themes serve as a reminder that while our efforts may not result in a desired outcome, God is nevertheless with us.

Living Our Mission

Fiscal year 2019–2020 was fast paced. I had moments in which to evaluate, reflect, and rest. I was ever mindful of a responsibility to live with public narratives that may not align with institutional realities and for which a response is often not appropriate. While the pace of the work, coupled with a commitment to quality, did not lessen, we implemented processes designed to address employee well-being (such as flexible work hours and the formalization of an employee recognition program) and assess them on an ongoing basis.

The initial twelve months of my presidency provided numerous opportunities for me to meet with students, alumni, donors, and prospective friends of the school. Whether impromptu or a planned visit, each interaction afforded me an invitation to listen carefully to what was shared, to reflect deeply on what was not articulated, and to acknowledge the ways in which each person makes it possible for Colgate Rochester Crozer to be faithful to its mission.

Higher education necessitates an ability to adapt to unforeseen circumstances with increasing agility that is marked by concern for students, faculty, and staff. A fall 2019 emphasis on strengthening the school's infrastructure, with specific attention to technological enhancements and obtaining approval to participate in the State Authorization Reciprocity Agreement (SARA) program to conduct distance education, subsequently made it possible, in response to COVID-19, to transition in mid-March 2020 from on-campus to remote instruction and operations as we continued to respond in a manner that was fiscally responsible and humane.

THIS FAR BY FAITH

Even in the shadow of a failed coup on January 6, 2021, the somber acknowledgment of more than 500,000 reported COVID-19-related deaths in the United States, and the nonindictment in the death of Daniel Prude, Colgate Rochester Crozer Divinity School had much for which to give God thanks and praise. As a community guided by our mission to form students in theological and multireligious studies to serve, care, and advocate for all peoples and the earth, the theme for fiscal year 2020–2021, "This Far by Faith," reminded us that formation is a communal endeavor. As we approached the one-year anniversary of a transition to remote operations, it was important to acknowledge faculty, staff, and students for their continued commitment to Colgate Rochester Crozer as evidenced in their response to changes in educational delivery, interactive engagement, and creativity.

While the pace of the work, especially when coupled with an ongoing expectation of quality, did not lessen, I was concerned about the effect of sustained Zoom fatigue on the health of employees, the school's most valued assets. I was equally concerned about a tendency to translate remote operations into a sense of false expectations regarding staff availability. To address this, we emphasized the following expectations and assessed them on an ongoing basis:

- Two-hour blocks of Zoom meetings to be followed by one hour of not being available by Zoom
- Not checking emails before 8:30 a.m. and after 4:30 p.m. (understanding that in case of emergency or time-sensitive matter, persons know how to reach the applicable staff member via phone)
- Reemphasizing the importance of checking email at least three times (at the beginning, middle, and end) in the workday
- The option to take a non-PTO mental-health day monthly

I experience Colgate Rochester Crozer as an institution comprised of people who, to borrow from James Weldon Johnson, the author and activist who penned the words to "Lift Every Voice and Sing" in 1900, "sing songs full of faith and hope." Johnson's work harkens to a time when mob rule and lynching were the order of the day in the United States. I exercise some creative license in my appropriation of a song recognized as the Black National Anthem as a reflective point of entry that pushes me to consider who inhabits Colgate Rochester Crozer during a time when increasingly the only persons who may not be at risk of having their humanity questioned are cisgender white heterosexual males or those who can pass as such. This very present threat to humanity and what it means to be fully human, when held in tension with issues of sexual orientation, identity, preference, and respect, seeks to disrupt every aspect of shared life. Thus, I am challenged to consider named and unnamed persons who directly and indirectly are present in various aspects of the school where I serve as the chief executive officer.

Personal experiences shared with me offer glimpses of former faculty, staff, and students who matriculated at a campus located in the Highland Park neighborhood on acreage that afforded perhaps the most beautiful panoramic view in all of Rochester. Accounts of student gatherings in the refectory and at professors' homes and of international relationships suggest a commitment to raise awareness around issues of justice. As I listened to these historical retellings, I was aware of the need for deep analysis and understanding of intersectional realities. These demand that we name and respond to systemic issues with which (particularly minoritized) people contend. These invisible, yet very present, persons who are in many regards "larger than life itself," dwell among us and invite us to consider what it means to live more faithfully into our vision to become a seminary of and for the communities to which we are connected.

I was attentive to current and prospective students' ability and desire to use Zoom and course management systems to narrow geographical divides. Simultaneously, faculty established and honored expectations that reflected Colgate Rochester Crozer's commitment to excellence in teaching and learning. Coming from varied socioeconomic backgrounds, faith traditions, and educational experiences, many of our students are multivocational and employed in a variety of contexts. They bring these experiences with them into the virtual and real classrooms and common areas—along with their ministry supervisors, episcopal leaders, parishioners, community members, family members, and more. In listening to them, I try to be careful not to translate, or perhaps interpret unfairly, their articulation of ministry concerns as appeals for absolute solutions to concrete presenting moral dilemmas. I want to stimulate, not stifle, their intellectual curiosity. Given the enormous responsibility that accompanies these student ministry appointments, Colgate Rochester Crozer's relationships with judicatories and other entities are of immense importance. As religious organizations continue to develop additional pathways to ministry, determining how we work together on behalf of students and their families, as well as the contexts in which our students serve may be a catalyst to move the church from a posture of survival to one of re-formation that repurposes and continues to value the cultivation of the mind as a spiritual discipline.

The importance of public perceptions about the institution reminded me to be considerate about expressions of grief as persons continue to process Colgate Rochester Crozer's decision to relocate to the Village Gate neighborhood. At the same time, this 2.5-mile migration to a mixed-use commercial park that runs adjacent to an operating railroad track highlights the significance of space and one's place in a particular locale. For we cannot ignore questions of whose lives matter. We must be seriously concerned about our Black, Asian, Latinx, LGBTQIAPK[1] students, employees, and their families. We cannot ignore the possibility that persons who dwell among us could be racially profiled or subjected to body shaming and harassment in a metropolitan area where approximately 75 percent of Monroe County's residents self-identify as white. And so our faculty continues to reflect on the question: What does it mean, and what is required, for Colgate Rochester Crozer to remain a safe sanctuary institution?

At the school's September 19, 2023, Christian Faith & LGBTQ+ Experience Lecture, given by four persons who self-identify as transgender, and one who is the parent of a young transgender child, consequences of antitransgender legislation were palpably apparent. Imagine hearing personal accounts from persons who sought refuge in western New York because they feared for their or their child's life in the state they previously called home. Their narratives gave nuanced meaning to the psalmist's question of *singing the Lord's song in a strange and foreign land* when one feels like a refugee in the land of one's birth. What makes western New York, and especially Rochester, a destination point is quality medical care afforded to transgender persons at Trillium Hospital. While this was not common information to many attendees at Colgate Rochester Crozer's fall 2023 lecture, one-on-one conversations with several of the panelists after the lecture suggest that in this particular moment when legislative initiatives threaten what some consider a basic right—access to quality health care—Colgate Rochester Crozer has an opportunity to consider how its understanding of place, space, and mission might inform an ethos and ethic of sanctuary.

When I consider administrative changes made during my initial two years, it was apparent that Colgate Rochester Crozer had to articulate its understanding of presence and what this means in regard to sustaining existing relationships and cultivating new ones. It required me to name and familiarize myself with institutional partners, stakeholders, and known and unknown key decision makers. I had to learn to imagine those not "physically" in the room but whose perspective may or should influence matters that affect our operations and ultimately our ability to thrive. Other issues included that of institutional identity informed by our location, a move toward multiple program delivery modalities in fiscal year 2022–2023, and the possibilities that may enrich learning experiences for multiple constituent groups.

A confessional moment: before I joined the Colgate Rochester Crozer community, there was a time when I did not accept invitations from "well-meaning" Euro-American students to address historical-contemporary manifestations of racism as this country's original sin. Instead, I used those student encounters to encourage them to name their discomfort or dis-ease and to engage in dialogue with my Euro-American progressive "liberal" faculty colleagues about social-historical accounts that are antithetical to the frequently colorless accounts that are often accepted without question. Given the resurgence of white Christian nationalism, I realized more than ever that now, as a seminary president, I do have a responsibility to create space in which students can reflect on ways in which they are both compelled to appeal to the moral conscience of the nation and articulate an ethical ecclesiology that demonstrates their understanding of the nature, purpose, and function of church and its relationship to Christ and white supremacy.

With this stance, I attempted to lead by example as an active participant in the life of Colgate Rochester Crozer. I took this stance cognizant of risks associated with speaking truth—for instance, to our board of trustees—about racism, sexism, and (to borrow a term from my colleague Dr. Valerie Bridgeman, vice president of academic affairs and dean at Methodist Theological Seminary in Ohio) homo-aggressiveness that is embedded deeply in our institution, as it is in most educational institutions in the United States. When I and others participate in this justice-infused work, we do so mindful of the ways in which Eurocentric thought and practice is often privileged in our degree programs. With this awareness and its accompanying dissonance, a repetition of preferred courses may be counterproductive to an institutional commitment that values other worldviews. How we communicate that this work is not exclusively the work of the faculty, but that of the entire community, is essential. Formation of students to serve, care, and advocate for all peoples and the earth is no easy task. For it requires time to divest ourselves of pre- and misconceptions, to cultivate a climate where all voices can be heard without fear of retaliation, to think about the costs/risks associated with some of our organizational partnerships and institutional collaborations, and to seek forgiveness when we get it wrong and unconsciously put others in jeopardy. In such a time as this there are lessons to be learned from the songs of voices within our community that are often muted and ignored.

FOR SUCH A TIME AS NOW (JEREMIAH 29:11)

Fiscal year 2021–2022's theme invited us to consider the significance of the prophet Jeremiah's letter to a people in exile. For almost two years, students, faculty, and staff had adapted to the realities of remote course delivery and seminary operations. While they had done so with remarkable grace, flexibility, and mutual concern, some of our students, particularly those in our MDiv and MA programs, clearly preferred campus-based course delivery. We approached the end of the academic year mindful that our ongoing response to COVID-19 required us to consider the impact of our campus work-space design, traffic flow, and ventilation, among many other things.

With the fiscal year priorities of new student recruitment, educational and operational technology, and a vision campaign in mind, Jeremiah's letter to the exiles in Babylon reminded us of the importance to build where we are. We recognized that we had yet to experience fully the plans the Lord had for us—plans for the school's welfare and not for harm, to give us a future with hope. The active engagement of students in the life of the school, the generosity of our donors, and the presence of our friends at school-sponsored events reminded us that God was with us yet.

Our participation in In Trust's Wise Stewards initiative affirmed the work we were doing to address needs assessment, board member training, and board member recruitment. An area of concern was candor and transparency between me as president and each governing and life trustee. To make a distinction between the complementary work of the board and the administration, we developed a new pattern of communication. At each October meeting, each VP would provide a high-level overview of their team; in February they would speak to opportunities; and in May they would each share a moment of celebration. Also, at the all-employee meetings I convene, I typically allow for what I describe as a "sound off." In response to the prompt, "*What one question would you like the board to address at its February 2022 meeting?*," I shared the following questions, which employees posed to the board, and suggested that we share them with all employees and students:

1. What does the board think about the relationship between space/place/accessibility, whether physical or digital, and the school's mission?

2. Have any board members attended any events sponsored by the Association of Theological Schools (or other agencies) to keep up with current trends?
3. How do we reflect our commitment to be a seminary of and for the community in how we make our classrooms as open and accessible as possible to the community, whether as matriculated students or as auditors? Who is sitting in our classrooms? What is our delivery system? Who matters?
4. How welcoming does the board perceive the institution to be?
5. The school's new $300 per month tuition plan is very helpful and has been a draw for students. This shift from $598 per credit hour with no internal financial aid to doctor of ministry students aligns with the school's commitment to equity and justice. What other similar initiatives might we create, and how might we scale the tuition plan to impact more people?
6. What is the board's concept of formation?

When I reflected on my initial three years as president of Colgate Rochester Crozer Divinity School, that fiscal year's theme—"For Such a Time as Now"—reminded me that our corporate prayer life deeply informs how we respond to pandemics, white supremacy, violence, and death. I presumed that each governing and life trustee, employee, and student had some form of prayer life. Now I wanted to encourage all of us to consider gathering intentionally as a community to discern God's plans for the school's future.

In that second year of remote operations and ongoing concerns about COVID infection rates, it was imperative that we decide what was required of each of us, individually and collectively, to ensure that Colgate Rochester Crozer would continue to thrive. For while enrollment numbers are indicators, they are only one factor in discernment of the Lord's plans for the school's welfare and hope-filled future. And while data influences decisions, the information it provides can also encourage and welcome a shift from what is to what might be. More broadly, the region in which we are physically located—and the wider world—needs Colgate Rochester Crozer, and we have many gifts and resources to contribute to the ongoing work of justice. Sometimes, I knew, it takes gathering in prayer *as a community* to identify who and what we can be and do, and to gather the courage to do it. We needed the focusing and reviving power of prayer to stop using COVID or past narratives and assumptions as excuses for inaction. Our world was depending on us for that.

REVIVE US AGAIN (EZEKIEL 37:1–14)

At my tenth board meeting at Colgate Rochester Crozer Divinity School in October 2022, I found myself with more questions than answers, more qualitative evidence that this learning community was and is in a season of rebirth, renewal, and revival than is supported by quantitative data alone. For instance, at the September 12 all-employee meeting, when asked what one word best described what they wanted the board to know about Colgate Rochester Crozer, faculty and staff shared the following: "fiscal-stewardship," "resilience," "relationships," "transformation," "innovation," "spiritual-formation," "viable," "spiritually rich," "creativity," "laboring," "invitation-to-partnership," "transition," "hopeful," "hope," "commitment," "undaunted," "revamping." When asked the same question, responses from approximately 25 percent of our students indicated they wanted the board to know they experience Colgate Rochester Crozer as: "family," "invigorating," "progressive," "informative," "galvanizing," "empowering," "prophetic," "challenging," "a charism," "inclusive." As we continued to adapt to the "yet unknowns" related to ongoing coronavirus mutations, I was mindful that the school's viability and stability depend heavily on public perception. An ever-present concern for me was how to balance budget realities in a manner that might yield a return on our investment in support of student recruitment and relationship cultivation. With an active faith, ever mindful of individual employees' concerns about health, and seeking to align our qualitative and quantitative data, we recognized a need to reengage in person, not only in the greater Rochester area but in other sectors of the United States and Canada. We realized how much representation matters.

As I concluded my fourth year of service at Colgate Rochester Crozer, the significance of one of the main Sankofa symbols, a mythical bird with its feet firmly planted facing forward and its head turned backward, reminded me to reflect on where we had been, what we had accomplished, and what we had learned, even as we moved into the future to which we were called. At our May 2023 meeting, I looked back intentionally to my first presentation to the board at its May 13, 2019, meeting. With an emphasis on "Living Our Mission: Past, Present, Future," I asked the board if we were "open to an invitation to participate in Colgate Rochester Crozer's rebirth."

Recognizing that numbers are always open to interpretation, the seminary's core challenges, from my then-outsider-looking-in perspective, were enrollment, operations, and endowment. Mindful that freestanding seminaries' greatest contribution to church and society is not to prepare persons to serve exclusively in congregations but rather to form people for ministry for a time that is yet unfolding, I wondered aloud whether Colgate Rochester Crozer could (re)define who we are fast enough to make a difference. What prompted this thought was the school's abiding commitment to peace and justice, potential for national and international collaborations, and embrace of a nonresidential "learner-centered" approach to graduate theological education.

I hold on to the promise that "our God is making all things new." We could not have imagined living out our mission during a global pandemic. However, if we look at any decade in the life of this school's two centuries, we notice that trustees, presidents, senior leadership, faculty, staff, students, alumni, and friends of Colgate Rochester Crozer have always lived out this institution's mission one day at a time, one prayer at a time, one individual and collective effort at a time. The work to which we are called in support of Colgate Rochester Crozer is not easy, but with trust, faith, and perseverance, it is indeed possible if we devote our time and resources to prepare the school to reach its next centennial.

GIVING THANKS IN ALL THINGS (1 THESSALONIANS 5:12–20)

As I reflect on my time as president, I give thanks for emerging signs that our efforts to strengthen our infrastructure were wise investments of time, resources, and energy. We reviewed policies and our commitment to apply them consistently. We made changes to align policy and practice with the school's core values. We worked to increase intentionality in modeling accountability and responsibility across the institution. This year's ten-year retrospective in the State of the School Report shows two of our four key metrics—enrollment and expense-to-full-time equivalency per student—trending favorably; one—annual giving—holding steady; and the fourth—endowment draw—indicating an area of concern that will begin to trend favorably as we continue our emphasis on both student recruitment and retention and donor/friend cultivation. This fourth metric—the draw on the endowment—is of most concern for me. As the school's only asset, the endowment is subject to factors, such as market trends, that are beyond our control. At the same time, this metric motivates us as we review existing programs and explore new ones. We are, after all, the only theologically progressive seminary in western New York. The biblical account of the multiplication of a few loaves of bread and fish to feed a multitude is a helpful metaphorical and spiritual illustration. This pericope invites us to consider whether the board is willing to step out on faith. In other words, will the board take some risks with our resources and share with others why Colgate Rochester Crozer merits consideration? Reflecting on those merits might convey what is needed for this 206-year-old school to thrive.

I remain grateful for the strides we have made to position the school well to respond to inevitable change. This is no small feat. Much is required of a staff of seventeen, and there are some moments that call for celebration even as we remember what is required of us to address current fiscal realities. We have, for example, made significant progress in student enrollment. By spring 2019, we were welcoming 71 students. And in spring of 2024, it was a joy to welcome 61 returning and 31 entering students. Of the 92 students enrolled that semester, 26 were in the doctor of ministry program, 3 in the master of arts program, 35 in the master of divinity program, and 28 in the graduate certificate program. This represented the highest entering spring class since 2017. That semester, 11 of the 19 students were in the doctor of ministry program; the other degree programs accounted for 8 students combined. Student recruitment, retention initiatives, and activities to cultivate relationships with donors and friends have all provided momentum in support of our goal of 140 students. But even with this growing student body, attention to fiscal realities remains a primary concern.

My presidency so far has not been easy, but with trust, faith, and perseverance, I give God thanks for what just might come forth from this investment of my and my team's efforts, along with the board, to position Colgate Rochester Crozer to thrive.

ATTENDING TO THE FRAGMENTS: A CONCLUDING THOUGHT

Writing four days before the conclusion of the United States' 2024 national election, I am mindful that effecting change in higher education requires leaders, faculty, trustees, donors, students, and other stakeholders to take inventory of an institution's history and to examine the school's defining moments. Leaders in higher education need to ask, "What time is it?" What time is it when a call for equity is unaccompanied by a call for accountability and responsibility? What time is it when the promise of equity, justice, and fairness is met with reluctance to dismantle systemic oppression, particularly at institutions of higher learning, that for centuries have privileged constructions of whiteness that are often reflected, for example, in admissions criteria, syllabi, and program learning outcomes? What time is it when leaders in higher education use this moment to reflect upon our vocation and communal implications of our research, work, and life? In this moment, leaders in higher education must reimagine the ways in which our collective efforts signal that for such a time as now we have an opportunity to assess the relevance of our institution's mission and core values, to evaluate methods by which we collaborate and engage with organizations and persons with whom we have shared values, to invest in our school's greatest assets—our students and employees—to be mindful of our hiring practices and to be clear that change and cultural shifts can be and often are painful and met with resistance. I am deeply committed to this work. At the same time, I also must acknowledge how fragments—sharp edges, irregular sizes, multihued—sometimes serve as a cautionary lesson to me to avoid a tendency to prioritize an institution's health to the detriment of my own well-being. Fragments—habits, routines, communities—should be examined regularly to avoid normalizing anxiety. Fragments—walking, immersing my hands in soil, pampering sessions—remind me to reclaim practices that allow me to connect with nature and with self. Fragments—life in all of its complexity—warn against unconsciously commodifying myself as I continue to respond to institutional demands. To be well is a gift I owe to myself and to my loved ones. Asé.

Dialogue

Angela Sims, Grace Y. Kao, Juan J. Molina Flores

Grace: Can you help us better understand the impact and significance of relocating the seminary? Your note about the move only being "2.5 miles" away suggests one thing, and yet you also talk about "ongoing internal and external conversations" and "expressions of grief" about the move. But if you don't mind my asking, what exactly was lost or grieved?

Angela: What was lost was nostalgia and a constructed sense of place. Those who grieve the most vocally were never fully vested financially in the maintenance associated with a facility that was 150-plus years old. While I hesitate to name this, I also recognize how a preference for a particular style of architecture most closely associated with primarily white colleges and universities built in a particular era, may inform how individuals mourn the loss of a campus that was an essential aspect of their student experience and central to their own sense of formation.

Grace: Ah—those are helpful clarifications! As an outsider I wouldn't have known any of this.

Angela: I hesitated to give voice to my observations as it is never my intention to minimize attachments that people have to institutions.

Juan: I appreciated your emphasis on the physical space. Maybe what you were also trying to say is that there was also a certain awareness that there were other issues or spaces as the move was happening, such as racism and gender issues that were emerging or you needed to be aware of. I say this because the description of the movements also seemed to suggest underlying issues.

It seems like you took a lot of risks here. Just accepting being the first woman president of the institution was a big risk. And then knowing that this institution was already going through that transition of moving was another risk as well. Moving is especially tough because, as you say, the physical spaces reflect or symbolize, among other things, a culture and other issues that are part of the institution. And so, as you're finding a space and moving into it, you're finding the way human resources are seen or appreciated, how alumni are also seen, all of that.

Grace: You are very tactfully, very diplomatically, naming so many different dynamics. Like, I appreciated your "confessional" note about the type of invitations you didn't tend to accept from "well-meaning" Euro-American students to talk about racism in ways they were hoping you would (prior to joining Colgate Rochester), but now as seminary president and the resurgence of white Christian nationalism, your sense of what you should do has changed. This thinking about what you, *qua* Angela Sims, want or should do and what you, *qua* seminary president, should do sounds like it could be exhausting at times.

Angela: Both individuals and organizations take on multiple identities as a way to navigate different spaces, different times. I think a lot about institutional identity right now. For me, it's always asking, "What are lessons that might be learned by an institution that is still going through a significant moment of change? What is it that we might learn if we begin to listen more closely and deeply to what's occurring around us as the only theologically progressive institution in this region, and respond in kind?" And I think about my personal identity, too, as I attend to the fragments and reconnect not just with the institution but with the soil, with myself.

Juan: Angela, I like the fact that you gave a theme to each movement, and that you were following a fiscal year. There is a lot there in terms of what your reflection and your executive leadership team's reflection process was—about the past and the future.

But there is also a sense of *enoughness*. At the end of the day, in five years you've accomplished so much. Not only personally, but also with the institution, especially if the board and most of your constituents are happy with your leadership and see themselves as well positioned for the near future.

Grace: As someone who works at a progressive UMC (United Methodist Church) seminary with deep ecumenical and multireligious commitments, I was struck by your understanding that an institution's "corporate prayer life" informs how they respond to various issues, including the pandemic and white supremacy. And how you wanted to encourage your seminary community to "gather intentionally . . . to discern God's plans for the school future"—meaning, you wanted to draw the community together in collective prayer. Given my multireligious context, I cannot imagine our faculty responding well to any president of ours wanting us to root our responses (to white supremacy or violence and so forth) to corporate prayer!

Angela: I think it is extremely important that each institution understand its mission and its vision. Our vision statement acknowledges a responsibility to be faithful to the school's distinctive Christian identity as we honor our commitment to practices of peace, service, and justice. While I have students who are not Christian and staff members who are spiritual but not religious, we gather once a week for corporate worship. In that space of worship, I believe that the Spirit is hearing those collective prayers, whether they are verbalized or not. I also think each president has a responsibility to cultivate a particular type of ethos. I think about prayer not as prescriptive but as a way that a community gathers to hear something other than their own voice.

Juan: To me, that—the way in which you are setting the tone for acceptance of new situations that may mean growing spiritually and humanly—is integral to the vision that you are embodying for the board and your community.

I have some questions that you might want to consider for your own leadership: What is behind that desire to be open to the Spirit, to try new and sometimes controversial prayer styles or practices, as well as other ways of welcoming students and staff? How can that desire and practice be more widely shared, so that they can continue to take root? It would be helpful for you to state those things so that staff and board can see how important those issues are for you and for the institution.

Grace: Angela, what I appreciate about so many of your responses in this conversation is your sense of CRCDS (Colgate Rochester Crozer Divinity School). Because of the school's tradition, history, and vision, you can do some things well while you recognize that the school is probably not positioned to do other things well. And you are also exploring future possibilities, like your note about thinking through what "ethos and ethic of sanctuary" CRCDS can provide for trans folks who find themselves going to western New York and Rochester for health care. I love how in acknowledging your school's financial pressures, you are looking to build on existing strengths given your mission—not trying to be all things to all people.

On another note, both you and Juan are in charge of institutions and are exercising spiritual authority over faculty, staff, and students. That sounds like a monumental task.

Angela: I don't see myself as exercising spiritual authority.

Grace: Well, the fact that you are calling the community to corporate prayer and that you're leading it at times is, to me, an expression of spiritual authority. For the record, I do none of that where I work—I have literally never even once preached in CST (Claremont School of Theology) chapel.

Juan: Angela, I think you provide this leadership with a distinctive and inviting humility. You know, at the beginning of your essay what caught me the most was that I hadn't even thought about giving my budget a title. It's just, it's called "Year so-and-so," and you're thinking of it in spiritual and biblical terms, what this means. I thought even if you are not very aware of your spiritual leadership, you certainly have a connection to the divine because that comes across just through your naming of those fiscal years. So there is certainly something there that people saw, and that "something" is also why they asked you to be the president! They had a certain trust that you would lead them into a good space. And you have.

10

¡Presentes! The Latinization of Theological Education

Joanne Solis-Walker

For many years I have found myself questioning the choices that my predecessors in Hispanic theological education made. Specifically, I questioned their decision to remain within primarily white institutions even when those institutions were not committed or loyal to them. Why did the Hispanic and Latine[1] communities on the United States mainland not launch even one seminary by and for the Latine community? Was there—is there—an advantage to this approach? After all, other ethnic groups have accredited seminaries that serve their respective communities. But Hispanics have none.

There are many reasons to pursue the establishment of a seminary created for Latines and by Latines. The census numbers speak for themselves.[2] The Latine church is new and young. It represents a rapidly growing church-planting movement[3] that extends life to withering Protestant and Catholic churches. Moreover, recent trends[4] reflect an increase in self-sufficient Hispanic church communities. In contrast to a few years ago, more Hispanic churches now opt to buy their own church facilities, many sharing those facilities with other Latine congregations, rather than negotiating for leasing and limited use of white church spaces.[5] The increasing independence of these faith communities helps explain the corresponding increased desire for accessible and culturally responsive theological education to support the growing number of self-sufficient Latine churches and congregations.

It is important to recognize the valuable presence of accredited seminaries in Puerto Rico and throughout Latin America. However, certain considerations often lead individuals to pursue education from institutions on the US mainland.[6] Likewise, while Hispanic Bible institutes (HBIs) have done life-changing work in forming leaders for the Latine church, they have not historically had the resources to offer the kind of education an ATS (Association of Theological Schools)–accredited and regionally accredited school can. Consequently, this growing and distinct community needs the support of a fully accredited theological institution, one tailored to the specific leadership needs of the diverse Latine community on the US mainland. However, it does not exist.

Or does it? Hispanic theological education entities do exist, only not in the traditional ways we are accustomed to experiencing theological education.

This essay considers how, while embedded in traditional ATS institutions, Hispanics developed a unique and independent theological education infrastructure designed to meet the needs of their communities. In general, those Hispanic-serving programs outside of ATS institutions have flourished thanks to their homegrown or *en casa* framework for theological education—an education that notably happens *en conjunto*, in community, in contrast to the more individualistic focus of most predominantly white institutions.

At its best, this Latine model of theological education therefore rejects the traditional Western models of formation, even as it overlaps with them. In this essay I hope to show how this model emphasizes the contributions of Hispanic-led organizations that have undergirded the Hispanic church, added value to Hispanic Bible institutes, and provided academic support and leadership development for students and scholars. This model has enabled Hispanics to celebrate their own thinkers and practitioners and their scholarly contributions on their own terms, without shoehorning them into another culture's entrenched model of education.

In response to recent funding opportunities, seminaries are developing what some of them regard as new theological programs for the Hispanic church. In certain ways such responses simply draw attention at last to the fact that Latine communities have long been *presentes*, successfully organizing their own forms of theological education. Those modes of theological education continue to thrive even without an accredited Latine seminary.

So, while for many constituencies the present chaotic state of theological education is concerning, this essay proudly shows how in fact Latine theological education is thriving—and thriving in many forms. There may be no traditional Latine seminary, but theological education is still happening—and it is happening on the Hispanic community's terms, valuing its particular traditions and respecting its distinctive wisdom.

¡Presentes, Presentes! Lessons Learned

I have spent most of my career within theological education building programs that are culturally responsive and accessible to, and attainable for, communities of color, particularly the Latine ecclesial communities. Launching these programs was my attempt to redress what I subconsciously considered to be a wrong: We did not have *our own* seminary.

Therefore, I set out to discover what immediate actions we could take to assert our presence in a continuously dismissive environment. This led to a deeper exploration of a larger, more complex issue surrounding our *presencia*, which continues to provoke conflicting responses and perpetuate a false narrative about the Latine community. As political scientist Abigail Golden-Vazquez appropriately observes: "Hispanics are not new to this country . . . [much of] Arizona, California, Colorado, Nevada, New Mexico, Utah, and Wyoming was handed over to the United States in the

Treaty of Guadalupe Hidalgo in 1848, making the Mexicans in those lands US citizens overnight. . . . The people living in those states did not cross the border—the border crossed them."[7]

The gap between this historical reality and the dominant political and social narratives fuels our ongoing struggle for *presencia*. Though this has been a persistent challenge within theological education, we must—and will—continue to expect more from a field that claims and seeks to deepen our understanding of God, the church, and culture.

This disconnect is why Latine pioneers in theological education confronted the significant challenge of invisibility. Despite their presence, they were often overlooked and, perhaps more troublingly, dismissed. This challenge persists today, but those of us who have inherited the lived experiences of Latine scholars continue to raise our voices. Persistence—a hallmark of our leadership—drives change. While progress may seem slow, we are nonetheless witnessing a meaningful shift in the landscape, amid the chaos.

THE CHANGING LANDSCAPE

On May 31, 2024, Latine religious scholars across the country watched as Iliff Theological Seminary in Denver awarded Rev. Joanne Rodriguez with an honorary doctorate. It marked a historic moment for Dr. Rodriguez, who for the past twenty-five years has led the Hispanic Theological Institute (HTI). It was also a momentous occasion for the broader Latine community. Many of us watching the event were overwhelmed with emotion: it was as if we ourselves were receiving the honor. And in many ways, we were. Yes, it was one scholar and leader, Joanne Rodriguez, receiving this well-deserved Doctor Honoris Causa degree. But she represented Latine scholars across theological education. Her recognition felt like our recognition, too.

In that moment, we listened to a leader who has passionately championed the educational rights of Latine scholars within theological education. Her efforts have contributed to the dismantling of systemic barriers within academic structures. She has cultivated inclusive environments and forged pathways of opportunity for Latine scholars, enabling them to excel in theological studies, honor their families and communities, and make significant contributions to their communities and the wider academic sphere.

For her, pursuing success as an administrator entailed forgoing the traditional path of completing a doctoral degree. While a degree was not required, the decision should not be misunderstood. This aligns with a work culture that demands more of its leaders of color. Despite not expecting to stay at HTI for so many years, she excelled in a system that, to its detriment, often neglects those in administrative roles. Her recognition by Iliff was both well earned and long overdue, and, as her community, we understood the importance of the moment.

Given our invisibility within theological education, these kinds of recognitions and accolades are not commonly directed toward Hispanic scholars. But in this hooding, we finally had a moment. One of our trailblazers in the *formación teológica* of our *gente* was being publicly acknowledged and validated. We *all* felt seen. We were—we are—*presente*.

ALTERNATIVE PATHWAYS: *GENTE DE LA LUCHA*

Hispanic theological educators have often remained invisible when serving predominantly white and Anglophone institutions because those institutions have failed to prioritize Hispanic educators' work with sufficient funding, respect, and recognition—such as an honorary doctorate. Yet, where else could we serve? There is no Latine seminary within the fifty states.[8] Could there be an advantage to staying within the very institutions that have suppressed our voices and visibility?

What might have seemed like a conflict and a limitation we, the Hispanic community, transformed into an opportunity: to embrace the spirit of Jeremiah's call to exiles to seek the welfare of the city in which they find themselves: "Build houses and live in them; plant gardens and eat what they produce. Take wives and have sons and daughters; take wives for your sons, and give your daughters in marriage, that they may bear sons and daughters; multiply there, and do not decrease. But seek the welfare of the city where I have sent you into exile, and pray to the Lord on its behalf, for in its welfare you will find your welfare" (Jer. 29:5–7 NRSV). On our own terms, we settled into the spaces of predominantly white institutions, building houses in various vibrant shades that reflect our diverse cultural communities. We planted gardens filled with native flowers from across Latin America, and we are now harvesting the fruits of those efforts. Our numbers are growing, not diminishing, as we actively seek the peace and prosperity of the seminaries, cities, and churches in which we find ourselves, praying that their flourishing will lead to our own. And we are entering with *ganas* those very same spaces that were once off-limits to our communities.

Despite the gap between housing a Hispanic program and inviting the Hispanics themselves to make the house a home, Hispanics have always appreciated the spaces white institutions have created. The larger (granted, predominantly white) arena of theological education has been a meeting place for scholars from different parts of Ibero-America. Latinx theologies were birthed through these *encuentros* in predominantly white spaces. These gatherings for critical theological reflection helped shape the cultural identities of our scholars.

There is no need to question whether such embeddedness led to significant losses. Consider the common scenario in which a seminary hires a single Hispanic leader charged with transforming the institution into a leading Hispanic-serving theological center. Despite this ambitious goal, the leader is often given minimal funding and administrative support to fulfill the mission the institution expects them to advance. This individual is then tasked with ensuring the institution's success, even though the seminary leadership lacks both the missional commitment and the knowledge to assist in the process—despite the institution's long dependence on the Hispanic community for its financial sustainability.

However, good intentions are not good enough.[9] There are no shortcuts. Effectively serving Latine communities requires significant investments of time, financial resources, relational capital, and clear missional direction. The absence of these elements results in stress, frustration, and unmet expectations, which negatively affect not only the Latine administrator but also the churches and communities the program aims to serve, as well as the seminary's leadership, faculty, staff, and students.

It is no secret: White institutions were not designed for Latines. While they often desired Hispanic students—especially in recent years, as they scrambled to meet enrollment and tuition-revenue goals—they have tended to lack the ability to recruit and retain Hispanic students, staff, faculty, and administrators. Many were overlooked for promotions because of their *Latinidad*. Others were denied tenure. Some peers treated their Latine counterparts with disregard while trying to discredit them. And though it happens discreetly, Hispanic programs were—and too often still are—the first to lose funding when there are budget cuts.

An uninformed and narrow view might suggest that our embeddedness was a poor decision. It certainly was a high price to pay, but ironically, it also created opportunities. Our community has been marginalized, overpowered, silenced, and rendered invisible, but as *gente de la lucha* we remain resilient, addressing and redressing the wrongs.

The recognition of Rev. Dr. Joanne Rodriguez's leadership is an acknowledgment of our *presencia* within theological education. While very significant, it also materializes one of the concrete ways we are advancing the broader field of theological education through the process of Latinization. We've done this without a seminary.

President Javier Viera[10] of Garrett Evangelical Seminary named this dynamic in a tribute to the leadership of Rev. Dr. Elizabeth Conde-Frazier. Viera remarked that Conde-Frazier never did gravitate toward the center; instead, "she brought the center to the margins," creating a space where others could feel welcomed and free from the pressures of being at the center.

So, while yet being deeply embedded within primarily white institutions, Latinx administrators and scholars like Conde-Frazier and Rodriguez learned to navigate those spaces. In unexpected ways, these *nuevos caminos* have made the embeddedness advantageous for Latine communities, shielding them from the pressure to conform to the traditional model of education, the one long designed and preserved for white male students that excluded women and people of color. The embeddedness forced the Hispanic communities to forge an "in-house" or "*en-casa*" path uniquely tailored to serve their own communities, and this has been liberating. This homegrown approach to theological education promotes doing theology *latinamente y en conjunto*[11]—two enormous advantages and strengths that merit more attention than this space allows.

NO LATINE SEMINARY? THE *EN-CASA* FRAMEWORK FOR THEOLOGICAL EDUCATION

Instead of creating a traditional seminary, Latine communities developed a framework of theological institutions tailored to their unique needs. In response to the evolving demands of Hispanic communities, Latine scholars in leadership roles established key organizations to serve their students and faculty. Despite starting small, they shared a vision for theological education that effectively addressed their communities. As a result, the Hispanic community quickly established its own contextual seminary through three key organizations: the Hispanic Summer Program (HSP) in 1989,[12] the Asociación para la Educación Teológica Hispana (AETH) in 1992, and the Hispanic Theological Initiative (HTI) in 1996. These independent organizations have trained hundreds of Latine scholars and practitioners who now serve the church, their communities, and the academy, forming our *en-casa* framework.

Research by Kenneth Davis and Edwin I. Hernandez reminds us of the vision of Latine scholars from decades past, when HSP, AETH, and HTI emerged in the theological sphere. Davis and Hernandez's book, *Reconstructing the Sacred Tower*, is not merely a historical account: it offers an understanding of the needs these scholars identified at the time, and of their efforts to invite ATS, denominations, seminaries, and theological schools to respond to the "challenge and promise of Latino/a theological education."[13] The book argues that the Hispanic church is a pivotal institution within the *barrio*. Given this significant role, the research underscores the urgent need for theological training of Hispanic pastors. To achieve this effectively, theological institutions must be willing to rethink their approach to equipping Hispanic leaders.

The book's recommendations were intended for the aforementioned entities, and it is possible that it did indeed empower some seminaries to serve the Latine community more competently. However, it also propelled HSP, AETH, and HTI into new levels of service, functioning independently from any of those theological institutions, denominations, and accrediting bodies. The fruit of this labor is visible in the number of Latine tenured faculty, professors, and administrators today and, perhaps most importantly, in the shaping of many students from Hispanic backgrounds doing *teología en conjunto* and *latinamente*.

Our *en-casa* framework resists and confronts implicit and explicit biases at the macro and micro levels. It has liberated us to reimagine theological education so we can view it through the lenses of the Latine communities. Hispanic leaders were empowered by the absence of opportunities within the white institutions in which they served, and this absence, marked by the open wounds and the scars of unfair and unjust systems, prompted us to engage in creative and strategic solutions to the problems. Without minimizing the efforts of many more leaders or oversimplifying the process, which involved an abundance of hard work, resilience, and dedication, the Latinization of theological education was significantly influenced by these three organizations, which fundamentally and structurally changed the landscape of theological education.

The Latinization of Theological Education

When I became associate dean at Candler School of Theology, leaders in the Hispanic theological movement urged me to lead from the margins and prioritize our community's needs. They cautioned against compromising my cultural values for a central position. This collective, community-focused approach is central to the Latinization of theological education, embodying the *en conjunto* and *en-casa* frameworks. The Latine way of theological education is *en conjunto*. Even when there is only one Hispanic in an institution, these frameworks enable connection, reflection, and collaboration, strengthening our *presencia* in theological education.

Without question, one of the greatest contributions to the Latinization of theological education is our emphasis on *teología en conjunto*. Drawing from the writings of Justo González, editors José David Rodriguez and Loida I. Martell-Otero laid the foundation in their compilation of chapters for *Teologia en Conjunto: A Collaborative Hispanic Protestant Theology*. "We use the term *teología en conjunto* to emphasize two fundamental aspects affecting Hispanic theology: its rich diversity and its integral collaborative spirit."[14] It is "a theology constructed in a shared way with a commitment to unity and communion."[15]

Teología en conjunto is about communities reflecting together theologically. The *en-casa* framework models this "togetherness" through a network that supports students and church leaders across institutions and communities, regardless of geographical location.

The phrase was more fully embraced in 1995 when "a group of Latina and Latino theologians, ethicists, sociologists of religion, pastors, teachers, and students gathered on the grounds of Princeton Theological Seminary to discuss the distinctiveness of our (Hispanic) theology in a collaborative way."[16] However, the term itself is characteristic of the community within and beyond theological education. It is also a common thread that weaves in and out of each one of the three organizations credited for major contributions to the Latinization of theological education.

The HTI Latinizes Theological Education

Since the aforementioned meeting at Princeton, HTI has continued to breathe life into this unique approach of *teología en conjunto*, and by doing so it has Latinized theological education. In addition to the value that it has added to students and to the Latine church, the HTI has developed standards that hold theological institutions accountable for their engagement with HTI fellows. The HTI ensures that doctoral advisors are not ignoring HTI students or giving them scant attention. In a real sense, they tell member schools, "*¡Ojo!* We're watching you!" and call them to look out for their HTI fellows. This shift is significant, as it moves Hispanic theological education from merely being embedded within white institutions to being visibly *presentes* and occupying its rightful and respected place within the ecology of theological education.

As a result, the HTI has supported 48 master's and 175 doctoral students. According to the 2024 HTI annual report,[17] most graduate schools have a 31 percent retention rate and their students take 9.3 years on average for doctoral completion. However, 92 percent of HTI students have earned their degrees in 5.5 years. Among them, 40 percent hold tenured positions, 23 percent are on the tenure track, and many serve in high-level administrative roles, including eleven deans and six current college presidents.

Theological education has changed as a result of HTI and will continue to evolve as HTI trains future generations of scholars and produces resources for the academy and the church.[18] The future includes appointing Latine women in senior leadership positions. Latinas in Leadership is a more recent training opportunity. It offers significant support to *mujeres* aspiring to become presidents or deans at seminaries, especially as they struggle to break the glass ceiling of the ivory tower.

Nonetheless, the number of Hispanic women presidents and deans serving at ATS member schools will, I expect, continue to increase, thanks to the contributions of HTI and the other two institutions of the *en-casa* framework. The truth is that this type of leadership already exists within our *en-casa* framework. At the helm of leadership for HSP, AETH, and HTI are Latina women who are not credited sufficiently for how they nurtured the vision and defined its purposes, growing each institution in itself and connecting the institutions in a network that serves the diverse Latine communities on their own terms, while also Latinizing theological education. In the leaders of these three organizations we already see strong Hispanic women leading at the level of deans and presidents.

The AETH Latinizes Theological Education

While not the firstborn organization of the three, AETH has paved the way in creating *presencia* for the Latine church within theological education by serving the Hispanic church and strengthening Hispanic Bible institutes (HBIs). The institutes have long been the primary space for formal theological education for *pastores y pastoras*, despite often being dismissed as not being credible. Yet, they represent the closest model to a Latine seminary and have produced some of the most gifted pastors and leaders in the Latine church, transforming the formation of laity. Many Latine scholars, including myself, began our theological education in HBIs. While HSP and HTI focused on Latine students and faculty, AETH positioned itself as a key resource for the Latino church.

The AETH's impact on the Latinization of theological education is also evident through its partnerships within the academy. Many institutions that have received Lilly Endowment funding for Hispanic programs have included AETH in their proposals—an unsurprising fact given that many Latine leaders from these schools were shaped by the *en-casa* framework and supported by AETH, HSP, HTI, or leaders influenced by them. These partnerships reflect our Latine approach to *teología en conjunto*.

The collaborative efforts also bring greater visibility to programs that, though *presentes* for many years, have gone largely unnoticed. Many of these programs have accomplished their work on a shoestring budget. Partnering with AETH enlarges the footprint and visibility of these institutions within the Latine community, which makes education more accessible. However, it still entails a risk. Primarily white institutions funded to do this work for the first time will be tempted to disguise the oppression and marginalization of our communities by projecting a false interest in the advancement of our *gente* when their real motive is their organizational success. The Latine community must proceed anyway, but we must do so with caution and a deep awareness of "the atrocities committed against our native ancestors . . . entire populations were wiped out, ancient civilizations destroyed, and million upon millions sacrificed on the altars of the invaders' thirst for gold, land, and glory."[19] While we must continue to take risks, the stakes are higher for white institutions. True, we in the Latine community have a stronger line of defense because of our *en-casa* ecology, but there is nonetheless much work we must continue doing. Fortunately, AETH stands on the front lines, stewarding the relationship of the academy with the church while educating and empowering our Latine church of the *barrios*.

One of the ways in which AETH has strengthened the Hispanic church while Latinizing theological education is by bringing visibility and credibility to Hispanic Bible institutes. This enterprise is built on the seminal work of Elizabeth Conde-Frazier, whose research focuses on the training of Hispanic pastors through *Institutos Biblicos*.[20] In a later work for the Theological Education between the Times series, *Atando Cabos: Latinx Contributions to Theological Education*, Conde-Frazier describes AETH as "a network of Bible Institutes, seminaries, and other theological entities"[21] seeking to resource the Hispanic church.

There is no such thing as a single or stand-alone Bible institute. Instead, there is an extensive network of Bible institutes, and AETH has been instrumental in shedding light on this hidden gem that forms such an important part of our *en-casa* framework for and network of theological education. Initially,

ATS-accredited seminaries and others refused to acknowledge the contributions and validity of HBIs. But eventually ATS heeded the call of Davis and Hernandez to reimagine the formation of the pastors of the *barrio*. Hispanic Bible institutes are not new. They have been *presentes* all along, even if not on the radar of certain (white) decision makers and leadership organizations.

In 2013, ATS and AETH entered into a partnership and created a pathway for AETH to offer a certification of Hispanic Bible institutes that allows certified institutes to go through a formal process similar to that of accreditation.[22] The AETH has been able to certify Hispanic Bible institutes from the Pentecostal, Lutheran, Evangelical Covenant, Disciples of Christ, Presbyterian, and Catholic traditions, among others. This has uniquely positioned it not only to serve the Hispanic churches of *el barrio* but to have a major, ongoing impact upon theological institutions, including ATS schools and ATS itself. After completing the requirements at *el instituto*, some students enroll in graduate degree programs at institutions accredited by ATS. It has also had a profound impact upon the value attributed to similar spaces, like the Catholic diocesan training opportunities for Hispanics that have been overlooked within the ecosystems of theological education. Some organizations like the Mexican American Catholic College (MACC) have been paving the way since 1972, choosing to fulfill their mission without conforming to the traditional modes of theological education.

The AETH is also the overarching support system of the Justo and Catherine González Resource Center, which houses the plethora of resources in Spanish and English written by Justo González. Some of these are academic resources, and others are Bible studies that help to bridge the gap between the church and the academy.

As a result of a partnership with Candler School of Theology, AETH has also launched a new initiative, Antioquia, that offers church and HBI leaders a place to engage in research and reflect together on their teaching. Together AETH and Candler have also launched La Biblioteca Digital Pitts, an online library space that makes a collection of English- and Spanish-language resources available to HBI students and faculty. While these initiatives are in their early days, they are already making an impact.

The HSP Latinizes Theological Education

Those serving at AETH during its initial years and within different seminaries could be considered the *orgullo*, the pride and joy, of HSP. At that point, AETH symbolized the growth and advancement of the community. It was the fruit of the labor of many, including HSP, an organization founded with the vision to Latinize theological education.

The HSP was a strategic response to the needs of the Latine theological community. It was the first of the three homegrown institutions to be established, and it made a way when there was no way. The vision for HSP was to exist as an external organization, and it continues to do so today. It was connected to theological education, but in a nontraditional way. Though hosted and housed each summer by a different school of theology, most of its funding sources were external, and this was important if it was to respond to the real needs that were surfacing as Latine students were enrolling in theological education programs. It responded to research led by Justo González, which reported that Latine students "needed an educational context that took seriously . . . the challenges and questions that derive from their context of ministry and religious experiences."[23]

While seminaries were not able to offer contextualized education to their Latine students, they still wanted to recruit and enroll them in their programs. Despite the challenges Latine scholars were facing in white institutions, the white schools of theology were responsive to the invitation extended by HSP to become sponsoring schools. Given the "absence of a full-fledged Hispanic seminary or Hispanic program of ministerial education and training, it was decided to have a two-week summer program whose character would be such that it would serve as a Latino seminary for that short period of time."[24] Though this was definitely not the traditional route for a seminary, and though it was a different path than the one taken by other ethnic groups, it has nonetheless served and continues to serve its purpose of enabling students to "do theology *latinamente*."[25] Students not only acquire the skills necessary to engage in theology from a Latinx perspective, but these practices are deeply integrated within the culture of their community. Upon returning to their institutions, students are equipped with both the knowledge and confidence to apply these insights effectively and *latinamente*.

Much has happened since the establishment of HSP in 1989. The organization was launched with the primary task of supporting Latine students and faculty from different seminaries. It offered intensive summer courses in theology and related disciplines to address the underrepresentation of Hispanics in theological education and ministry leadership. It immediately became a place to build community among the diverse Latine and Latine-at-heart. The relationships built transcended the two weeks of in-person contact. However, that was just the beginning.

During its thirty-fifth anniversary celebration in 2024, HSP announced its new name: the Hispanic Scholars Program. It will continue to offer two-week intensives to graduate degree students as part of its summer program, but it has expanded to include Hispanic students enrolled in undergraduate degree programs. However, the new name points to the growth that it has experienced during the past thirty-five years and the many ways it continues to be *presente*.[26]

Through Hispanic Eyes (THE) is a pedagogical training course that HSP offers to non-Hispanic faculty and administrators. It "seeks to tangibly change theological education through developing cohorts of individuals committed to pursuing practical projects at their home institutions that are in service of Latinx communities."[27] All THE participants are guided through complex discussions on cultural competency, with the aim of equipping them to design projects that improve conditions for Latinx students and colleagues within their institutions. This initiative represents one of the most significant ways in which HSP has contributed to the Latinization of theological education.

The HSP's partnership with the Lake Institute on Faith and Giving addresses a critical challenge for Hispanic leaders: fund-raising. Securing financial resources is essential for the sustainability of Hispanic-serving programs, which have traditionally relied on grants, creating a dependency that threatens their longevity. Budget cuts often target these programs first. By offering training in fund-raising, HSP highlights and enhances the competence of Latine leaders, who have historically been overlooked for senior positions due to a lack of experience in this area.

At the helm of leadership of HSP is the Reverend Dr. Daisy Machado, whose history significantly weaves in and out of two of the three organizations. Dr. Machado also served as the first HTI director, originally housed at Candler School of Theology, Emory University. The Latinization of theological education is part of her legacy.

The En-Casa *Framework*

We do not call any of them a seminary, but HSP, AETH, and HTI each has its own version of micro seminaries embedded within its organization. The AETH has Hispanic Bible institutes, which provide theological education for Hispanic pastors who do not require a graduate degree for ordination. The HSP has the Hispanic summer program, which trains Latine graduate degree and undergraduate students theologically during the annual two-week intensives. The HTI has its Latinx cohort of primarily PhD students and students pursuing a master's degree.

Each of these three institutions creates educational materials and resources that serve the broader theological education ecology. The AETH publishes book series written from a Hispanic perspective, and it also manages the Justo and Catherine González Resource Center. The HTI contributes through its platforms, including the *Perspectivas* journal, Open Plaza, and the Dissertation Project. Likewise, the HSP has launched La Colectiva Teológica Latina (LCTL), which enables Latina ministers and scholars to produce educational content for seminaries, adding to the collective body of resources in the field.

The Latinization of theological education owes much to the contributions of these organizations, which have been central to the development of Latine scholarship and leadership. Theological education more broadly has much to learn about the Latine *comunidad* and the collectivist approach to formation *en conjunto*. While we Latines remain grateful for the funding sources and the opportunity to launch programs, in many ways we are not discovering something new. We've been investing in ourselves for a long time. The funding sources did not make us. Long-delayed recognition from the ATS did not create us. We were *presentes* long before these developments, and through it all God has led us in creating educational pathways for our *gente*.

¡PRESENTES!

In 2023, CaminoRoad, A Development Company, an organization that I help lead, presented the research findings of an appreciative inquiry project commissioned by the ATS that mapped the landscape of Hispanic and Latinx theological education.[28] One outcome of the research was to name needs that, if addressed, could advance the theological formation of Hispanic/Latinx ecclesial leaders. The research also called for making the presence of Hispanic theological education more publicly known by articulating accomplishments that have contributed to the Latinization of theological education—in short, making the invisible visibly *presente*.

¡Presentes! names the ways in which we, as a Latine people, have shown up to the theological education scene over the years. *¡Presentes!* means we are not new to theological education but have instead been shaping and confronting theological education for years from within. *¡Presentes!* includes a leadership development component that has allowed us to grow and form our own Latine scholars.

Recent funding from the Lilly Endowment Pathways for Tomorrow Initiative provides theological schools with the opportunity to enhance their programs in response to the evolving challenges of ecclesial leadership. Several grant recipients have proposed initiatives focused on creating new programs and diverse learning opportunities for Hispanic communities. For example, Candler School of Theology at Emory University launched La Mesa Academy for Theological Studies, and Northwest Nazarene University's School of Theology introduced the first ThD program in Spanish. These initiatives are already transforming Latinx theological education.

The CaminoRoad study particularly emphasizes the significance of fostering emotional, physical, and holistic well-being. This happens in many ways. El Día de la Raza, celebrated internationally in October, honors the diverse cultures within the Hispanic and Latinx communities. At our event at Candler School of Theology, the atrium becomes a vibrant plaza filled with traditional food, *artesanía*, and students in cultural attire. The atmosphere transforms as Latine students take over the space, singing and dancing to salsa, merengue, and reggaeton, with deans, faculty, staff, and students joining in. This moment marked a significant cultural shift, showing that these first-year students felt safe, welcomed, and like they truly belonged. They were *presentes* and their *presencia* has continued to Latinize the Candler community.

CONCLUSION

In *The End of Theological Education*, Ted Smith describes the need for "theological education in this time between the times."[29] The Latinization of theological education is a prime example of what has been happening "in this time between the times." Something is taking place that others, including some within our own Latine community, have not seen—but it is happening, and happening in "*el presente*" (in the here and now), and we are invited to be *¡pre-*

sentes! "Look at the new thing I am going to do. It is already happening. Don't you see it?" (Isa. 43:19a New Century Version).

The Latine communities within theological education did not choose the route of founding their own schools. Instead, they started programs like AETH, HSP, and HTI, among many others, to work within predominantly white structures. This decision has perhaps made these efforts less visible. Nonetheless, Latine communities have been present all along. And because they were and continue to be *presente* in the predominantly white system, they have helped to transform—to Latinize—theological education. Those involved in theological education should pay close attention and seek to learn, not only from the Latine communities but also from other cultural groups invisible within this ecology who are likewise transforming theological education.

Why has the Hispanic and Latine community in the United States mainland not launched even one seminary by and for the Latine community? Simply put: it did, but in its own way. The community has not established and may never establish a fully accredited seminary on the US mainland that is designed specifically for and by us. However, we did something greater. We have fostered a scholarly community and influenced predominantly white institutions and theological education through our unique approach. Reminiscent of the exilic experience described in Jeremiah, we may not officially control the space, but we created networks of institutions that transform many spaces and disrupt the empire.

The Latine model of theological education does not follow the traditional norms and forms of a seminary, but it exists and is thriving, thanks to its homegrown, *en-casa*, *en-conjunto* model that will continue to Latinize theological education.

Dialogue

Joanne Solis-Walker, Juan J. Molina Flores, Matthew Wesley Williams

Juan: Thanks for writing the essay and staying true to the theme you selected from the beginning. I appreciated the diplomatic way you addressed the topics of *presencia* and Latinization. Your constructive approach led to a time of personal reflection. It's clear that writing has been a spiritual journey for you, not just a theological exercise.

I also value the significance of you tracing your formation to a Hispanic Bible institute; it gave you a voice in the conversation and made you a part of the movement.

Joanne: Though not intentionally, this became a chance to position myself within Latine theological education, as a Latine student, minister, scholar, and administrator. The outcome was unexpected and increased my appreciation of our communities.

Juan: I particularly appreciated how you included Rev. Dr. Joanne Rodriguez of HTI in your narrative. Using her as an example was fitting, as many Latines share similar experiences. Her accomplishments resonated deeply, reflecting the struggles we've faced as Latine scholars over the years. Your focus on celebrating her achievements highlighted the collective experience of the Latine community.

Another key contribution was your portrayal of the challenge Latines face in establishing a theological seminary. The idea of having a seminary is often seen as a prized jewel, but this isn't necessarily the case. As someone who has questioned this perspective, I appreciate how your narrative addresses this issue, and it reflects MACC's long-standing inquiry into whether a seminary is truly the "prized jewel."

Matthew: Are these schools really the prize? I've come to regard the COVID-19 pandemic as an apocalypse, an unveiling, especially in theological education. The long arc of destabilization of traditional forms of theological education that escalated during that time indicates to me that this form is dying, if not dead. So, Juan's question becomes really important: Is this the prize? We've been sitting on acres of diamonds, while longing to be included in a form of theological education that has long been in decline.

Joanne: In full transparency, early on, I was one of those people who viewed "having" a Latine seminary as a prized jewel—only to realize that this perspective was limited in understanding our broader role within theological education. Because we are sitting on acres of diamonds, the embeddedness has been *puro fuego*, refining fire.

Matthew: Your essay is a subtle confession in recognizing that at one point, you were asking, "Why don't we have what they have?" But then comes the awareness that the Latine communities have been doing theological education in a different form for a very long time.

Juan: Your very cohesive narrative also communicates an important message about the margins and the center. Since they didn't want us (I am speaking in a corporate sense for Latines here) at the center or would not accommodate us, we created alternative opportunities that have been life-giving to us and our communities.

Matthew: What Javier Viera said about Elizabeth Conde-Frazier ["She brought the center to the margins,"] was right on point because the academic institution thinks of itself as the center of the universe. It reminds me of the novelist Toni Morrison, who says about her writing of *Beloved*: "I went to the margins, claimed it as the center, and waited for the rest of y'all to catch up with me."

Elizabeth has always held her own center. She went to Esperanza and was very clear: "I'm still doing theological education. I'm just not doing it in the forms that y'all recognize. The forms you recognize are illegitimate for my people and my context."

Juan: It is not easy to be alone on the margins, doing theology in a different way. Sometimes it seems as if people do not look at you with high regard, as if they don't value you, even though we've been doing this work for a long time and it has had an impact. But it is important to claim a space even there, in the margins.

As you discussed the three organizations, which in many ways represent the Hispanic seminary model, I kept thinking about MACC. In the San Antonio area and within the Catholic tradition, MACC represented an alternative path. It could have been integrated with another religious entity, but it chose a different path in 1972. This date is significant because it highlights how organizations like MACC were already considering their place and identity, asking: Where do we belong?

We Hispanics have long sought to create spaces we can call home. While some found their place within mainstream organizations, others realized that mainstream institutions were not suitable and chose to forge new paths. I appreciated not only the narrative you provided but also the historical context, including the founding dates of the three organizations, which clarified how we, including MACC, have collectively contributed to shaping our own kind of seminary.

Joanne: I'm curious about how many other organizations, like MACC, have significantly contributed to the Latinization of theological education. Although I couldn't explore this fully, it would be valuable to map these institutions on a historical timeline to understand their roles and longevity. There isn't a central database tracking this work, and ATS doesn't account for programs in Spanish or those serving the Latine community. We lack a clear picture of who has been present and for how long. I hope this essay sparks interest in uncovering this history.

Matthew: When you talked about visibility, I wondered: Visible to whom? What struck me as I kept reading was that it's visible in itself. Latine theological education is proven, not experimental—it's older than some historic seminaries. There's an entire ecosystem here, and bringing that to visibility gives the body more access to itself. That's a beautiful thing—an inflection point in the ecosystem's awareness and its capacity to build on what it's already done.

Juan: Things are different. We are looking at theological education as in between the times. We are pointing to a culture within theological education that has sometimes been limiting. My impression is that ATS's focus is on accredited institutions and institutions that exist for a specific purpose: get people ordained or make them professors. Now that theological education is being seen differently, it is time for things to be done differently. That's why the awareness your essay brings of what else has been there that we haven't been able to see is important. It puts us on the map.

Matthew: This point Father Juan makes—about not being on the map—is entirely valid. This question of cartography, of how we draw the world, is key. We've been drawing our world through the lenses of somebody else's imagination. Operating on somebody else's maps has us thinking of ourselves in a deficit model.

This essay addresses those concerns but from an asset-based mind-set. Instead of highlighting what is not, it makes others aware of a system that's already been in place, but not understood by conventional theological education and perhaps without the Latine community being fully self-aware of the brilliant models they have created.

Joanne: In many ways, our communities have been rendered invisible. This is why I write—to enhance the visibility of our efforts and the individuals we support. It is essential that we be recognized for the contributions we are making to theological education, but it is equally important for our Latine community to be proud of the many ways we have been and continue to be *presentes*.

Juan: You discuss three well-known organizations in our field, and I thank you for that. But we should also ask the social justice question: Who else is missing from the table? We need to identify not only other Latina organizations but other ethnic and cultural groups within theological education that remain invisible. As proponents of multiculturalism, we must recognize the value of others.

Matthew: Father Juan's comment about those missing from the table offers the opportunity to thank you for the ways you celebrated the transformational leadership of Elizabeth Conde-Frazier, Joanne Rodriguez, and Daisy Machado. This deserves its own attention, and it is long overdue.

Joanne: It felt important to highlight the crucial role of women leaders in this movement. Theological education has changed, not just for Latinos, but much more broadly, thanks to their leadership. Just as the impact of these organizations on the Latinization of theological education is often underestimated, we can no longer overlook the vital role of these women leaders. It's important for everyone in theological education, including the women leading these organizations, to recognize them and other notable women like Dr. Loida Martell, Dr. Doris Garcia, and Dr. Elsie

Miranda, who have been "the first Latinas" serving in executive leadership roles.

Matthew: One last comment. When you go down the line of how many folks HTI has supported, and the retention and completion rates compared to others, it echoes a question Martin Luther King asked Harry Belafonte: "I wonder if we are integrating our people into a burning house?" Communities like HTI, HSP, and AETH have been crucial in preventing folks from getting lost in the sauce. The shedding of old maps is a kind of detoxification that can only be sustained in community, and this essay gives the community more voice around that question. It brings the whole ecosystem into another level of historical subjectivity. Thank you, Joanne.

11

The Vocation of the Black (Theological) School

Matthew Wesley Williams

In a 1974 essay entitled "The Vocation of the Black Scholar and the Struggles of the Black Community," the late historian and activist Vincent G. Harding challenged Black scholars to reframe their scholarly vocation not as a commitment to the academy for its own sake but as a calling to provide the intellectual underpinnings for the cause of Black liberation in the United States, in the African diaspora, and on the African continent. Harding wrote: "For it is finally that community-in-struggle which *calls*. It is that community through which vocation, purpose, direction, and life itself are most fully known and lived. . . . For it is only within the context of the long fight for freedom of the black community that we are ultimately moved towards a true sense of ourselves." Harding went on to say: "For the life and work of the black scholar in search of vocation, the primary context is not to be found in the questionable freedom and relative affluence of the American university. Our essential social, political, and spiritual context is the colonized situation of the masses of the black community in America."[1]

Four years earlier, in his essay "Toward the Black University," Harding similarly called upon Black educational institutions to provide "an education shaped by our necessities, authenticated by our life, filled with our uniqueness and devoted to our freedom."[2] Harding penned these epistles to Black institutions and intelligentsia roughly a century after the genesis of historically Black colleges, universities, and seminaries. Since their inception, historically Black colleges, universities, and seminaries have made bricks without straw, educating generations despite chronic underfunding and relative institutional fragility. Against all odds, these cherished institutions consistently "punch above their weight," delivering educational pathways and economic outcomes that rival, and in some cases outpace, many of their well-resourced historically white peer institutions.[3] Yet, Harding's use of "Toward" in the title implies that, after more than a century, he believed that Black scholars and schools had not yet met the high calling of education for Black liberation.

This essay responds to Harding's call once again to bind the vocation of the Black scholar to the struggles of the Black community. Echoing his imagining of "the Black university," it asks of Black (theological) schools what Harding asked of Black scholars, namely: How might we reimagine the vocation of the Black (theological) school in light of the present and emerging struggles that face African-descended people in the United States and abroad?

Central to this discussion is the relationship between institutional vocation and design. Specifically: How does the design of our institutions—beyond curriculum, pedagogy, and programming—affect their ability to advance Black liberation? In the spirit of design thinking, I resist the urge to prescribe an institutional model that answers these questions. Instead, I pose important questions with a few bread crumbs from history and personal experience that may inform experimental efforts to redesign legacy systems and craft new approaches to this work.

I put the term "theological" in parentheses to signal an analysis of Black theological education within the broader context of Black higher education in the United States. Understood in this historical and sociopolitical context, we can better appreciate the long-standing aspirations, questions, and contradictions that have fueled the formation of Black theological education within and beyond Black theological institutions.

I come to this inquiry after four years of leading a historically Black theological school whose mission explicitly identifies the school as an Africentric[4] Christian institution that cultivates leaders who practice liberation, peace, and justice. This mission has been revised over time, an indicator of an evolution in the institution's identity and intellectual contributions over the previous sixty-plus years. My tenure as president of my graduate alma mater provided me a unique opportunity to view simultaneously, from the inside out, the state of a single historically Black theological school, the broader ecosystem of Black theological education, and (as a member president in the United Negro College Fund network)[5] the larger landscape of Black higher education.

This essay aims to map our current position within the long history of Black education. Where are we? What time is it? How might we assess the vitality of our educational tradition that understands education as a means to freedom? How might we begin to recalibrate the alignment between what we say we are about and what we are doing?

I am interested in what the design of Black educational institutions reveals about their vocations, either in the interests of Black liberation or some other aim. Not: What do we say we do? Nor: What do we intend or desire to do? But: What are our institutions designed to do? This is a question of institutional design that ultimately determines our institutional vocation-in-action.

THE SAME ENTERPRISE?

Early in my tenure as president of the Interdenominational Theological Center (ITC), we hosted on campus a meeting of diverse leaders in theological education, organized by two beloved colleagues. This meeting was part of a funded project that sought to envision the future of theological education amid destabilizing shifts in the field. One morning during the consultation, I listened intently to a conversation about the future of faculty in theological education. These conversations about the future of the field have long been focused on the "2040 question," shorthand for racial and ethnic demographic shifts in theological education that are expected to make white students a numerical minority by that year.[6] For over twenty years, the ecosystem of predominantly white institutions has been chasing its tail, wondering what to do about the insurgency of Black and brown bodies in their schools and pews. This meeting reflected that ongoing struggle, with discussions spiraling into familiar patterns of hand-wringing and indignation.

> "*I'm so tired!*" expressed the pain and disappointment of faculty of color who experience incessant microaggressions and overt racism in predominantly white schools that profess to value diversity.
>
> "*What about us?*" expressed the need to change curricula to reflect the bodies of knowledge that speak to the diverse contexts from which an increasing number of theological students come.
>
> "*I didn't know!*" expressed the utter shock and confession of ignorance from well-meaning white colleagues who were oblivious to the trauma they actively inflicted or passively allowed.
>
> "*We've done fairly well*" expressed the self-congratulatory observation of a predominantly white school that has outdistanced others in terms of representational diversity among its students or faculty, or both.

The more I listened, the more frustrated I became. My frustration was twofold. The first frustration I then voiced in the room. I said, "With due respect to my colleagues in the room, I find this to be an incredibly frustrating conversation. I've spent the last fifteen-plus years in these field-wide conversations in which we have been asking the same questions about diversity and inclusion, reiterating the same sentiments, and repeating the same mistakes. It seems that we aren't learning anything. I would expect that at the least our questions would be a bit more nuanced, that they would have evolved to some degree."

Beneath the drive toward representational diversity, which governs most diversity, equity, and inclusion (DEI) conversations and efforts, persistent assumptions linger about the nature and purpose of education. Our understanding of the nature and purpose of theological education is grounded in too-often-unexamined cultural norms and unspoken sociopolitical commitments. Very few of our conversations descend to such depths. These conversations tend to stay at the surface level of diverse representation, focused on which predominantly white institutions *appear* to be racially diverse and on the right side of racism. Rarely do we give attention to whether they have actually cultivated the institutional conditions in which students and scholars of color can thrive.

Postcolonial theologian W. Anne Joh named this dynamic clearly, noting that "well-meaning institutions tell students from communities of color that they are inclusive and have a commitment to diversity, but they neither cultivate institutional will for justice-oriented diversity nor forge new institutional habits. As a result, students and faculty of color are often left to work as individuals within institutions whose wills and habits are in opposition to, or in direct conflict with, the lived worlds of these scholars." Joh goes on to name the human cost of this negligence, arguing that "being 'included' or folded into such unchanged institutions is to experience violence at close range."[7] The echo of Joh's searing insight resounded in that room. We scholars and students of color know this violence intimately, in our own bodies.

The second source of my frustration was a question that I did not raise in that room, in part because it was still only an embryonic inkling at the moment. I needed more time to let the gut feeling form into a clear question. The words eventually formed to match that gut instinct: "*Are we even in the same educational enterprise?*" The questions of diversity, equity, and inclusion that dominated this conversation are typically framed to assess Black and brown folks' proximity to and participation (inclusion) in historically white institutional spaces. But I was leading a historically Black institution whose mission and vision were explicit about its commitment to Black liberation within the global context of African diaspora.

We use the same language to describe our institutions and see ourselves as colleagues within the same field. Yet, I cannot help but wonder if we are up to completely different educational endeavors. Liberation is an altogether different institutional impulse than inclusion.

Black (Theological) Education in Historical Context

Vocational discernment, whether individual or institutional, requires a reckoning with our roots. Critical reflection on ancestry, heritage, history, and bloodline charisms helps us to identify the core intentions that define our being and drive our work. Our consideration of the vocation of Black (theological) education must take seriously the origin story of this distinctive educational enterprise. To neglect this puts us in danger of misunderstanding the work of this distinct tradition as a mere photo negative of its historically white counterparts.

Currently, the Association of Theological Schools (ATS) accredits six historically Black theological schools: Payne Theological Seminary, Hood Theological Seminary, Shaw University Divinity School, Howard University School of Divinity, the Samuel DeWitt Proctor School of Theology at Virginia Union University, and ITC. Increasingly, historically white theological schools boast of student bodies predominantly composed of people of color. In some cases, these schools also claim a critical mass of Black and brown faculty. These demographic shifts among students and, to a significantly lesser degree, among scholars at white schools have stirred conversations about the continuing relevance of historically Black schools. Such questions assume that the principal purpose of Black theological schools, and Historically Black Colleges and Universities (HBCUs) broadly, was and is to respond to racial exclusion due to segregation in higher education. However, the mission and vision of these schools articulate proactive possibilities for flourishing, rather than mere reactive responses to discrimination. With one exception, the schools explicitly name liberation, justice, and freedom as core institutional aims. The roots of this shared focus run deep.

The origins of Black theological education in the United States lie not in the halls of the American academy nor in the sanctuaries of the mainline Protestant church, but in the clandestine spaces where Black literacy was a revolutionary and criminalized enterprise. Black theological education in the United States began as an extra-institutional endeavor. Using the tools of the New World in tandem with ancient African religious and theological traditions, enslaved and "unslaved" Africans conjured new religious cultures in the "invisible institution."[8] Enslaved and free Black communities facilitated theological education and formation through an orchestra of practices including, but not limited to, ritual, mysticism, conjure, hymnody, and preaching.[9]

In the early nineteenth century, the seeds of graduate theological education in the United States were taking root at Andover Theological Seminary and at other early institutions that followed its educational template. Meanwhile, in the South, antiliteracy laws criminalized education for Black people. Any form of Black education was an act of defiance and self-assertion, which involved the reading both of texts and of the times.[10]

Slavers and the enslaved alike widely understood Black literacy as a threat to Black subjugation. As historian Jarvis Givens stated simply, "The literate slave was akin to a fugitive slave."[11] Givens relates Frederick Douglass's famous account of an instance in which he overheard his white overseer, Hugh Auld, scolding his wife for her efforts to teach Douglass to read in hopes that Douglass would learn to read the Bible. Auld protested, "If he learns to read the Bible it will forever unfit him to be a slave. . . . If you teach him how to read, he'll want to know how to write, and this accomplished, he'll be running away with himself." Douglass cited Auld's diatribe against his education as an awakening. He decided that he would endeavor to "run away with himself." He determined to learn to read, write, and, in so doing, *unfit* himself to be a slave.

Douglass's narrative expresses a deeper theme in the lineage of Black education in the United States: Education is a constitutive element of the project of Black freedom. Givens describes the transgressive pedagogical strategies forged in the fires of enslavement as *fugitive pedagogy*. Fugitive pedagogy is a "metanarrative of black educational history. It is a social and rhetorical frame by which we might interpret black Americans' pursuit to enact humanizing and affirming practices of teaching and learning."[12]

This, however, is not the only theme running throughout Black education. Historian Carter G. Woodson, known as "the Father of Black History," coined the term "miseducation" to describe the ways in which formal education had been weaponized against Black flourishing and freedom. Woodson exposed the insidious ways in which inclusion in white institutions and formation in schools established *for* Black people often served to reinforce master-slave power relations and to "fit [the Negro] again" for subjugation in other forms. Speaking of theological education in his 1933 landmark book, *The Mis-Education of the Negro*, Woodson warns Black clergy against theological education that is deliberately designed to disable them from leading in service to the interests of Black people: "In schools of theology Negroes are taught the interpretation of the Bible worked out by those who have justified segregation and winked at the economic debasement of the Negro sometimes almost to the point of starvation. Deriving their sense of right from this teaching, graduates of such schools have no messages to grip the people whom they have been ill-trained to serve."[13]

The establishment of the African Institute (later Cheney University) in 1837 marked the beginning of HBCUs. After the end of the Civil War, these schools began to proliferate throughout the former slave states as an integral element of emancipation for formerly enslaved Africans. These HBCUs were founded and funded through a convergence of the interests of white philanthropic paternalism and Black self-determination.[14] In many cases, the earliest iterations of these institutions were schools of religion, theology, and ministry. They were institutional expressions of an answer to two perennial sociopolitical questions: What should the education of Africa's offspring include? And what does it require?

The founding and the development of Black educational institutions were deeply intertwined with contested economic and political interests. The Southern education movement[15] powered the proliferation of HBCUs at their founding and has shaped their development ever since. In the aftermath of the Civil War, the Southern education movement was chiefly concerned with how the education and socialization of "the Negro" could contribute to the postslavery economic order of the New South after the Civil War. The contentions that shaped the Southern educational movement vacillated between the aspirations of emancipated Africans, lower-class whites, the Southern planter classes, Northern philanthropic interests, and others. This was a discourse informed by labor interests,[16] specifically the survival needs and economic aspirations of the emancipated Africans and the self-interests of other influential actors in the emerging American empire who sought to sustain and advance their standing and self-image after losing the golden goose of legal slavery. The education question was (and is) an economic and political question.

Historian Peniel Joseph described this era as the first of three Reconstruction periods in the United States. Drawing from W. E. B. Du Bois's legendary work *Black Reconstruction in America*, Joseph noted that this first Reconstruction following the Civil War was not merely an attempt to establish the American democratic experiment on the foundation of equality; it was essentially the second founding of the nation. Joseph outlined these three epochs as follows:

> The first Reconstruction era, 1865 to 1898, was followed by decades of Jim Crow, with its mendacious principle of "separate

> but equal." The Second Reconstruction spanned the heroic period of the civil rights era—from the May 17, 1954, Supreme Court decision in Brown v. Board of Education of Topeka to Dr. Martin Luther King Jr.'s April 4, 1968, assassination. And in our time, we have come to the Third Reconstruction, the period from the election of Barack Obama as president in 2008 through the recent Black Lives Matter (BLM) protests and all that they have entailed.[17]

Each of these periods reflects a cycle of progress toward multiracial democracy that met with intense backlash. Joseph argued that this pattern reflects an archetypal conflict between American reconstructionist and Confederate redemptionist political visions that attempt to answer the core issue that fueled the Civil War: the value and standing of Black life within the American empire.

Both of the first two Reconstruction periods also marked the founding and growth of Black educational and advocacy institutions that embodied aspirations for survival, freedom, full citizenship, economic access, and community sovereignty. The development of Black institutions in both of these prior periods was seen as a means to establish Black standing and value within the American empire. The six accredited historically Black theological schools are products of these first two periods. What then will be the institutional legacy of this third Reconstruction? What are the underlying assumptions that will inform how Black institutional life evolves in this period?

BLACK (THEOLOGICAL) EDUCATION IN THE THIRD RECONSTRUCTION

The rallying cry "Black Lives Matter" and the movement it represents have profoundly influenced the theo-ethical foundations of the third Reconstruction. This affirmation of the inherent value of Black lives indicts theological, political, and economic systems that violate Black dignity and well-being. The abolitionist commitments of the Black Lives Matter movement hold that the legacy systems we have inherited are designed to produce what they have consistently produced over time: inequity, injustice, and indignity, not by happenstance but by design. Thus the abolitionist desire of Black Lives Matter is not only for an analysis and reformation of legacy systems but an intentional cocreation of new systems that embed Black joy, dignity, and well-being into the very core of their design.

The racial reckoning in this third Reconstruction runs concurrently with a period of destabilization in higher education generally, and in theological education in particular. While the nation reckons with the fundamental questions of its founding, this moment of destabilization invites theological schools to return to the fundamental questions about their nature and purpose within the sociopolitical sandbox in which North American theological education sits.

Black theological education has always been an enterprise rife with sociopolitical significance, one closely tied to the question of the "problem of the Negro" in this country. Like its two predecessors, this Reconstruction period calls for imaginative institutional development. Such development may include the reformation of legacy institutions, but it also calls for the design and development of new institutional forms in the interest of Black liberation.

In each Reconstruction period, the core debate around the nature and purpose of Black (theological) education reflects the difference between what education looks like when it is designed *for* "the Negro" in the interests of others versus what it looks like when it is designed *by* "the Negro" in our own self-interest. That said, Black education has long been marked by contention over whether our self-interested freedom dreams are best served by gaining access to the rights and privileges of the American empire as is, or whether the freedom dreams of our people call for a complete reimagining of the social order, both within the United States and the broader African diaspora.

At each of these pivotal moments, the nature and purpose of education for Africa's offspring are a question that has been and must be painstakingly revisited. This requires us to return to the contested and complicated consensus upon which our inherited institutions are built.

ON DESIGN

During a 2013 national consultation on doctoral theological education hosted by the Fund for Theological Education (FTE), Dr. Juan Martinez described the current and emerging landscape of theological education. "The consensus which gave rise to the structures of which we are a part is fractured," he observed. Dr. Martinez's prescient observation emphasized the need to address not just visible demographic shifts but the deeper consensus—the implicit agreements and underlying assumptions that currently shape theological education.

All design is born of a consensus, a set of implicit and explicit agreements reflecting a shared imagination about who and what aims a given product, program, or institution will serve. Considering theological education and its institutions within the framework of design removes our institutional forms and educational models from the realm of inevitability. It enables us to recognize that our inherited systems reflect someone's choices, agreements, and, most importantly, imagination. This is the stuff of the "consensus" around which the institutions we now inhabit were designed.

Yet more than mere structure, design is the link between the visible and unseen dimensions of our institutional lives. Design helps us to notice how unseen imaginaries, ideologies, narratives, and cultures animate our visible structures, programs, and institutional arrangements. Avoidance of this level of inquiry runs the risk of reproducing the very results we say we don't want. This is the level of inquiry that makes real transformation possible. This is the level at which design takes place.

In July 2019, I was appointed interim president of ITC to begin a process of institutional overhaul, commonly dubbed ITC 2.0. Prior to my appointment, I had led a seven-month task force process that sought to assess the condition of the institution and its prospects for the future in light of the changing landscape of theological education. Like many theological schools, ITC was in a fragile place, reckoning with the irreversible shifts in the landscape that have further shaken the stability of our institutions. The stakes were clear: transform or die.

Transformation is not a tweak: it is a comprehensive process that requires an honest deep dive to discover root causes. That discovery then demands the courage to ask tough questions, follow where the logic leads, and imagine again what we are called to be and do, not for mere survival but for the realization of our shared mission and vision. As Vincent Harding wrote, "It is more than obvious that nations, no less than individuals, are best known and most clearly marked by the questions they choose not to ask."[18] The same is true of institutions. Transformation requires us to transgress taboos and ask the hard questions we typically avoid.

Transformation, therefore, focuses our attention on systems rather than symptoms. Our attention to the relationship between the parts and the whole of our institutional systems enables us to avoid fixating on broken parts (symptoms) alone. Focusing on the whole system and the logic underlying its design also helps us to see beyond episodic moments of upheaval. We gain perspective that enables us to notice the underlying patterns and mental models that, for better or for worse, generate consistent outcomes over time. This is never the work of a single heroic individual. Nor is it possible without the shared imagination and effort of a village. As the proverb reminds us, "Many hands make light work."

Village Visioning: Whose Imagination?

Early in my tenure as president, I walked into the chapel to observe the community as it gathered for ITC's Village Visioning

Day. We called together the village, a representative sample of the ecosystem of institutional stakeholders. Students, alumni, faculty, deans, colleagues from neighboring schools in the Atlanta University Center, surrounding community members, local pastors, and others gathered to engage our collective imagination. We invited the village to imagine together what ITC 2.0 might entail and require.

We organized the day's deliberations around three questions:

- What do our communities and churches need/desire from ITC now?
- How is ITC uniquely gifted and positioned to address those needs and desires?
- If ITC were fully flourishing to meet these needs and desires, what would that look like?

Driving these questions and this process were the principles of *design justice and human-centered design*. Design justice centers the perspectives and well-being of the most vulnerable among us and examines how design either perpetuates or challenges systemic inequalities.[19] In tandem, human-centered design enlists impacted communities as designers of innovative solutions to their own problems. These solutions must pass the triple test of desirability, feasibility, and viability.[20] Human-centered design first seeks to understand desirability—the needs and desires of end-users and beneficiaries. Feasibility then asks what we can do better than anyone else, whether due to unique capability, perspective, or positioning. Finally, viability integrates end-user needs and organizational aptitude with an assessment of the environment to determine what solutions may be sustained under current and future marketplace conditions. At the intersection of these three inquiries—desirability, feasibility, viability—lies the heart of human-centered design.

Throughout the day, we employed various participatory methods—dialogue, graphic facilitation, movement, guided visualization, and more—to tap into the collective wisdom and imagination of the village. We grounded the day in a concept called the Two Loops Theory of Change.[21] This systems-change framework begins from the premise that all human systems, including institutions, are not mechanical structures but living systems, subject to the cycles of life, death, and rebirth. These cycles don't operate in a linear fashion. In living systems, new life coexists in a symbiotic relationship with that which is dying. Like a nurse log, nutrients in the dying systems nourish new life that seeks to sprout. This framework helps us to let go of the false dichotomies between legacy and innovation. What is past is present. And the future is already now.

Grounding itself in this framework, the gathered village began to release the typical tension between the old and the new and reorient our sense of time. We settled into the Akan principle and practice of Sankofa, which means to "go back and fetch" the best of your people's past to forge a promising future. The Sankofa symbol is a bird whose legs and body are moving in a forward direction while its long neck bends backward over its body to reach into the past. Looking back, the bird's beak holds an egg that represents its future. Digging into the best of our shared legacy, we began to imagine what seeds we may carry into the future.

The imagination of the village yielded a new vision of institutional life and impact, including:

- Becoming a community and civic asset reintegrated with Atlanta's Westside community
- Developing a campus without walls or gates, driven by Afrofuturist visions of Black flourishing
- Serving as an intergenerational incubator for community leadership fostering Beloved Community
- Creating a cyber community for learning, activism, and faith formation
- Establishing an ecologically sustainable campus that serves as a living laboratory for faith-rooted solutions in affordable housing, climate resilience, and environmental justice

- Acting as a communal social impact hub addressing issues such as mass incarceration, food systems, health equity, climate resilience, and environmental justice

The visions that emerged from the village and subsequent processes reflected the possibility of a transformed institution. This new vision drew from the best of ITC's legacy while aligning itself with its mission and vision. It tapped into the "extra-institutional" roots of Black (theological) education, which has historically served the project of Black liberation. By engaging our imagination, we began forming a new consensus from which a fresh institutional design could emerge.

At its core, theological education is a formation of the imagination. Perhaps the most important question we can ask is: *Whose imagination* is informing our institutional models?

Adrienne Maree Brown named the importance of imagination precisely, arguing that "we are in an imagination battle. Trayvon Martin and Mike Brown and Renisha McBride and so many others are dead because, in some white imagination, they were dangerous. And that imagination is so respected that those who kill, based on an imagined, racialized fear of Black people, are rarely held accountable. . . . Imagination gives us borders, gives us superiority, gives us race as an indicator of capability. I often feel I am trapped inside someone else's imagination, and I must engage my own imagination in order to break free."[22]

Envisioning Black (Theological) Education: Bread Crumbs and Questions

The visions articulated by the ITC village reflected a deep-rooted understanding of education as "*the process by which a community builds its capacity to solve its problems and co-create its future.*"[23] It is not merely an individual initiation into a privileged class of credentialed intellectuals. Education in this view is not confined to admission and graduation from a graduate theological school but is a continuous process embedded within the everyday ecosystem of institutions that shape us theologically. This institutional ecosystem includes but is not limited to the church.

Theological education, as a formation of the imagination, provides traditions and tools for learners to undergo *metanoia*—a transformation of consciousness toward the kin(g)dom of God. This prophetic imagination allows us to reimagine ourselves and our world in the image of God and of the Beloved Community.[24] Theological education at its best invites "the *ekklēsia*" to imagine and embody alternative ways of being in community, rooted in the Way of Jesus.

The vision that emerged from the ITC village amplified the need, previously affirmed by the board of trustees, for a comprehensive institutional overhaul to include ITC's board governance, institutional operations, and educational model. Such an innovative vision requires institutional conditions that facilitate its emergence. New wine does not fare well in old wineskins.

This vision also stoked the development of a renewed educational aim: the cultivation of "prophetic problem-solvers." I coined the term "prophetic problem-solvers" to describe a type of faith-rooted leadership that integrates prophetic imagination with human-centered problem-solving methodologies. These leaders are learners and listeners formed through critical theological study situated in community. Prophetic problem-solvers facilitate the cocreation of systems-level solutions that are informed by theological visions of justice and peace that address the perennial flesh-and-blood problems of our communities. Leaning into public listening more than public speaking, they listen well enough to hear the voice and vision that emerge from an affected community. In so doing they curate indigenous theological visions for our lives that bring us closer to the kin-dom of God. These are not individual heroes that swoop in to save the day. Prophetic problem-solvers are accountable cocreators and choreographers who facilitate access to the inherent power, resources, relations, and assets already among us.

The late homiletician Miles Jerome Jones once defined Black liberation as "a new self-understanding in relationship to the Eternal."[25] If Black theological education is to be a liberative enterprise, this "new self-understanding" must be at the core of our educational aim. This begs the question of how we come to understand ourselves and our relationship to the Creator, cosmos, creation, and community. Liberative Black (theological) education recognizes that theological formation takes place in the everyday practices of socioeconomic and political life. Flesh-and-blood questions of how we feed, shelter, clothe, educate, and govern ourselves are intrinsically theological questions that shape our sense of power, agency, worth, and relationship to the sacred.

As a pastor, especially with youth and children, I often accompanied young people and their families as they navigated various systems of socialization: school, sports, and family, among others. Reflecting over time with young people on their spiritualities, theologies, identities, gifts, vocational aspirations, fears, and disappointments, I came to a disheartening awareness: that the theologies of the young people I pastored, and of their families, were being shaped more by the economies and ecologies in which they were growing than by the rhetoric and rites of the church. In a real sense, every sermon, youth group gathering, Bible study, service project, and counseling session was an intervention in a theological framework already in development. Their theologies had been shaped by the stuff of everyday life. Their understanding of their relationship to themselves, their communities, their Creator, and creation was primarily formed by the intrinsic assumptions of the financial, family, education, and other systems they inhabited.

Black theological education must enable faithful learners and leaders to understand critically and engage constructively the everyday ecosystems that are actively shaping our people's "self-understanding in relationship to the Eternal." Educational institutions then must reimagine their relationship and partnerships with the diverse institutions that make up these everyday ecosystems as partners in formation and education, again not only the church. This kind of education in theo-praxis builds in faith-rooted leaders a capacity to design theologically grounded alternatives that reshape how we work to sustain Black life, and in turn reshape the theological underpinnings that drive the systems we inhabit. Such education must also offer the critical tools to excavate and examine the oppressive ideologies baked into those systems, stir the prophetic imagination, and facilitate the cocreation of alternatives. This focus reinforces the nature and purpose of Black theological education as an enterprise that is ultimately accountable to God's desire for the freedom and well-being of Black people. This necessitates a broader institutional recalibration, rather than mere programmatic or curricular revision.

If we recalibrate our institutions to this North Star, and follow where its logic leads, then we will inevitably have to face the tough questions we tend to avoid. What constitutes good governance for a liberation-focused educational institution? How might we sustain our mission in alignment with our values so our survival doesn't depend on student debt? How might we better prepare students to make a difference while making a living? In what ways does accreditation facilitate or inhibit our ability to imagine new institutional forms? How might we develop assessment methodologies and tools that measure impact rather than merely outputs and outcomes? How might we rethink academic reward systems to incentivize faculty to prioritize praxis as the preferred aim of teaching and learning? In what ways do our investment strategies reflect our institutional vocation? How might we build values-based revenue strategies that leverage our capital and cultural assets for social impact? How do our land use and campus operations strategies align with our mission, educational aim, and vision? These reconsiderations lead us to wrestle with structural and strategic questions, but they don't stop there. They inevitably push us to revisit existential institutional questions: Who are we? Why do we exist? Whom do we serve? And, what are the ultimate aims of our efforts?

Adrienne Maree Brown encourages us to learn our way forward: "We embody. We learn. We release the idea of failure because it's all data."[26] We come to know who we are and how we are called together by imagining, trying, failing, learning, and trying again.

In September 2023 I ended my tenure at ITC after over four years of arduous work, which at times felt impossible. I cannot overstate the toll of taking on an institutional overhaul amid the COVID-19 pandemic. While we made significant strides toward the vision of ITC 2.0, the realization of that vision remains in process. Meanwhile the future of the institution, like so many in our field, faces significant headwinds that require difficult discernment and decision making.

I offer these reflections to similarly situated colleagues who wrestle daily with the dissonance between our inherited models and the changing landscape we must traverse. This moment calls us toward a new way rooted in ancestral wisdom. I believe another way is possible, even if we have yet only witnessed glimpses of it.

Vincent Harding's challenge to Black (theological) schools more than fifty years ago is as relevant today as it was in 1970. He wrote, "Black schools face a momentous challenge. They are no longer needed as poorer, carbon copies [of white schools]. [On the contrary,] the total disarray in which the [white] 'models' find themselves may present a moment of great opportunity for black schools . . . to become models themselves—models of blackness, models of the university's total commitment to the life of its community and its world."[27]

Dialogue

Matthew Wesley Williams, Angela Sims, Joanne Solis-Walker

Angela: I was excited when I read the words, "This essay responds to Harding's call once again to bind the vocation of the Black scholar to the struggles of the Black community. . . . How might we reimagine the vocation of the Black (theological) school in light of the present and emerging struggles that face African-descended people in the United States and abroad." For me, it's a similar question that I've asked of the Society for the Study of Black Religion. It's a question that's future-oriented.

Then there was this key question, "How does the design of our institutions—at a level beyond curriculum, pedagogy, and programming—affect their ability to advance Black liberation?" For me, this is a key question that I think needs to be explored in conjunction with the realities of accreditation. Thus: What does it mean to be an *accredited* theological school that is designed to advance the cause of Black liberation?

Matthew: Yes! These questions implicate the guilds and agencies that influence, fund, and regulate this field. We can't really address these questions in our institutions without asking similar questions of the ecosystem.

Angela: Yes, then there's the cultivation of prophetic problem-solvers. This seems to be a model that runs the risk of putting new wine in old wineskins unless simultaneous energy is allocated to birthing this new imagination from which prophetic problem-solvers emerge. How do you hold this in tension with some of the realities and constraints around accreditation and funding? And it's not just a question of figuring out a new model. It's a question of who will exercise the moral courage to bring that model into existence!

Joanne: I think your call for prophetic problem-solvers is closely linked to that question. You're calling people not only to address symptoms but to change systems.

Angela: This question really became clear when reading about those Village Visioning deliberations. The imagination of the village yielded a new vision of institutional life and impact. This is exciting because it is an invitational model that bridges and intersects multiple communities. But again the question for me is: Who will midwife this imagination into reality?

Matthew: *That* is the question! Or maybe it's a question of who will serve as the doula for this kind of rebirth. In many cases, doulas operate outside of, or alongside, conventional medical institutional spaces. So that's a perfect, perfect metaphor. Thank you.

I was in a conversation recently with a group of pastors about sacred memory and innovation. We discussed how innovation calls for a model of leadership that is much more doula than director. It's about paying attention and creating the conditions to support the new life that wants to emerge.

Angela: When we get to design, you talk about how the stakes were clear as you reentered ITC as president: transform or die. This prescient comment prompts me to ask the question: Do we need to rethink our views and understandings of death as a gift from which new birth can emerge? Perhaps transformation is too soft, and that death really *is* death. Our willingness to die and allow for new birth may be what is really at stake. This is scary, and it is hard!

Joanne: Matthew, one of my pet peeves when I'm grading papers is that when a writer asks a question, they have to provide an answer. You've woven these questions into your essay in such an intriguing way that I found myself searching for answers to each one.

What your essay sparked in me was *curiosity*. You were drawing me in with all the questions, creating a sense of urgency. . . . Like, all these questions need answers!

And you provided us with an abundance of material to start addressing them. You made this powerful statement: "Liberation is an altogether different institutional impulse than inclusion."

Matthew: Joanne, I appreciate how you picked up on the way I hoped to use these questions. A couple of years ago, I coauthored a book with two colleagues, Dori Baker and Stephen Lewis, called *Another Way: Living and Leading Change on Purpose*. It tells a story of what we learned in ten years of experimentation at the intersection of leadership formation and vocational development, particularly with young people and the institutions that support them. We outlined and described four care practices, abbreviated to the acronym C-A-R-E, that are core to the work that we've been doing. The *A* in that acronym stands for "asking self-awakening questions."[1]

And that's what I intended to do in this chapter—ask self-awakening questions. These are questions to which we don't necessarily know the answers, but we know they need to be asked to expand our self-awareness and imagination. They call us to curiosity and hopefully to some urgency and experimentation. I refused to try to prescribe a simple answer to these complex questions. The questions invite others to be curious, and to play and experiment with potential solutions. I'm glad it stimulated your curiosity in that way.

Joanne: One question it raised is, what are we liberating ourselves from? It also emphasized that not only must theological education and theological institutions adopt this approach of liberation, but there must also be a liberation within those who have experienced theological education for a complete transformation to occur.

Matthew: Yes! Absolutely!

Joanne: Otherwise, those who have gone through that experience will keep replicating these theologies and practices. When you mention theo-praxis, what occurred to me is that our people are already doing ministry in their own community spaces, just not within the institutional church. And so you shouldn't lose sight of that realm because it's relevant to what you're proposing in terms of institutional design. You're calling that out, and so it provides an opportunity to call us all to reimagine how theological education may be designed to take place inside and outside of traditional institutional spaces.

Matthew: Joanne, you are right on point as you're considering whether a new model and new design of theological education will be possible inside and outside of existing institutions. One of the things I said to the faculty when I was at ITC was that to take up this notion of prophetic problem solving as an educational aim and model requires a disavowal of the dominant value system of theological education. The reward system that the guilds uphold and our institutions enforce would have to go out of the window if theo-praxis were our focus as an institution.

These questions have been with me for a while now. As I write in the essay, some of them began to take shape while I was a pastor. There's a longer story that I chopped down for brevity. It comes from being a youth pastor, walking with young people who were dealing with questions of theodicy in light of the struggles and trauma their families were experiencing. In particular, in walking with one young woman, I recognized that she had already shaped and formed a way of thinking theologically around evil and suffering that actually undermined her humanity and her agency. My pastoral experience with my youth groups and that young woman's situation in particular made a profound impact on my thinking and practice.

Joanne: Meaning their theologies were shaped and reinforced by their everyday experience, ecosystem, and economy.

Matthew: Precisely! And this little intervention that I was making with her and the youth group a few times a week seemed like a drop in a bucket. I can't tell you how powerless I felt.

Joanne: Matthew, I had all kinds of emotions when I read your piece. You wrote this amid an internal struggle and real transition. And I read you as not only talking about the community in struggle but about ways you see God taking your experience and your ability to see the fruit of the whole difficult process. I may have had a little tear in my eye at some point. Thank you for having the courage to step into that space and to produce a piece like this.

Matthew: Joanne, somehow you caught a lot of what I did not say explicitly. Yes, I was writing through grief. And I think it's important to name that explicitly, because what is inevitably going to attend these processes, whether transformation or death or some combination of the two, is grief.

For those of us who have been shaped by and through these institutions, we have to be honest: as much as we critique them, they are a part of who we are.

My grief had to do not just with my institution. My experience in that role helped me to view the promise of and the threats to the future of Black education more broadly. Yes, this was somewhat therapeutic, but again, it was important for me to write in a way that did not focus only on ITC. This really is a bigger set of questions that I was holding before my time in leadership at ITC, and now I'm holding differently since my departure.

I can't thank both of you enough for your empathic reading and responses. I'm deeply grateful.

For Further Thought

Ted A. Smith and Corwin Malcolm Davis

Ted: All the books in the Theological Education between the Times (TEBT) series have ended with a brief section inviting readers to further thought. Different authors have done different things with this section. For some, it is a list of suggested readings—the kind of thing a bibliography might supply, but in a more curated form. For other authors, it is a kind of coda. But it is always invitational. With what invitations would you close this volume?

Corwin: I am grateful that this collection offers readers so many different directions they can go, but all united around common themes. I think one of the more specific invitations that I would offer is to extend the contextual analyses that so many of these chapters present. Whether they currently serve in churches, or nonprofits, or the more formalized "academy," where do readers see theological education happening right where they are? What insights might others glean from the work being done organically and faithfully even in the unsung places? And, connecting back to your citing of Keri Day's words in the introduction, how might readers testify in their own way to that?

Ted: I appreciate your invitation to readers to expand the contexts and identities from which reflection on theological education is happening. The TEBT series could be twice as long as it is and still not begin to feature voices from all the relevant contexts. Comprehensiveness was never an option. That's one reason to bring the project to a close now: to leave the conversation radically, obviously incomplete, and so to invite others to extend it in their own ways. Or to start a new conversation entirely.

I think of David Nacho's insight about the importance of the recognition of our "non-self-sufficiency" as theological educators. I feel called to account especially by his contrast between "the high-minded crossing of boundaries that always includes a kind of condescension" and "a recognition of the teacher's own needs for the other." That's a recognition that has grown in me over the course of the project, not least through the teaching of people like David. And you. And the gift of getting to overhear a conversation like the one between Matthew Wesley Williams, Angela Sims, and Joanne Solis-Walker on the vocation of a Black theological school. In the language Janette Ok's essay gives us, their teaching reveals anew my lack, and so cultivates my desire for understanding.

I give thanks for the many wise teachers I have met in the course of this project. But even these encounters have not made me—or the project more broadly—self-sufficient. The conversations remain in need of completion by others. Concluding the series, then, is itself a kind of invitation to those others. It is also an expression of trust in God. For all the words of this book and of this whole series have not accomplished the renewal of theological education for which we hope. This does not mean that we should keep talking until we get it right. We can't hasten that day with a little more effort. Instead, we can fall silent with the confidence that the Word of God will do—and has already done—what our words cannot. Ending the series at this time therefore offers not only invitations, but also prayers of supplication and praise.

Corwin: Amen. I hear your reflections on this book, and on the entire series, as informed by an eschatological vision. The work that all the authors have done throughout the series has been between the times of the "already" and the "not-yet." Each vision is an attempt of theological education to inch a bit further toward the God who desires to be known, even as that God has drawn near to us. I think your prayers of supplication and praise—and, really, the whole work of the series—are the fruit of that drawing near of God.

As a scholar and practitioner who is still early in his career, this project has been an enriching opportunity for me to consider the work to which I am called. The shifting place of theological education in our broader world is something that I think about daily as I try to locate my own place in it. The beauty of these dialogues is that we are all learning from each other about some of our shared hopes, while honoring our unique responses to them. It is noble work, and it is holy work. And I feel so fortunate that all of us—the authors, readers, and communities—are doing the work *together*.

Contributors

Corwin Malcolm Davis is assistant professor of Africana religions, theologies, and culture at Pacific School of Religion. He serves as the associate director of the Theological Education between the Times project. His writing has appeared or is forthcoming in journals such as *Religions*, *Theology and Sexuality*, and *Political Theology*. Rev. Davis is an ordained itinerant elder in the AME Church, where he has served in congregational ministry and at the AME Publishing House.

Grace Y. Kao is professor of ethics, the Sano Chair in Pacific and Asian American Theology, and a founding codirector of the Center for Sexuality, Gender, and Religion at Claremont School of Theology. She has authored or coedited four books, including her latest monograph, *My Body, Their Baby: A Progressive Christian Vision for Surrogacy* (2023). In addition to teaching and keeping an active speaking schedule, Dr. Kao serves as a board member in two Asian Pacific Islander scholarly organizations: the Pacific, Asian, and North American Asian Women in Theology and Ministry network (PANAAWTM) and the Asian Pacific American Religions Research Initiative (APARRI). A lay member of the Presbyterian Church (U.S.A.) since her late twenties, she grew up attending a monoethnic Taiwanese American evangelical church. You can read more about her and her work at drgracekao.com.

John Kartje is a Catholic priest of the Archdiocese of Chicago. He has served in both parish and university ministry. In 2015 he was appointed rector/president and associate professor of biblical studies at Mundelein Seminary, near Chicago.

Ann Killian, OP, is a Dominican Sister of Peace and assistant professor of English at the University of Notre Dame. She holds graduate degrees from Yale University and the University of Oxford and was the inaugural Public Humanities Fellow for the Medieval Institute at Notre Dame. Her publications on literature and theology have appeared in *Spiritus: A Journal of Christian Spirituality*, *Speculum: A Journal of Medieval Studies*, and *Studies in the Age of Chaucer*. She has written for *Commonweal*, *Global Sisters Report*, and *Notre Dame Magazine*. She currently serves on the National Council of Pax Christi USA, the national Catholic peace movement, and on the Futuring Leadership Team of the Dominican Sisters Conference.

Caleb Maskell is an associate national director of Vineyard USA, responsible for the Vineyard's national initiatives in theology and education. Involved in the Vineyard movement for his whole adult life, Caleb has served variously as a church planter, pastor, worship leader, and all-purpose volunteer at Vineyard churches in Chicago, New Haven, New York City, Philadelphia, and Denver. Since 2010 he has helped to lead the Society of Vineyard Scholars. Trained as a historian of Christianity, Caleb holds an AB from the University of Chicago, an MDiv from Yale Divinity School, and a PhD from Princeton University. He is passionate about developing leaders and institutions that will help to produce a healthy, courageous, and hospitable future for the church in the twenty-first century.

Juan J. Molina Flores is a priest of the Catholic Archdiocese of San Antonio and the fifth president of the Mexican American Catholic College (MACC). Before coming to MACC, he served as a parish priest and as director of the Collection for the Church in Latin America and as Foreign Policy Advisor for Latin America and Global Trade in the Office of International Justice and Peace, both at the United States Conference of Catholic Bishops (USCCB). Prior to his service at USCCB, he worked with Catholic Relief Services. He has given many talks on the moral dimensions of the economy, foreign policy, and the work of solidarity of the Catholic community. Among many other publications, he is the author of *The Impact of Remittances in Developing Countries: Saving, Investment, and School Enrollment.*

David Nacho is an ordained Bolivian/Canadian Baptist pastor and a PhD candidate at the Oxford Centre for Mission Studies. He served as interim director and then academic dean at the Community for Interdisciplinary Theological Studies (CETI) between 2010 and 2020. During that time, he also served as adjunct faculty at the Bolivian Baptist Seminary and Carey Theological College (Vancouver, BC). He is currently serving as director of Street Ministries at First Baptist Church, Vancouver. He recently joined the Vancouver School of Theology as a research associate and Regent College as a community representative in its senate.

Janette H. Ok is associate professor of New Testament at Fuller Seminary and an ordained pastor at Ekko Church in Anaheim, California. Her research interests include 1 Peter, 1–3 John, the Catholic Epistles, and the formation of early Christian identity, with an emphasis on Asian American, intersectional, feminist, and social-scientific approaches to biblical interpretation. Janette is the author of *Constructing Ethnic Identity in 1 Peter: Who You Are No Longer* (2021) and coeditor of *The New Testament in Color: A Multiethnic Bible Commentary* (2024). Currently, she is writing a commentary on the Letters of John and a book on reading the New Testament as Asian Americans. Janette is passionate about forming wise leaders for the church.

Julian Davis Reid (MDiv, Candler School of Theology) is a child of God, husband, father, son, brother, and Black artist-theologian of Chicago. His academic and musical work focuses on rest and Black music as eschatological hope and lived reality. Alongside having founded his contemplative-musical ministry Notes of Rest, Julian is a consultant with Fearless Dialogues and a touring musician. A pianist, producer, and composer, Julian has released projects with his own ensemble, Circle of Trust, and with the jazz-electronic fusion group he cofounded, The JuJu Exchange. He has performed with Jennifer Hudson, Chance the Rapper, Andrew Bird, Keyon Harrold, Isaiah Collier, Tiff Joy, and Jamila Woods, and his work has been covered in the *New York Times*, *Forbes*, and *Sojourners*. Prior to his graduate studies, Julian served as a pastor at a nondenominational church and in interdenominational undergraduate campus ministry. He hopes that his offering helps you listen deeper still.

Angela Sims is the thirteenth president of Colgate Rochester Crozer Divinity School. She is the seminary's first woman president and the first Black woman president to lead any Rochester-area college. Sims takes seriously the prophetic imperative "to do justice, love mercy, and walk humbly with God." As a womanist social ethicist, her research examines connections between faith, race, and violence with specific attention to historical and contemporary ethical implications of lynching and a culture of lynching in the United States. Sims is the author of *Lynched: The Power of Memory in a Culture of Terror* (2016) and coeditor with Emilie M. Townes, Stacey Floyd-Thomas, and Alison P. Gise Johnson of *Walking Through the Valley: Womanist Explorations in the Spirit of Katie Geneva Cannon* (2011). In 2024 she was elected to the presidential line of the American Academy of Religion.

Ted A. Smith is Charles Howard Candler Professor of Divinity and associate dean of faculty at Emory University's Candler School of Theology. He also serves as director of the Theological Education between the Times project. Smith is the author of three books: *The End of Theological Education* (2023), *Weird John Brown* (2015), and *The New Measures* (2007). Together these books try to think theologically about core American Protestant institutions, practices, ideals, and rhetoric in the time of their unraveling. Ordained to ministry in the Presbyterian Church (U.S.A.), Smith served as pastor to two small-membership churches prior to his doctoral studies.

Joanne Solis-Walker serves as the associate dean of La Mesa Academy for Theological Studies and Professor in the Practice of Leadership at Emory University's Candler School of Theology. La Mesa is a transformative initiative providing accessible, contextually relevant theological training to equip leaders for diverse and dynamic settings. Joanne is a visionary builder who has contributed to Christian higher education by innovating theological programs tailored to meet the needs of various cultural contexts. She has a PhD in organizational leadership and development, specializing in ecclesial leadership, and is a highly respected practical theologian whose career spans leadership, teaching, and ministry. As the cofounder at CaminoRoad, A Development Company, she applies her expertise in organizational development to help institutions and communities flourish.

Matthew Wesley Williams served as the eleventh president of the Interdenominational Theological Center (ITC) from July 2019 to September 2023. Prior to his leadership at ITC, his graduate alma mater, Williams served as the Vice President of Strategic Initiatives for the Forum for Theological Exploration (FTE), formerly known as the Fund for Theological Education. There he coauthored with Stephen Lewis and Dori Baker *Another Way: Living and Leading Change on Purpose* (2020), a highly acclaimed book on innovative leadership and change. An ordained ruling elder in the Presbyterian Church (U.S.A.), he holds degrees from

Florida A&M University and ITC. He currently serves as Senior Vice President for Community Development, Marketing and Communications with Groundswell, a nonprofit organization that builds community power through equitable solar solutions, clean energy programs, and pioneering research initiatives that help facilitate a just transition to a clean energy future.

Notes

Introduction

1. Here and elsewhere in this introduction, quotations from the Bible are from the NRSVue. We have added italics for emphasis.

2. Here we want to acknowledge the similarity between the title of the present volume and that of the extraordinary journal *@ This Point: Theological Investigations in Church and Culture*, edited by Mark Douglas of Columbia Theological Seminary. The title for the present book emerged out of the group's reflections on John Kartje's meditation and on longer conversations about what it means to live "between the times," rather than direct reference to the journal. But we think the two titles reflect some shared theological sensibilities, and we want to be sure to direct readers to the journal.

3. Ted A. Smith, *The End of Theological Education*, Theological Education between the Times (Grand Rapids: Eerdmans, 2023).

4. Keri Day, *Notes of a Native Daughter: Testifying in Theological Education*, Theological Education between the Times (Grand Rapids: Eerdmans, 2021), 2.

5. Willie James Jennings, *After Whiteness: An Education in Belonging*, Theological Education between the Times (Grand Rapids: Eerdmans, 2020), 35.

6. Jennings, *After Whiteness*, 34.

Chapter 1

1. Elizabeth Lin, "The Loneliness of the Progressive Asian American Christian," *Salt Collective*, December 22, 2016, reprinted on Liz Lin's

personal website: https://tinyurl.com/yup3z9kk, and then reposted on January 9, 2017, at *HuffPost* as "It's Lonely Being a Liberal Asian-American Christian," at https://tinyurl.com/bdwefmr5.

2. Lin, "The Loneliness of the Progressive Asian American Christian."

3. See Liz Lin, "Still a Progressive Asian American Christian, Now a Lot Less Lonely," My Name Is Elizabeth, May 30, 2017, https://tinyurl.com/bdeh6yj5, and the "About" section of the PAAC website at https://tinyurl.com/rw5dne2n.

4. For example, consider this June 2017 post with the tag "fun thread time" that received 553 comments: "What are some 'tells' or 'dog-whistles' that you are walking into a theologically conservative church? I'll start: 1. When the youth pastor brags to a room full of high-schoolers about how hot their wife is and how AMAZING and AWESOME sex is . . . but was designed by God to be purely within the boundaries of marriage. 2. Intensely emotional altar calls where people start crying when the music shifts into minor key."

5. The list of PAAC regional groups included Atlanta, Chicago, DMV (DC, Maryland, Virginia), Los Angeles, New England, New York City, Orange County (CA), Philadelphia, Portland, San Diego, San Francisco Bay Area, Seattle, Texas, and the Twin Cities.

6. The conference was held at the City Hope Community Center June 16–18, 2017, and recordings of key sessions were made available for members unable to attend.

7. The prominent themes and questions that emerged according to a January 2018 "PAAC superthreads" shared Google doc included soteriology, reproductive justice, women's issues, Asian American masculinity, reading the Bible, sex, deconstruction, mental health, and LGBTQIA.

8. Many members celebrated the commercial success of this film that centered Asian and Asian American lives and found relatable the central conflict between romantic love and family obligation (even if they weren't "crazy rich"). Others expressed concerns about the film's representation of South Asians and reacted differently to the accusations that star Awkwafina had culturally appropriated Black culture by adopting a blaccent.

9. All episodes were housed on Spotify as well as on PAAC-affiliated sites (https://www.paachristians.org).

10. Progressive Asian American Christians, *Diverging*, https://www.paachristians.org/diverging.

11. Josie Huang, "Asian American, Christian, Progressive and Lonely. Is There a Church for You?" *LAist*, May 9, 2019, https://tinyurl.com/2p8s3tcb.

12. In the interest of full disclosure, I had also been asked to serve as an expert for the first cohort, tentatively agreed to do so for the second cohort but ultimately recommended several others to take my place since I wanted to maintain more peer (fewer professor-student) relationships with the PAAC community.

13. Mike Ferguson, "Progressive Asian American Christians Co-Founder Discusses How and Why the Group Helps Support Its Growing Community," Presbyterian News Service, October 4, 2023, https://tinyurl.com/2b4udvww. Some of these difficulties likely stemmed from generational differences. For instance, a recent article about punctuation usage in a casual context contained the following subhead "To Younger People, Putting a Period at the End of a Casually Written Thought Could Mean That You're Raring for a Fight." See Max Harrison-Caldwell, "No More Periods When Texting. Period." *New York Times*, June 29, 2021, https://tinyurl.com/3xftanj4.

14. The need for moderation also arose when some men questioned why so many Asian American women were paired with white partners or spouses—did their choices imply racial self-hatred (e.g., that women have internalized negative cultural stereotypes about demasculinized Asian American men)? Others found offensive the implication that such women were race-traitors or that they "belonged" in the first place to Asian American men.

15. Ferguson, "Progressive Asian American Christians Co-Founder Discusses How and Why the Group Helps Support Its Growing Community."

16. These group norms continued to evolve as the group did. As a moderator explained in an October 2018 post, newly added to the list of banned topics or comments were "negativity about Asian women in relationships with white men and all posts and comments praising Asian men dating white women." The rationale provided was that these comments were grounded in heteronormative assumptions and caused harm to both women in the group and to multiracial members (many of whom were the children of white male/Asian women pairings).

17. This "mod [moderator] note" would also invite anyone giving a recommendation to share what they knew about the racial-ethnic composition of the church (e.g., "predominantly Filipinx").

18. All PAAC podcasts can be found at https://www.paachristians.org.

19. Each PAAC sermon began with a rationale explaining the series: "Since most people who identify as progressive, Asian/Pacific Islander/ Desi American, and Christian don't have access to a pastor who shares all these identities, PAAC started offering a monthly sermon. On the first Sunday of every month . . . we have an hour-long virtual gathering where we share a 20-minute sermon . . . , followed by a 30-minute coffee conversation." The PAAC leadership welcomed donations by Venmo so they could pay speakers a flat rate of $350 to "cover the costs of preparing, recording, and delivering the sermon" and also provide speakers with an additional $100 to stay for the post-livestream online community coffee hour.

20. See, for example, Byungkyu Lee, Kangsan Lee, and Benjamin Hartmann, "Transformation of Social Relationships in Covid-19 America: Remote Communication May Amplify Political Echo Chambers," *Science Advances* 9, no. 51 (2023), DOI: 10.1126/sciadv.adi1540.

21. Justin Nortey, "More Houses of Worship Are Returning to Normal Operations, but In-Person Attendance Is Unchanged Since Fall," Pew Research Center, March 22, 2022, https://tinyurl.com/yc69khuc.

22. Private correspondence with Liz Lin, May 19, 2023.

23. I was one of the persons who volunteered and have since hosted two Los Angeles/Orange County–area PAAC regional meet-ups.

24. Katie Paul, "Meta's Facebook Says It Is Attracting Most Young Adults in 3 Years," Reuters, May 31, 2024, https://tinyurl.com/3yxd2uv2. Note that PAAC's concerns about remaining on Facebook predate founder Mark Zuckerberg's announcement in January 2025 that Meta would be ending "fact-checking" in the aftermath of the 2024 presidential election.

25. More information about these two churches can be found here: https://tinyurl.com/5f6ne955.

26. The Newbigin House of Studies (renamed the Center for Church Innovation [https://churchinnovation.org/]) had previously been PAAC's fiscal sponsor (i.e., where people would send their checks and where PAAC would hold their money for scholarships). This is because cofounder Lydia Shiu was originally a pastor at City Church, San Francisco, where the Newbigin House of Studies was formerly housed.

27. For these statistics, see Milan Vaishnav and Nitya Labh, "Asian Amer-

icans in California: Results from a 2022 Survey," Carnegie Endowment for International Peace, October 17, 2023, https://tinyurl.com/3e5xep8p.

28. See, for instance, "Religion Among Asian Americans," Pew Research Center, October 11, 2023, https://tinyurl.com/2njz5j85; David Leonhardt, "Asian Americans, Shifting Right," *New York Times*, March 6, 2023, updated March 9, 2023, https://tinyurl.com/5n7pnw7e; James Zarsadiaz, "What Did the Asian American Vote This Year Tell Us?," *Los Angeles Times*, November 10, 2024, https://tinyurl.com/3udd9dub.

Chapter 2

1. In the modern Catholic seminary system, the term "formator" is generally reserved for those faculty members who serve as spiritual directors or pastoral mentors/advisors (every seminarian is assigned a personal spiritual director and formation advisor), whereas the term "teaching faculty" is reserved for those on the faculty whose primary role is classroom teaching. Insofar as every faculty member is to some degree responsible for the formation of the students, here I am applying the title "formator" to any seminary faculty member.

2. There are, to be sure, often early indicators in a seminarian's behavior of the type of priest he *might* turn out to be. Yet, for all but the most obstinate or problematic cases, it can be easy for a faculty person to convince themselves that such behavior will be "reformed" before ordination or within the first few years of priesthood.

3. Julie Hanlon Rubio and Paul J. Schutz, "Beyond 'Bad Apples': Understanding Clergy Perpetrated Sexual Abuse as a Structural Problem & Cultivating Strategies for Change," 2022, https://tinyurl.com/28sf59uf.

4. Catherine Clifford, "Crisis and Hope," in *Priestly Ministry and the People of God: Hopes and Horizons*, ed. Richard R. Gaillardetz, Thomas H. Groome, and Richard Lennan (Maryknoll, NY: Orbis Books, 2022), 62.

5. *Optatam Totius* (1965), par. 5, Vatican website, https://t.ly/4IH4n.

6. Congregation for the Clergy, *The Gift of the Priestly Vocation* (2016), par. 92, https://t.ly/LXJxj (emphasis added).

7. The ideas developed in this section and the next draw heavily on the fruit of collaboration with my colleague at Mundelein Seminary, Dr. Marie Pitt-Payne.

8. For a concise discussion of the history of the philosophical concept of "person," see Juan Manuel Burgos, *Personalist Anthropology: A Philosophical Guide to Life*, trans. Benjamin Wilkinson with James Beauregard (Wilmington, DE: Vernon, 2022), 15–42.

9. Dietrich von Hildebrand, *The Heart: An Analysis of Human and Divine Subjectivity* (South Bend, IN: St. Augustine's Press, 1965/2007), 4.

10. Robert L. Anello, MSA, "In the Beginning Were the Bells: The Development of Human Formation for Priests," *Seminary Journal* 19 (2013): 51.

11. For a detailed exploration of changes in Catholic seminary formation around the time of the Second Vatican Council, see Katarina Schuth, *Seminary Formation: Recent History, Current Circumstances, New Directions* (Collegeville, MN: Liturgical Press, 2016).

12. *Gaudium et Spes* (1965), par. 12, Vatican website, https://t.ly/zC3mL (emphasis added).

13. Karol Wojtyla, "Inaugural Papal Mass Homily" (1978), Vatican website, https://t.ly/AEd_k (emphasis added).

14. Juan Manuel Burgos, "Wojtyla's Personalism as Integral Personalism," *Quaestiones Disputatae* 9 (2019): 91–111.

15. Burgos, "Wojtyla's Personalism," 108–9.

16. Anello, "In the Beginning," 56.

17. *Pastores Dabo Vobis* (1992), par. 43, Vatican website, https://t.ly/l3trx.

18. Thomas Cheruparambil, "Priestly Formation According to Pastores Dabo Vobis," *Catholic Theology and Thought* 75 (2015): 322.

19. *Pastores Dabo Vobis*, pars. 43–44.

20. *Ratio Fundamentalis*, par. 110.

21. *Pastores Dabo Vobis*, par. 23. The phrase "pastoral charity" occurs fifty times in the document.

22. *Pastores Dabo Vobis*, par. 23.

23. *Lumen Gentium* (1964), par. 24, Vatican website, https://t.ly/DcF8f.

24. United States Conference of Catholic Bishops, *Program of Priestly Formation*, 6th ed. (USCCB, 2022), par. 100. This document governs priestly formation in all Catholic seminaries in the United States.

25. For example: "There is a reciprocal relationship between spiritual and intellectual formation. . . . Intellectual formation is integral to what it means to be human." *Program of Priestly Formation*, par. 261.

26. Karolin Kuhn and Hans Zollner, "Teaching Theology in a Way

That Fosters Human Formation and Safeguarding," *ET-Studies* 11, no. 1 (2020): 123.

27. Kuhn and Zollner call for several "paradigm shifts" in intellectual formation so that the academic classroom might become a major focus for human formation. These include implementing student-centered teaching and learning and more use of real-life scenarios. Such methodologies provide opportunities for the students to engage in authentic encounters with each other and the teacher, providing an experiential base upon which the self-knowledge/self-possession/self-gift dynamic can operate.

Chapter 3

1. Helen Prejean, *Dead Man Walking: The Eyewitness Account of the Death Penalty That Sparked a National Debate* (New York: Vintage Books, 1994), 6.

2. Diarmuid O'Murchu, *Religious Life in the 21st Century: The Prospect of Refounding* (Maryknoll, NY: Orbis Books, 2016), 13, notes that following Christ has always been the *why* behind the vows throughout the long history of religious life. Juliet Mousseau, *Prophetic Witnesses to Joy: A Theology of the Vowed Life* (Collegeville, MN: Liturgical Press, 2021), 3, discusses Pope Francis's writings on the call of religious life, which repeatedly emphasize the presence of joy.

3. Sandra M. Schneiders, *Finding the Treasure: Locating Catholic Religious Life in a New Ecclesial and Cultural Context* (New York: Paulist, 2000), 303–4, describes the charism of religious life as the "single-minded quest for God to the exclusion of any other primary life commitment." Schneiders distinguishes between the charism of religious life as a whole and the charism of particular orders.

4. Chrys Geraets, Dan Roach, and Alfonso ViaReque, "The Spirit of the Dominican Vocation" (Adrian, MI: Dominican Generalate, 1973). Written in Santa Cruz, Bolivia, and dated December 1, 1972.

5. Thea Bowman, Address to the US Bishops' Conference, June 1989, United States Conference of Catholic Bishops, https://tinyurl.com/222xjk4s.

6. Smith, *The End of Theological Education*, 171.

7. On the realities of consecrated life today, see Maria Cimperman, *Religious Life for Our World: Creating Communities of Hope* (Maryknoll, NY: Orbis Books, 2020), 19–21. Updated statistics published annually in the CARA Report; see Center for Applied Research in the Apostolate, cara.georgetown.edu.

8. See the crucible exercise in Cimperman, *Religious Life*, 125–26.

9. All the faithful are called to practice the evangelical counsels in their own form of life; see the *Catechism of the Catholic Church*, sec. 915. "Christ proposes the evangelical counsels, in their great variety, to every disciple. The perfection of charity, to which all the faithful are called, entails for those who freely follow the call to consecrated life the obligation of practicing chastity in celibacy for the sake of the Kingdom, poverty and obedience. It is the profession of these counsels, within a permanent state of life recognized by the Church, that characterizes the life consecrated to God." "Forms of Consecrated Life," United States Conference of Catholic Bishops, accessed February 26, 2025, https://tinyurl.com/44tm6h6z.

10. *Julian of Norwich, Showings*, ed. E. Colledge and J. Walsh, Classics of Western Spirituality (New York: Paulist, 1978), 241, 338.

11. *The Nine Ways of Prayer of St. Dominic*, ed. and trans. Simon Tugwell (Dublin: Dominican Publications, 1978), 30.

12. Colleen Mary Mallon, *Inclusivity and Institutional Change in Education: A Theologian's Journey*, Theological Education between the Times (Grand Rapids: Eerdmans, 2023), connects the Dominican charism of "embodying *veritas* [truth]" to the work of antiracism, diversity, and equity.

13. On the open table of Eucharist as a call to anti-racist commitment, see Anita Baird, "Transforming Religious Communities to Be Intercultural and Anti-Racist," *Horizon: Journal of the National Religious Vocation Conference* 46, no. 2 (2021): 3–6.

14. Francis, *Laudato Si'* (Vatican City: Vatican Press, 2015), sec. 240, see https://tinyurl.com/nhjxrm2s.

15. On the history of racist practices in US-based congregations of women religious, see Shannen Dee Williams, *Subversive Habits: Black Catholic Nuns in the Long African American Freedom Struggle* (Durham, NC: Duke University Press, 2022), 103–33.

16. Kayla Bennett, "Dominican Sisters' 'I Was Here' Event Is in Memory of the People They Enslaved," *Record*, September 30, 2022, https://tinyurl.com/29c7ujus.

17. Day, *Notes of a Native Daughter*, 103.

18. Day, *Notes of a Native Daughter*, 103.

19. Francis, *Evangelii Gaudium*, sec. 87, Vatican website, https://tinyurl.com/mr2we3ab.

20. Francis, *Laudato Si'*, sec. 24.

21. For example, on the fifth anniversary of *Laudato Si'* in 2020, sixteen congregations of Dominican Sisters in the United States pooled more than $46 million in investments for an initial seeding to create the Climate Solutions Funds, which finances projects to address climate change and assist communities adversely affected by its effects. See Brian Roewe, "Dominican Sisters Commit $46 Million to Seed New Climate Solutions Funds," *National Catholic Reporter*, June 18, 2020, https://tinyurl.com/3n2bn37s.

22. My own congregation, the Dominican Sisters of Peace, has placed over 2,000 acres of land in conservancies that prohibit development—605 acres in St. Catharine, Kentucky; approximately 1,500 acres in Ponchatoula, Louisiana; and 37 acres in Plainville, Massachusetts.

23. According to Sr. Claire McGowan, Land Justice Futures works with congregations "to explore their potential to make their sacred lands available to groups historically deprived of land—in other words to contribute concretely to the healing of racial and ecological injustice." They conduct research to identify the land's original inhabitants, then provide training and resources for building relationships with local indigenous and Black groups. "Imagine the impact on U.S. society if 10 or 15 or more congregations were to find ways to voluntarily return some of the land that was stolen by our ancestors from their ancestors." McGowan asked, "Might part of our legacy as we diminish be our incarnation of land justice for the future?" Quoted with permission from Claire McGowan, OP, Talk to Free-Formed Mission Group, April 5, 2024. See the Land Justice Futures website: https://www.landjusticefutures.org/.

24. See Sharon Therese Zayac, *Earth Spirituality: In the Catholic and Dominican Traditions* (San Antonio, TX: Sor Juana Press, 2003), and other publications by Sor Juana Press, a project of Santuario Sister Farm, a ministry sponsored by the Adrian Dominicans, at https://tinyurl.com/2mmwt24t.

Dialogue

1. Henri Nouwen, *¡Gracias! A Latin American Journal* (Maryknoll, NY: Orbis, 1983, 1993).

2. Jennings, *After Whiteness*, 6.

Chapter 4

1. This posture of reflection on the charisms given in the founding era very much rhymes with the approach recommended in Pope Paul VI's Apostolic Exhortation on the Renewal of Religious Life. See Pope Paul VI, "Evangelica Testificatio," in *Vatican Council II: The Conciliar and Postconciliar Documents*, ed. Austin Flannery, OP (Collegeville, MN: Liturgical Press, 2014), 685–86.

2. For an introduction to this phenomenon, see Lester Ruth, *Worshiping with the Anaheim Vineyard: The Emergence of Contemporary Worship* (Grand Rapids: Eerdmans, 2017).

3. Over the years, Vineyard leaders have turned primarily to a number of key Scriptures in the New Testament to underwrite this emphasis. Examples include Matt. 10; Luke 9; 1 Cor. 12–14; and Eph. 4. A canonical Vineyard take on the pastoral impact of practicing these texts is John Wimber, *Power Evangelism* (San Francisco: Harper & Row, 1986).

4. Some of the better studies of the Vineyard movement include Donald Miller, *Reinventing American Protestantism: Christianity in the New Millennium* (Oakland: University of California Press, 1997); T. M. Luhrmann, *When God Talks Back: Understanding the American Evangelical Relationship with God* (New York: Knopf, 2012); and Jon Bialecki, *A Diagram for Fire: Miracles and Variation in an American Charismatic Movement* (Oakland: University of California Press, 2017). The first admirable attempt at a Vineyard history written by a movement insider is Bill Jackson, *The Quest for the Radical Middle: A History of the Vineyard* (Bowie, MD: Vineyard International Publishing, 1999). The Vineyard has also often made cameo appearances in synoptic histories of both American evangelicalism (e.g., Douglas A. Sweeney, *The American Evangelical Story: A History of the Movement* [Grand Rapids: Baker Academic, 2005]) and

global Pentecostalism (e.g., Allan Heaton Anderson, *An Introduction to Pentecostalism*, 2nd ed. [Cambridge: Cambridge University Press, 2014]).

5. The phrase "new paradigm churches" comes from Donald Miller's *Reinventing American Protestantism*.

6. John Wimber, "Staying Focused: The Vineyard as a Centered-Set," in *John Wimber's Pastoral Letters*, ed. Derek Morphew (Bowie, MD: Vineyard International Publishing, 2019), 161; John Wimber, "Who Are We and Where Are We Going? (Part I)," in Morphew, *John Wimber's Pastoral Letters*, 6. Characteristically, John Wimber favored the theology of the kingdom of God precisely because he believed that it was the chief theological paradigm taught by Jesus Christ.

7. See George Marsden, *Reforming Fundamentalism: Fuller Seminary and the New Evangelicalism*, 2nd ed. (Grand Rapids: Eerdmans, 1995), 245–98.

8. Alexander Venter, a South African Vineyard pastor and practical theologian, recounts a fascinating anecdote in which John Wimber told him that when he died, he would like his tombstone to read, simply, "He equipped the saints." See Alexander Venter, *Doing Church: Building from the Bottom Up* (Bowie, MD: Vineyard International Publishing, 2000), 190.

9. See, for example, the 1993 essay "Leading and Developing Foot Soldiers," in Morphew, *John Wimber's Pastoral Letters*.

10. Wimber, "Who Are We and Where Are We Going? (Part I)," 10.

11. E.g., Luke 10:9.

12. Some elements of this section are drawn with permission from Caleb Maskell, "Healing Power," *Christian History* 142 (2022): 41–43.

13. John Wimber and Kevin Springer, *Power Healing* (San Francisco: HarperOne, 1991), 51. All the following details of this paradigmatic story can be found in *Power Healing*, 44–55.

14. Wimber and Springer, *Power Healing*, 51.

15. For a sophisticated (and astonishing) philosophical, biblical, and historical study of Christian miracle stories, see Craig Keener, *Miracles: The Credibility of the New Testament Accounts* (Grand Rapids: Baker Academic, 2011).

16. John Wimber, "Zip to 3000 in Five Years," in *Signs and Wonders Today* (Winchester, VA: Christian Life Missions, 1983), 14. For an account of some of these healing stories, see Carol Wimber, *John Wimber: The Way It Was* (London: Hodder & Stoughton, 1999), 131–58.

17. Wimber, "Zip to 3000 in Five Years."

18. Wimber and Springer, *Power Healing*, xviii, 55.

19. Wimber and Springer, *Power Healing*, xviii, 55.

20. The magazine was expanded and republished the following year as a book, entitled *Signs and Wonders Today* (Winchester, VA: Christian Life Missions, 1983).

21. C. Peter Wagner, *Wrestling with Alligators, Prophets, and Theologians: Lessons from a Lifetime in the Church* (Bloomington, MN: Chosen Books, 2011), 128.

22. Michael J. McClymond, "Charismatic Renewal and Neo-Pentecostalism: From North American Origins to Global Permutations," in *The Cambridge Companion to Pentecostalism* (New York: Cambridge University Press, 2014), 41.

23. Marsden, *Reforming Fundamentalism*, 294. For a perceptive study on MC510, see Jon Bialecki, "The Third Wave and the Third World: C. Peter Wagner, John Wimber, and the Pedagogy of Global Renewal in the Late Twentieth Century," *Pneuma* 37, no. 2 (2015): 177–200.

24. John Wimber, "The Five-Fold Ministry," in Morphew, *John Wimber's Pastoral Letters*, 177.

25. Wimber, "The Five-Fold Ministry," 177.

26. Wagner to Wimber, February 24, 1992, C. Peter Wagner Collection, Fuller Theological Seminary, Box 32.

27. These disputes have been little known, even among those who followed both men closely, in part because the bulk of both disputes took place in private correspondence, some of which has only just become available for research.

28. On the phenomenon of strategic-level spiritual warfare, see David Walker McConeghy, "Geographies of Prayer: Place and Religion in Modern America" (PhD diss., University of California Santa Barbara, 2013), and Matthew D. Taylor, *The Violent Take It by Force* (Minneapolis: Broadleaf, 2014).

29. On the New Apostolic Reformation, start with John Weaver, *The New Apostolic Reformation: History of a Modern Charismatic Movement* (Jefferson, NC: McFarland, 2016).

30. C. Peter Wagner, *Apostles Today: Biblical Government for Biblical Power* (Bloomington, MN: Chosen Books, 2006), 9.

31. C. Peter Wagner, *The New Apostolic Churches* (Raleigh, NC: Regal, 1998), 20.

32. Wimber, "The Five-Fold Ministry," 183.

33. Wimber, "The Five-Fold Ministry," 182.

34. Wimber, "The Five-Fold Ministry," 179.

35. Wimber, "The Five-Fold Ministry," 189.

36. I am indebted to Rev. Dr. Todd Kennedy for this apposite capsule phrase concerning the work of ecclesial discernment.

37. Wimber, "The Five-Fold Ministry," 189.

Chapter 5

1. Elizabeth Conde-Frazier, in *Atando Cabos: Latinx Contributions to Theological Education*, Theological Education between the Times (Grand Rapids: Eerdmans, 2021), has also developed the idea of what I later describe as "in-between" institutions being part of a Protestant ecosystem that feeds the different parts, and which is beneficial to all the parts. See pages 87 to 102 of her book for context and explanation.

2. For a good understanding of why an institution like MACC came into being and the journey many Mexican Americans experienced during that time, see these two helpful resources: Virgilio Elizondo, *Galilean Journey: The Mexican-American Promise* (Maryknoll, NY: Orbis Books, 2005), and Virgilio Elizondo, *The Future Is Mestizo: Life Where Cultures Meet*, rev. ed. (Denver: University Press of Colorado, 2000).

3. Elizabeth Conde-Frazier and others have discussed how interdisciplinary education is not all that is needed; contextual and intergenerational education that speaks to different kinds of people and ages is also needed. See *Atando Cabos*, 83–90, for a fuller discussion on this topic. Maria Liu Wong, *On Becoming Wiser Together: Learning and Leading in the City*, Theological Education between the Times (Grand Rapids: Eerdmans, 2023), 1–10, also speaks of the intergenerational nature of learning in most contexts nowadays.

4. All names and identifying information have been changed to protect the privacy of each person in these stories.

5. Pope Francis, for example, has used this term to mean that humanity and the church are facing unprecedented challenges that require unprecedented ways of facing them. See Francis, *Evangelii Gaudium*, November 24, 2013, Vatican website, https://tinyurl.com/mr2we3ab.

6. Those of us doing ministry in different contexts, for example, have realized that it is not the same thing to minister in an immigrant community as it is in a mainly older, established congregation. The fact that a parish has a great number of younger families with children makes a big difference to how ministry must happen. And if parishioners come from a diversity of ethnic and linguistic backgrounds, ministry among them will also be particular to their needs.

7. In psychology, for example, some studies focus on how uncertainty gives the person some time to explore situations in a different way. And this way of looking at uncertainty has been popularized by digital magazines, such as *Psyche* (see, for example, Richard C. Sha and Nathan Harshman, "Uncertainty Isn't a Human Flaw, It's a Feature of the World," *Psyche*, April 18, 2023, https://tinyurl.com/ynessdka).

8. Parenting can be seen in this context as well. It is a distinct vocation with a sacramental dimension that can be understood as separate from the public life of a career, yet also enhancing public service and ministry in the church.

9. This is a basic principle or axiom of studies in spirituality in the Christian tradition. Saint Augustine referred to this desire in several of his works, especially in his lesser known *Cassiciacum Dialogues*. Other saints have referred to it in such ways as "healing the wound," with God being the one who both causes the wound and is the only remedy (see, for example, the works of Saint John Baptist of the Conception, a saint from the Golden Age of Spain).

10. Augustine of Hippo, *Confessions* 1.1.

11. Frederick Buechner, *Now and Then: A Memoir of Vocation* (San Francisco: HarperOne, 1991), presents a really beautiful meditation that speaks of this.

12. Examples of the kinds of "in-between" institutions are the clubs and associations in civic life and movements such as the charismatic movement or the religious congregations in the Roman Catholic Church.

13. Kathleen A. Cahalan and Gordon S. Mikoski, for example, offer a great introduction to one of these fields in *Opening the Field of Practical Theology* (Lanham, MD: Rowman & Littlefield, 2014).

14. Elizabeth Conde-Frazier, in *Atando Cabos*, has a good story and discussion about the emergent *comunidades de práctica*. See pp. 36–39 and 72–78.

15. Stephen Bevan, *Models of Contextual Theology* (Maryknoll, NY: Orbis Books, 2002), gives an overview of the emerging discipline of contextual theology.

16. While there is no unified theory of ways in which humans know, there are several sources one can reference to begin to understand modern theories of knowledge. One author from the field of spirituality and chaplaincy is John Ehman, who writes about four "widely accepted" epistemological categories of "ways of knowing" in https://tinyurl.com/2t99f6xw. Another author is Kurt C. Stange; see, for example, his article "Ways of Knowing, Learning, and Developing," *Annals of Family Medicine* 8, no. 1 (January 2010): 4–10.

17. For a very interesting and quite compelling explanation of how even reading the Bible in different ways (with different media) can influence the way the faithful create images of biblical characters, see Michael Patella's presentation at MACC titled "Revitalization of Imagination in Biblical Exegesis: The Saint John's Bible, Art and the Hispanic Legacy." A streaming of the presentation can be found on Facebook. One can also read Patella's book *Word and Image: The Hermeneutics of the Saint John's Bible* (Collegeville, MN: Liturgical Press, 2013) to get a good idea of this basic point.

18. Wong, *On Becoming Wiser Together*, presents some good ideas regarding ministry in urban settings and how this kind of ministry is best done by bringing different generations together.

19. Juan Carlos Scannone, SJ, for example, is a good expositor and editor of books that speak of a "theology of the people" in which much emphasis is given to the "faithful people of God." This last term refers to the people who, while simple in their theological understandings, are faithful in the church and in their devotional practices. See, for example Scannone's book in English, *Theology of the People: The Pastoral and Theological Roots of Pope Francis* (New York: Paulist, 2021). A shorter article about this same topic is "Pope Francis and the Theology of the People," *Theological Studies* 77, no. 1 (2016): 118–35.

20. The early Christian experience was not as intellectual as it became starting in the Middle Ages. The patristic synthesis of learning, for example, had a different flavor than medieval theology achieved in the universities. And one of the brilliant insights of Vatican II was to recognize this. The current use of mystagogy with those recently received into the church at Easter is perhaps an acknowledgment of this point.

Chapter 6

1. I will say more about CETI (Comunidad de Estudios Teológicos Interdisciplinarios) in the second part of this essay. For now, let me just say that CETI was founded in 1982 with the mandate to facilitate theological education characterized by dialogue with context, "a radical evangelical perspective, an integral mission intent, and a focus on the formation of all Christians through interdisciplinary dialogue, communal design, and implementation." Ruth Irene Padilla De Borst, "Integral Mission Formation in Abya Yala (Latin America): A Study of the Centro de Estudios Teológicos Interdisciplinarios (1982–2002) and Radical Evangélicos" (Boston University, 2016), vii.

2. "As presented by John, the Pharisees were a learned group who had influence with the people because they were accepted by them as guides in Jewish behavior and belief. As such they were community leaders, perhaps with some direct power in both the synagogue and government council in Jerusalem, and certainly with great influence." Anthony J. Saldarini, "Pharisees," *Anchor Yale Bible Dictionary*, 5; Accordance edition, 298.

3. Padilla De Borst, "Integral Mission Formation," 239. Padilla De Borst refers to Paul G. Hiebert, "The Missionary as Mediator of Global Theologizing," in *Globalizing Theology: Belief and Practice in an Era of World Christianity*, ed. Craig Ott and Harold A. Netland (Grand Rapids: Baker Academic, 2006), 307.

4. For a broad overview of the way in which neoliberal policies have shaped educational systems in Latin America, see Euclides Padilla Caíña, "Neoliberalismo y Educación," *Revista de Lenguas Modernas* 20 (2014): 337–70. Also see José Ramón Alcántara Mejía, "Sean transformados mediante la renovación de su mente," in *Presencia Cristiana en el Mundo Académico: El Testimonio Evangélico Hacia el Tercer Milenio; Palabra, Espíritu y Misión*, ed. Sidney Rooy (Buenos Aires: Kairós, 2001), 94.

5. Leopoldo Cervantes-Ortiz, "Theological Education and Public Education in Latin America," *Ministerial Formation* 111 (November 2008): 29.

6. Matthias Preiswerk, "Hacia un Descentramiento de la Educación Teológica," in *Otra Educación Teológica es Posible: Nuevos Sujetos y Campos*, ed. Nicolas Panotto and Matthias Preiswerk (Buenos Aires: Servicios Pedagogicos y Teologicos, 2017), 15.

7. Cecilia González-Andrieu, "The Good Education: Accessibility, Economy, Class and Power," in *Teaching Global Theologies: Power and Praxis*, ed. Kwok Pui-lan, Cecilia González-Andrieu, and Dwight Hopkins, Kindle edition (Waco, TX: Baylor University Press, 2015), location 1173. González-Andrieu embraces the line of the Latin American Conference of Bishops (CELAM), which defines education in these terms: Education humanizes and personalizes a human being when it makes it possible for him or her to develop fully in thought and in freedom, allowing these to bear fruit in habits that lead to understanding and that initiate a communion with the totality of what is real. In this way, the human person humanizes the world, produces culture, transforms society, and builds up history.

8. Matthias Preiswerk et al., "Manifesto of Quality Theological Education in Latin America," *Ministerial Formation* 111 (November 2008): 45.

Chapter 7

1. Min Jin Lee, *Pachinko* (New York: Grand Central, 2017), 275

2. Lee, *Pachinko*, 276.

3. Lee, *Pachinko*, 276.

4. Lee, *Pachinko*, 276, 308.

5. Sarah Eleazar, "Teachers Must Get to Know Students and Then Learn How to Teach Them: Spivak," *Express Tribune*, October 26, 2014, https://tinyurl.com/yvda9nh4. See also Gayatri Chakravorty Spivak, *Death of a Discipline*, twentieth anniversary ed. (New York: Columbia University Press, 2023), 101; Spivak, "Righting Wrongs," *South Atlantic Quarterly* 103, nos. 2–3 (2004): 523–81.

6. Walter Brueggemann, "Covenanting as Human Vocation," *Interpretation* 33, no. 2 (1979): 115–29, 125.

7. James K. A. Smith, *You Are What You Love: The Spiritual Power of Habit* (Grand Rapids: Brazos, 2016), 1–25.

8. James K. A. Smith, *Desiring the Kingdom: Worship, Worldview, and Cultural Formation* (Grand Rapids: Baker Academic, 2009), 46, 54–63.

9. Smith, *Desiring the Kingdom*, 67–69, 70–72.

10. Anne W. Stewart, *Poetic Ethics in Proverbs: Wisdom Literature and*

the Shaping of the Moral Self (Cambridge: Cambridge University Press, 2014), 135.

11. I will refer to the author of Proverbs primarily as "teacher" and to its addressees as "students" in the plural, even when the text addresses a singular male student.

12. Stewart, *Poetic Ethics in Proverbs*, 135.

13. Scriptural translations are mine unless otherwise indicated.

14. Stewart, *Poetic Ethics in Proverbs*, 149.

15. Smith, *You Are What You Love*, 12.

16. Stewart, *Poetic Ethics in Proverbs*, 162, 149.

17. Alice Ogden Bellis, *Proverbs*, Wisdom Commentary (Collegeville, MN: Liturgical Press, 2018), 77.

18. Sehee Kim, "The Call of Woman Wisdom—Proverbs 8," in Bellis, *Proverbs*, 79.

19. Bellis, *Proverbs*, 10.

20. Bellis, *Proverbs*, 10.

21. Bellis, *Proverbs*, 90, in 8:34.

22. Bruce K. Waltke, *The Book of Proverbs, Chapters 1–15* (Grand Rapids: Eerdmans, 2004), eBook, chap. 9.

23. Waltke, *Proverbs*, eBook, chap. 9.

24. Funlola Olojede, "Being Wise and Being Female in Old Testament and in Africa," *Scriptura* 111, no. 3 (2013): 472–79, 476.

25. Olojede, "Being Wise," 476–77.

26. Stewart, *Poetic Ethics in Proverbs*, 138–39.

27. Stewart, *Poetic Ethics in Proverbs*, 139.

28. Waltke, *The Book of Proverbs*, eBook, chap. 9.

29. Stewart, *Poetic Ethics in Proverbs*, 139.

30. Michael V. Fox, "The Pedagogy of Proverbs 2," *Journal of Biblical Literature* 113 (1994): 241.

31. Sun Myung Lyu, *Righteousness in the Book of Proverbs*, Forschungen zum Alten Testament 2 (Tübingen: Mohr Siebeck, 2012), 65.

32. Stewart, *Poetic Ethics in Proverbs*, 163.

33. Stewart, *Poetic Ethics in Proverbs*, 162.

34. Stewart, *Poetic Ethics in Proverbs*, 143.

35. bell hooks, *Teaching to Transgress: Education as the Practice of Freedom* (New York: Routledge, 2014), 7. Hereafter, page references from this work will be given in parentheses in the text.

36. Uli Chi, *The Wise Leader* (Grand Rapids: Eerdmans, 2024), 14.

37. Chi, *The Wise Leader*, 14.

38. hooks, *Teaching to Transgress*, 199.

39. Mark D. Jordan, *Transforming Fire: Imagining Christian Teaching*, Theological Education between the Times (Grand Rapids: Eerdmans, 2021), 6.

40. Jordan, *Transforming Fire*, 35.

41. Augustine, *Confessions* 12.14.17.

42. Jordan, *Transforming Fire*, 35.

43. Jordan, *Transforming Fire*, 156.

44. Smith, *The End of Theological Education*, 126, 201.

45. Smith, *The End of Theological Education*, 201.

Chapter 8

1. Saint Augustine, *Confessions*, trans. Henry Chadwick (Oxford: Oxford University Press, 2009), 153.

2. Amiri Baraka, *Blues People: Negro Music in White America* (New York: William Morrow, 1963), 80.

3. *The Sound of Music*, directed by Robert Wise, music composed by Richard Rodgers and Oscar Hammerstein II (1965).

4. James Cone, *The Spirituals and the Blues*, 4th ed. (Maryknoll, NY: Orbis Books, 1997), 121.

5. James Cone, *The Cross and the Lynching Tree* (reprint, Maryknoll, NY: Orbis Books, 2013), 3.

6. Cone, *The Cross and the Lynching Tree*, 161.

7. Tricia Hersey, *Rest Is Resistance: A Manifesto* (New York: Little, Brown Spark, 2022), 117.

8. Delores Williams, *Sisters in the Wilderness* (Maryknoll, NY: Orbis Books, 1993), 33.

9. Walter Brueggemann, "Exodus," in *The New Interpreter's Bible Commentary*, vol. 1, *Introduction to the Pentateuch, Genesis, Exodus, Leviticus, Numbers, Deuteronomy*, ed. Leander E. Keck, illustrated ed. (Nashville: Abingdon, 2015), 812–16.

10. Abraham Joshua Heschel, *The Sabbath* (New York: Farrar, Straus & Giroux, 2005), 89.

11. Hersey, *Rest Is Resistance*, 132.

12. M. Eugene Boring, *The New Interpreter's Bible Commentary*, vol. 7, *The Gospels and Narrative Literature, Jesus and the Gospels, Matthew, and Mark*, ed. Eileen M. Schuller (Nashville: Abingdon, 2015), 486.

13. Amy-Jill Levine, "Gospel of Matthew," in *Women's Bible Commentary*, ed. Carol A. Newsom, Sharon H. Ringe, and Jacqueline E. Lapsley, 3rd ed., revised and updated (Louisville: Westminster John Knox, 2012), 477.

14. Hersey, *Rest Is Resistance*, 117.

15. Tiya Miles, *Night Flyer: Harriet Tubman and the Faith Dreams of a Free People* (New York: Penguin Press, 2024), 54–55.

16. Miles, *Night Flyer*, 200.

17. Gail R. O'Day, "Gospel of John," in Newsom, Ringe, and Lapsley, *Women's Bible Commentary*, 523.

18. Barbara A. Holmes, *Joy Unspeakable: Contemplative Practices of the Black Church*, 2nd ed. (Minneapolis: Fortress, 2017), 1.

19. Christina Sharpe, *In the Wake: On Blackness and Being* (reprint, Durham, NC: Duke University Press Books, 2016), 116.

Chapter 9

1. Lesbian, gay, bisexual, transgender, queer, intersexual, asexual, pansexual and polygamous, and kinkiness.

Chapter 10

1. While each of the terms used in this essay has meaning attributed by each person, the terms "Hispanic" and "Latine" are used interchangeably, with limited mention of "Latinx" and the gendered noun endings, such "-as" and "-es." For more information about the diversity of terms, see "Hispanic, Latino, Latinx or Latine? 2 Professors Share Their Own Preferences," Georgetown University, October 14, 2022, https://tinyurl.com/mu5s8nkv.

2. The Hispanic population in 2023 was over 65 million, which accounts for one-fifth of the entire population in the United States. "New Estimates Highlight Differences in Growth Between the U.S. Hispanic

and Non-Hispanic Populations," press release, United States Census Bureau, June 27, 2024, https://tinyurl.com/3jmxxvbb.

3. Alejandra Molina, "US Hispanic Protestant Churches Are Young, Growing and Largely New to the Country," *Roys Report*, January 31, 2023, https://tinyurl.com/3kncfsun.

4. In 2022, a Lifeway study found that only 14 percent of Latine research participants attended Hispanic services in white churches.

5. Aaron Earls, "U.S. Hispanic Protestant Landscape Full of Growing, Vibrant Churches," Lifeway Research, January 24, 2023, https://tinyurl.com/mv4effv6.

6. The considerations range from access to transcripts and credit transfers to degree validation, as well as differences in ecclesial practices between other countries and how Hispanics conduct church on the US mainland. Language is another important factor to consider since many on the US mainland are not bilingual or Latine but English-speaking.

7. Abigail Golden-Vazquez, "The Invisible Latino in America," Aspen Institute, February 1, 2019, https://tinyurl.com/58fmks3v.

8. A search within the ATS website member schools confirms that there is no ATS-accredited Hispanic/Latine theological school within the fifty states. "Discover Our Schools," Association of Theological Schools, accessed March 4, 2025, https://tinyurl.com/3bufvs6m.

9. Carolyn M. Shields, *Good Intentions Are Not Enough* (Lanham, MD: Rowman & Littlefield, 2003).

10. President Javier Viera is an HTI alum.

11. "Doing theology *latinamente*" is a term and phrase coined by the Hispanic Scholars Program. See "Doing Theology ¡latinamente!," Hispanic Scholars Program, accessed March 4, 2025, https://tinyurl.com/mppbr55x. *En conjunto* is a widely used term but coined as a phrase by HTI. See "HTI Scholars," Hispanic Theological Initiative, accessed March 4, 2025, https://tinyurl.com/4aew3hwv.

12. Now called the Hispanic Scholars Program.

13. Kenneth Davis and E. I. Hernandez, *Reconstructing the Sacred Tower: Challenge and Promise of Latino/a Theological Education* (Scranton, PA: University of Scranton Press, 2003), title page.

14. José David Rodriguez and Loida I. Martell-Otero, eds., *Teología en*

llaborative Hispanic Protestant Theology (Louisville: West- ı Knox, 1997), 1.

/in David Aponte and Miguel A. De La Torre, *Introducing Latinx* *›s* (Maryknoll, NY: Orbis Books, 2020), 80.

. Rodriguez and Martell-Otero, *Teología en Conjunto*, 80.

17. *Hispanic Theological Initiative, 2024–2025*, Hispanic Theological ıitiative, accessed March 4, 2025, https://tinyurl.com/y3futj4c (citing "Ph.D. Completion Project," Council of Graduate Schools, accessed March 4, 2025, https://tinyurl.com/48urkkbt), 6.

18. Through the Book Prizes and the HTI scholars' dissertations, the HTI has helped to produce resources written by, for, and about the Latine communities. Open Plaza is a public-facing platform that produces articles and podcasts for the broader community, and the *Perspectivas* journal continues to be a resource for academic communities.

19. Justo L. González, foreword to Rodriguez and Martell-Otero, *Teología en Conjunto*, ix.

20. Elizabeth Conde-Frazier, *Hispanic Bible Institutes: A Community of Theological Construction* (Scranton, PA: University of Scranton Press, 2004).

21. Conde-Frazier, *Atando Cabos*, 92.

22. Asociación para la Educación Teológica Hispana, *Hispanic Bible Institute Certification Manual* (Orlando: AETH, 2022), 3.

23. "Our History," Hispanic Scholars Program, accessed March 4, 2025, https://tinyurl.com/4d5u99su.

24. "Our History."

25. "Doing Theology ¡latinamente!"

26. Hispanic Scholars Program programs include HSP Summer Session, Through Hispanic Eyes, Latinx Discernment Workshop, Pedagogy Workshop, HSP Exchange, El Semillero. "Programs," Hispanic Scholars Program, accessed March 4, 2025, https://tinyurl.com/yc86htku.

27. "Through Hispanic Eyes" Hispanic Scholars Program, accessed March 4, 2025, https://tinyurl.com/zeb5vr7x.

28. CaminoRoad, A Development Company, *Mapping the Landscape of Hispanic/Latinx Theological Education*, *Hispanic/Latinx Pathways Research Project*, 2023, https://tinyurl.com/yjd3t7ka.

29. Smith, *The End of Theological Education*, 97.

Chapter 11

1. Vincent G. Harding, "The Vocation of the Black Scholar and the Struggles of the Black Community," in *Education and Black Struggle: Notes from the Colonized World*, ed. Vincent G. Harding (Cambridge, MA: Harvard Educational Review, 1974), 6.

2. Vincent G. Harding, "Toward the Black University—Part 1," *Ebony*, August 1970.

3. K. M. Saunders and B. T. Nagle, "HBCUs Punching Above Their Weight: A State-Level Analysis of Historically Black College and University Enrollment and Graduation" (2018).

4. The school's spelling of "Afri"-centric intends to tie the school's cultural orientation and concern to the *Afri*-can continent and diaspora, rather than using the cultural signifier "Afro," which can be more broadly applied to culture, products, style, etc.

5. The United Negro College Fund (UNCF) is the largest private provider of scholarships to Black and brown students in the United States. UNCF is a membership organization consisting of thirty-seven private historically Black colleges and universities. The Interdenominational Theological Center (ITC) is the only graduate theological school among its members.

6. Juan Martínez, "It's Already 2040 at a Seminary Near You," USC Center for Religion and Civic Culture, April 2, 2014, https://tinyurl.com/y46bdb9m.

7. W. Anne Joh, "On Diversity, Institutional Whiteness, and Its Will for Change," *Religious Studies News*, May 15, 2014, https://tinyurl.com/ye5zfccv.

8. Albert J. Raboteau popularized this term first used by E. Franklin Frazier to refer to the informal, clandestine religious practices and formation of enslaved Africans in the antebellum South. See Albert J. Raboteau, *Slave Religion: The "Invisible Institution" in the Antebellum South* (New York: Oxford University Press, 1978).

9. Jason R. Young, *Rituals of Resistance: African Atlantic Religion in Kongo and the Lowcountry South in the Era of Slavery* (Baton Rouge: Louisiana State University Press, 2007).

10. Heather Andrea Williams, *Self-Taught: African American Educa-*

and Freedom (Chapel Hill: University of North Carolina

s R. Givens, *Fugitive Pedagogy: Carter G. Woodson and the Art eaching*, Kindle ed. (Cambridge, MA: Harvard University Press, ocation 11.

. Givens, *Fugitive Pedagogy*, 11.

3. Carter Godwin Woodson, *The Mis-Education of the Negro* (Tren-n, NJ: Africa World Press, 1990), 2–3.

14. The late legal scholar Derrick Bell coined the term "interest convergence" in his analysis of the Supreme Court's 1954 *Brown v. Board of Education* decision. This theory asserts that positive social change for oppressed groups only occurs in historical moments when the interests of the oppressed converge with the interests of the ruling group. See Derrick A. Bell, "Brown v. Board of Education and the Interest-Convergence Dilemma," *Harvard Law Review* 93, no. 3 (January 1980): 518–33, https://doi.org/10.2307/1340546.

15. James D. Anderson, *The Education of Blacks in the South, 1860–1935*, Kindle ed. (Chapel Hill: University of North Carolina Press, 1988), location 81.

16. Anderson, *The Education of Blacks*, 81.

17. Peniel E. Joseph, *The Third Reconstruction*, Kindle ed. (New York: Basic Books, 2021), location 13.

18. Harding, "The Vocation of the Black Scholar," 3.

19. Sasha Costanza-Chock, *Design Justice: Community-Led Practices to Build the Worlds We Need*, Kindle ed. (Cambridge, MA: MIT Press, 2020), location 39. For a deeper dive into the ten principles of Design Justice, see Design Justice Network, https://tinyurl.com/4d8hebab.

20. Lauren Landry, "What Is Human-Centered Design?," *Business Insights Blog*, December 15, 2020, https://tinyurl.com/26vtk4fx.

21. This theory of change was first articulated by the Berkana Institute with the publication of the article, M. J. Wheatley and D. Frieze, "Using Emergence to Take Social Innovation to Scale" (2006), https://tinyurl.com/227bvhke.

22. Adrienne Maree Brown, "BALLE 2015 Closing Plenary Speech," June 12, 2015, https://tinyurl.com/58jedkju.

23. Matthew Wesley Williams, "Toward ITC 2.0" (unpublished ad-

dress, Eleventh Presidential Installation, Interdenominational Theological Center, November 19, 2021).

24. First coined by philosopher Josiah Royce, this term was popularized by Martin Luther King Jr. as an alternative articulation of the kingdom of God. King's Beloved Community is a global vision in which the triple evils of racism, militarism, and poverty are eradicated through the realization of justice, peacemaking, and shared wealth on an international scale.

25. Miles Jerome Jones, "Digging Deeper Wells" (unpublished lecture, Trinity United Church of Christ, Chicago, March 1994).

26. Adrienne Maree Brown, *Emergent Strategy*, Kindle ed. (Chico, CA: AK Press, 2017), locations 20, 161–62.

27. Harding, "Toward the Black University—Part 1," 157.

Dialogue

1. Stephen Lewis, Matthew Wesley Williams, and Dori Baker, *Another Way: Living and Leading Change on Purpose* (St. Louis: Chalice, 2020).